BEGINNER'S
CHECHEN
WITH ONLINE AUDIO

BEGINNER'S
CHECHEN
WITH ONLINE AUDIO

Kheda Garchakhanova
& John Lechner

Hippocrene Books
New York

**Audio files available at
www.hippocrenebooks.com**

For information, address:
HIPPOCRENE BOOKS, INC.
171 Madison Avenue
New York, NY 10016
www.hippocrenebooks.com

Cataloging-in-Publication data available from the Library of Congress.

ISBN 978-0-7818-1447-8

For our parents

Acknowledgements

This book would not have been possible without our first teachers of Chechen; they know who they are. Milana Mizayeva and Sarah Slye read and edited this text with expert insight, while Valentina Michelotti provided crucial structure for the book at the beginning. Malika Shaykhidova, a Chechen language teacher residing in Chechen Republic helped us with dialectal dialogues. Aida Vidan, who has written excellent Croatian and Serbian courses in this series, inspired us to write. Finally, we are incredibly grateful to our editor, Priti Gress, for taking a chance on this project.

CONTENTS

Introduction 1
  About this Course 1
  More on Chechen 2
  Some Features of Chechen Grammar 3

Pronunciation 8
  The Chechen Alphabet 8
  Dipthongs 10
  Difficult Consonants 11

Lesson 1: Arrival 13
  Dialogue I: At the Grozny Airport 14
  New Words 15
  Dialogue II: Meeting a Friend 16
  New Words 17
  Grammar: Noun Classes, 17; Chechen Pronouns, 20;
          The Question Particle -й and Question
          Words, 21
  Culture: Chechen Greetings 22
  Exercises 23

Lesson 2: At Home 27
  Dialogue I: At Hwava's Home 28
  New Words 29
  Dialogue II: At the Table 30
  New Words 31
  Grammar: Absolutive Case, 32; Present Progressive
          Tense, 34; The Allative Case and a Locative
          Form, 37; Saying "I have," "You have," etc.,
          37; The Negative Form of д.у "to be," 38
  Culture: As a Guest in a Chechen Home 39
  Exercises 39

Lesson 3: Going to University 43
   Dialogue I: At Hwava's House 44
   New Words 45
   Dialogue II: On the Phone 46
   New Words 47
   Grammar: Genitive Case, 48; Personal Pronouns:
              Adding the Ergative and Dative, 49; The
              Present Tense, 51
   Extra Vocabulary: Adverbs 53
   Culture: Months of the Year 54
   Exercises 55

Lesson 4: At the University 59
   Dialogue I: At the University 60
   Dialogue II: At the Library 60
   New Words 62
   Grammar: Ergative and Dative Case, 63; Future Tenses,
             66; More on Irregular Verbs, 68
   Days of the Week 69
   Cardinal Numbers 1 to 20 69
   Ordinal Numbers 1st to 20th 70
   Telling Time 71
   Culture: Borrowing of Russian Words 73
   New Words: School Related 74
   Exercises 74

Lesson 5: In the University Hallways 79
   Dialogue I: Meeting Another Student 80
   Dialogue II: In the Classroom 82
   New Words 84
      Family Members 86
      Adjectives Describing People 86
   Grammar: Past Tenses, 87; Imperatives: Making
             Commands, 90; Nouns: Instrumental Case, 91
   Exercises 93

Lesson 6: At the Market   97
Dialogue I: At the Market   98
Dialogue II: At the Stall   100
New Words   104
Grammar: The Substantive Case, 106; The Comparative
Case, 107; Chechen Cases: Declensions, 109;
Chechen cases: Pronouns, 115; Modal Verbs,
115; Preverbs, 117; Chechen Numbers 21 to
10,000   118
Culture: Expressions   119
Exercises   119

Lesson 7: At the Store   123
Dialogue I: At the Store   124
Dialogue II: At the Bookstore   126
New Words   128
Grammar: Present Perfect Tense, 130; Verbs: The
Real Conditional Mood, 132; Declining
Question Words, 132; Forming Nouns from
Verbs and Adjectives, 133; Syntax: Saying
"Why," "While," 135; Subordinate Clauses,
135; Saying "we two," "you too," etc., 136;
Declining Adjectives with Nouns, 137; Free
Adjectives, 137; Some Particular Adjectives,
139; Prepositions: Saying "about," 139
Exercises   140

Lesson 8: Renting an Apartment   143
Dialogue I: Renting an Apartment 1   144
Dialogue II: Renting an Apartment 2   146
New Words   150
Grammar: Other Uses of the Present Perfect Tense, 153;
Plural Verbs, 154; Word Building with Verbs,
156; Postpositions, 160; Syntax: "Where"
Clauses, 161
Exercises   162

Lesson 9: At the Wedding 167
Dialogue I: At the Wedding 168
Dialogue II: Old Man speaking about Chechen Nation 170
New Words 171
Grammar: Iterative Aspects of Verbs, 173; Word-
building: Causative Verbs, 174; Possessive
Pronouns, 175; Reflexive Pronouns,
176; the Present Gerund, 178; Declining
Demonstrative Pronouns, 178
Exercises 179

Lesson 10: Going to the Mountains 183
Dialogue I: Going to the Mountains 184
Dialogue II: At the Mountains 186
New Words 188
Grammar: Past Continuous Tense, 191; Unreal
Conditional Mood,191; -за Construction,
192; аьлла Construction, 192; Declining
Definite and Negative Pronouns, 193
Exercises 194

Lesson 11: A Tour of Grozny 199
Dialogue I: A Tour of Grozny 200
Dialogue II: Grozny—At the Mosque 202
New Words 204
Grammar: Participles, 206; Word-building: Nouns, 208
Exercises 209

Lesson 12: Excerpts from Chechen Literature 213
Poetry 214
New Words 214
Newspaper Article Excerpt 215
New Words 216
Grammar: Verb Conjugation Review 217
Exercises 218

Key to Exercises   223
Chechen-English Glossary   240
English-Chechen Glossary   251
Audio Track List   261

 **Audio files available at
www.hippocrenebooks.com**

Долор
INTRODUCTION

About this Course:

This course is designed for speakers of English to learn the basics of the Chechen language. Historically, the only Chechen language learning manuals available to students were in Russian; resources in English on the language were limited to phrasebooks, grammar sketches, and dictionaries. This course endeavors to fill that gap. To do so we have made a few assumptions based on the Chechen learners we have met over the years.

The most important assumption is that students have a *very* basic knowledge of the Cyrillic alphabet. Chechen is written in Cyrillic, but the pronunciation of spoken Chechen differs from the literary standard. Luckily, these differences, with time, are easy to recognize. For the dialogues in the first few lessons, we provide both literary standard Chechen and a transliterated spoken version based on a Latin alphabet created by the linguist Johanna Nichols.

Second, most students interested in Chechen are either linguists or life-long language lovers. Chechen is typically not the first foreign language students learn. Thus, we sometimes provide examples from other commonly taught languages—German, Romance languages, or Russian—to help explain grammatical concepts. A basic command of Russian is helpful given the number of loanwords in the language.

That said, anyone can take this course! We have tried to keep all technical vocabulary to a minimum and aim to achieve two goals: speaking as quickly as possible and gaining an overall knowledge of how Chechen works.

More on Chechen:

The Chechen language is spoken by 1.4 million people, most of whom reside in the Chechen Republic of the Russian Federation. That said, there are many speakers outside of Chechnya proper; thousands of Chechens live throughout Russia and there are sizable populations of Chechens living in Europe. Chechens also continue to live in Kazakhstan and Kyrgyzstan, ever since Stalin deported the nation in 1944. In the Middle East, especially Jordan and Turkey, the descendants of Chechen refugees from Russia's 19th-century conquest of the Caucasus still speak a distinct dialect.

Chechen—along with closely related Ingush, and more distantly related Bats—form the Nakh branch of the Northeast Caucasian language family (Nakh-Dagestani). Northeast Caucasian is one of three indigenous language families in the Caucasus. The other two are Northwest Caucasian (e.g. Kabardian, Adyghe, Abkhaz) and Kartvelian (Georgian, Mingrelian, Svan, and Laz). Most linguists agree that the Nakh-Dagestani and Kartvelian language families are unrelated to each other, and convincing evidence of a shared ancestry for Northeast and Northwest Caucasian has proven elusive.[1]

Chechen has many dialects that fit broadly into two groups: lowland speech and highland speech. The literary standard is based on the lowland dialects in and around Grozny, the capital city of the Chechen Republic. Many Chechens consider the highland dialects—with less vowels in their phonetic inventory, and less Russian and Turkic loanwords—a "purer" form of the language.[2] In the Republic of Georgia's Pankisi Gorge, less than 10,000 Kists speak a Chechen dialect that requires a few days of practice for lowland speakers to understand.[3]

Chechens and Ingush, though they speak mutually unintelligible languages, form a single speech community, *Vainakh* (lit. *our people*). Despite their differences, many Chechens and Ingush have a passive understanding of the other's language.

[1] Greppin, John A. C, and Alice C Harris. *The Indigenous Languages of the Caucasus.* Delmar, N.Y: Caravan Books, 1991.

[2] https://slaviccenters.duke.edu/sites/slaviccenters.duke.edu/files/file-attachments/chechen-grammar.original.pdf

[3] Jaimoukha, Amjad M. *The Chechens : a Handbook.* New York: RoutledgeCurzon, 2004.

The first script for Chechen came with the spread of Islam. Sufi sheikhs used the Arabic script for their manuscripts on philosophy and jurisprudence in the early 18th century.[4] At the time, the various Chechen dialects were simply the language of the village. Arabic was the language of religion and Kumyk—a Turkic idiom—the language of inter-ethnic communication.[5]

With the arrival of the Russians to the Caucasus, Qedi Dosov and Baron von Uslar developed a Cyrillic script in 1862. The Soviets initially followed Tsarist-era policies of Russification. But in 1923 an abrupt change in policies brought a Latin-based script.[6] The rise of a fellow Caucasian, Josef Stalin, however, saw a return of Russification policies and Chechen orthography switched back to Cyrillic in 1937.[7]

Following the collapse of the Soviet Union, President Dzhokhar Dudaev, as part of his nationalist bid for an independent Chechnya, promoted a new Latin script. Independence and a Latin script were short-lived and Cyrillic was restored in 1999.

Some Features of Chechen Grammar:

Chechen has several unique phonetic (how it sounds) and grammatical features that can make it difficult to learn. It is worthwhile, therefore, to give some context to the grammar and phonology that you will find in this book. Of course, if you would prefer to learn it as you go, feel free to skip this section!

Sounds: Chechen has a few sounds that can be difficult for speakers of English. Perhaps the most difficult, at first, will be the *unaspirated* or *ejective* consonants (t', k', p', q', etc.). For example: prepare to make the sound "t." Right before pronouncing it, close your glottis (throat), then "eject" the sound. If you've heard languages like Georgian, Navajo, or Amharic, then you should already be familiar. If not, no worries. The accompanying audio will provide plenty of practice.

Sentence Structure: Chechen sentence structure, or syntax, centers on the verb. The most important aspect of the Chechen verb is whether it is

---

[4] Ibid.
[5] Ibid..
[6] Ibid.
[7] Ibid.

transitive or intransitive. You may remember from middle school English classes that a transitive verb takes a direct object. Thus:

John	walks	the dog.
subject	*verb*	*direct object*

An intransitive verb does not take a direct object:

The dog	walks	in	the park.
subject	*verb*	*preposition*	*object of preposition*

Noun Cases: Chechen has eight cases. A noun's case is a way of indicating its relationship to other parts of the sentence. Chechen cases include the Absolutive (Nominative), Genitive, Dative, Ergative, Instrumental, Substantive, Comparative, and Allative/Locative (which we will treat as one "case"). In addition, there are several more "cases" that behave more like postpositions (a preposition comes before the noun, a postposition after). Many of these cases function similarly to their counterparts in other languages, so we will focus on the two most important for our current purposes: Chechen's Absolutive and Ergative cases.

English is an Indo-European language, related to languages as diverse as Russian, Spanish, Hindi, Greek, and Armenian. Many of these languages retain a case system, which would be familiar to anyone who has studied Ancient Greek, Latin, Russian, or German.

English cases were lost centuries ago, so now English speakers can only tell whether a noun is the subject, direct object, or indirect object by its place within the sentence (word order). In other Indo-European languages, word order is freer because the case of the noun tells us whether it is a subject (Nominative), direct object (Accusative), indirect object (Dative), belongs to something (often Genitive), in a location (Locative or Prepositional), or with or by means of something (Instrumental).

In these languages, the Nominative case is often unmarked, i.e., it does not take an ending (we will use '*0*' to describe 'unmarkedness' here). Let's look at the above example, but in Russian:

John (*0*)	vygulyvaet	sobak-u.
John (*Nom.*)	walk (*3Pres.*)	dog (*Acc.*)
John	walks	the dog.

And intransitive:

Sobak-a	gulaet	v	park-e̲.
Dog (*Nom.*)	walk (*3Pres.*)	in	park (*Loc.*)
The dog	walks	in	the park.

What did we notice? The case ending for the dog (*sobaka*) lets us know when it is the subject (Nominative: *sobaka̲*) or the direct object (Accusative: *sobaku̲*).

Chechen has a case system, but it differs from Russian in how it marks subject and object. Rather than mark the object with a different case—i.e., *sobaka* vs. *sobaku*—Chechen marks the subject in a different case, leaving the object alone. Linguists call this phenomenon ergativity, and believe it or not, it is quite a common feature in the languages of the world. Let's look first at the intransitive in Chechen:

Zhwala (*0*)	d.oedu	park-ehw.
Dog (*Abs.*)	walk (*Pres.*)	park (*Loc.*)
The dog	walks	in the park.

K'ant (*0*)	v.oedu	park-ehw.
Boy (*Abs.*)	walk (*Pres.*)	park (*Loc.*)
The boy	walks	in the park.

But:

K'ant-a	leel-d.o	zhwala (*0*).
Boy (*Erg.*)	walk (*Pres.*) (*lit.* 'makes walk')	dog (*Abs.*)
The boy	walks	the dog.

Instead of the dog taking a case ending, it stays in the Absolutive, and the subject (the boy) takes a new case ending, the Ergative case. Sometimes Chechen textbooks will use the term "Nominative" for the Absolutive case. The term "nominative" comes from classical grammars, and is fitting for describing many languages, but awkward for Chechen. Many linguists, therefore, prefer to describe the default case of the noun—i.e., the form that is unmarked—as the "Absolutive case," which we will do going forward.

Noun classes: You probably noticed above that the word "walks" changed from *d.oedu* to *v.oedu* when the subject switched from "dog" to "boy." This is the other important feature of Chechen: noun classes. Chechen has six noun classes. Only the first two—considered the human class—function similarly to Indo-European gender. Here are all six below. They are frequently listed using the present tense form of "to be."

	Human class		Other things			
	Masc. (I)	*Fem. (II)*	*III*	*IV*	*V*	*VI*
sing.	vu *is*	ju *is*	du *is*	ju *is*	bu *is*	bu *is*
pl.	bu *are*	bu *are*	du *are*	ju *are*	bu *are*	du *are*

About 30 percent of Chechen verbs agree with noun class.[8] Since "boy" is masculine and singular, "the boy walks" becomes "*k'ant v.oedu.*" "Dog" belongs to the fourth class of nouns; "the dog walks" therefore is "*zhwala d.oedu.*" Now let's look at these two sentences:

K'ant-<u>a</u>	leel-**d**.o	zhwala (*0*)
Boy (*Erg.*)	walk (*Pres.*) (*lit.* 'makes walk')	dog (*Abs.*)
The boy	walks	the dog.

Zhwal-<u>o</u>	leel-**v**.o	k'ant-<u>0</u>
Dog (*Erg.*)	walk (*Pres.*) (*lit.* 'makes walk')	dog (*Abs.*)
The dog	walks	the boy.

What happened? The verb in Chechen will always agree with the Absolutive case, the unmarked noun. It does not matter if the noun in the Absolutive case is the subject (of an intransitive verb) or the object (of a transitive verb).

---

[8] Nichols, Johanna, and A. D Vagapov. *Chechen-English and English-Chechen Dictionary*. London: RoutledgeCurzon, 2004.

Given these features of Chechen, to build sentences effectively you need a certain amount of information about both nouns and verbs. In our vocabulary section we provide the singular and plural forms of each noun, as well as its noun class. For verbs, we've borrowed a tool from Ancient Greek textbooks, the concept of principal parts of the verb. The principal parts of a verb are the key verb forms, or verb stems, from which other forms can be derived. For Chechen, we classify the infinitive, present stem, recent past stem, and present perfect as the principal parts of the verb. We will introduce these principal parts throughout the beginning of the textbook, then provide all four for each new verb thereafter.

Now you understand the three important features of Chechen and how they interact. Chechen verbs form the basis of sentence structure and determine which case the nouns will take. In turn, verbs (and adjectives) will often reflect which class the noun belongs to. Chechen grammar is the relationship between verb, case, and class.

You're not expected to learn all these complexities of Chechen right away. Rather, this section is only meant to give you a bit of an overview, so that when something unfamiliar pops up, you'll be ready with the big picture.

There's good news though: if you can understand these three concepts in Chechen grammar, then you are already more than halfway to learning this fascinating language!

 **PRONUNCIATION**

The Chechen Alphabet

Listen to the accompanying audio for each letter. Vowels can be both short (one syllable) and long (two syllables). Consonants can be both single and double.

Cyrillic	Cursive Cyrillic	Translit	English Equivalent	Notes
A a	*A a*	A a	c<u>ar</u>	
Аь аь	*Аь аь*	Ae ae		Similar to German ä in Mädchen
Б б	*Б б*	B b	<u>b</u>ad	
В в	*В в*	V v	<u>v</u>et *or* <u>w</u>olf	
Г г	*Г г*	G g	<u>g</u>arden	
ГӀ гӀ	*ГӀ гӀ*	Gh gh		French <u>r</u>ecommender German <u>r</u>ot
Д д	*Д д*	D d	<u>d</u>ad	
Е е	*Е е*	Je je	<u>y</u>es	
Ё ё	*Ё ё*	Jo jo	<u>yo</u>!	Same as Russian ё. This letter exists only in words that are borrowed from Russian
Ж ж	*Ж ж*	Zh zh	monta<u>ge</u>	Same as Russian ж
З з	*З з*	Z z	<u>z</u>oo	
И и	*И и*	I i	b<u>ee</u>	
Й й	*Й й*	J j	New <u>Y</u>ork	
К к	*К к*	K k	coo<u>k</u>	

Кх кх	*Кх кх*	Q q		к but further back in your throat. Similar to Arabic q in Quran
КІ кІ	*КІ кІ*	K' k'		See "ejectives" page 11
Къ къ	*Къ къ*	Q' q'		See page 11
Л л	*Л л*	L l	<u>l</u>emon	
М м	*М м*	M m	<u>m</u>other	
Н н	*Н н*	N n	<u>n</u>ice	
О о	*О о*	O o	<u>o</u>range	
Оь оь	*Оь оь*	Oe oe	b<u>ur</u>n	Similar to German ö in mögen
П п	*П п*	P p	<u>p</u>enny	
ПІ пІ	*ПІ пІ*	P' p'		See page 12
Р р	*Р р*	R r		Similar to Russian p in работа or Spanish <u>r</u>adio
С с	*С с*	S s	<u>s</u>port	
Т т	*Т т*	T t	<u>t</u>ime	
ТІ тІ	*ТІ тІ*	T' t'		See page 11
У у	*У у*	U u	m<u>oo</u>n	
Уь уь	*Уь уь*	Y y	m<u>u</u>te	
Ф ф	*Ф ф*	F f	<u>f</u>ile	Only in loanwords
Х х	*Х х*	X x	Scottish lo<u>ch</u>	Same as Russian x
Хь хь	*Хь хь*	Hw hw		Similar to Arabic ح
ХІ хІ	*ХІ хІ*	H h	<u>h</u>i	
Ц ц	*Ц ц*	C c	oven mit<u>ts</u>	Same as Russian ц

Цl цl	*Цl цl*	C' c'		See next page
Ч ч	*Ч ч*	Ch ch	<u>Ch</u>echen	
Чl чl	*Чl чl*	Ch' ch'		See next page
Ш ш	*Ш ш*	Sh sh	<u>sh</u>e	
Щ щ	*Щ щ*	Sch sch		Only found in Russian loanwords
Ъ	*Ъ*			Shwa that sounds like "a" in English "compass"
ы	*ы*		-	Only found in Russian loanwords
ь	*ь*			Same as Russian ь
Э э	*Э э*		p<u>e</u>t	Same as Russian э
Ю ю	*Ю ю*		<u>u</u>se	Same as Russian ю No longer in use
Юь юь	*Юь юь*		m<u>u</u>te	No longer in use
Я я	*Я я*			No longer in use
Яь яь	*Яь яь*			No longer in use
l	*l*	W w		See next page

Diphthongs

A diphthong is formed from two vowels pronounced together. Listen to the accompanying audio and practice each diphthong. Diphthongs can also be short or long.

Vowel	English Equivalent	Example
аь	<u>ai</u>r	аьтто
оь	b<u>ur</u>n	оьпа
ов	b<u>ow</u>l	ловзу
ой	<u>oi</u>l	ойла
уь	m<u>u</u>te	уьстагl

ей	<u>a</u>te	дейтта
ев	n<u>o</u> (*British accent*)	девзу
ай	d<u>ie</u>	дай

Difficult Consonants

The following consonants are unfamiliar to English speakers. Perhaps the most difficult to pronounce are the ejective consonants. To form an ejective, put your tongue and lips in position to pronounce the consonant as you would in English, but keep your throat closed. Then push the consonant through. This will give the consonant a small "pop." Listen to the accompanying audio and practice each sound and example.

Consonant	Notes	Example
ТӀ тӀ	Place your tongue as if you are going to say "t" but hold the air in your throat, then push the air out	ТӀам, тӀо
КӀ кӀ	Place your tongue as if you are going to say "k" but hold the air in your throat, then push the air out	КӀеза, кӀант
Кх кх	Equivalent to the sound found in Arabic (ق). Like a "k" but further back in your throat	Кхокха, токхе
Къ къ	The ejective form of кх. Same sound as Georgian ყ	Къолам, мукъам
Ӏ Ӏ	Equivalent to Arabic (ع).	Ӏалам, воӀ
ЧӀ чӀ	Place your lips and tongue as if you are going to say "ch" but hold the air in your throat, then push the air out. Equivalent to Georgian ჭ	ЧӀара, чӀаба
ЦӀ цӀ	Place your lips and tongue as if you are going to say "ts" but hold the air in your throat, then push the air out. Equivalent to Georgian წ	ЦӀазам, муцӀар

| Пl пl | Place your lips and tongue as if you are going to say "p" but hold the air in your throat, then push the air out. Equivalent to Georgian ვ | Пелг, плендар |

Корта I: Схьакхачар
Lesson 1: Arrival

Knowledge Check: In the following lessons this paragraph will review what we have previously learned.

Lesson Plan:
- Noun classes
- Chechen pronouns
- The question particle -й
- Greetings

ДИАЛОГ I: Сольжа – ГӀалан Аэропортехь

Таможенник:	Ваш паспорт, пожалуйста.
Джон:	Де дика хуьлда!
Таможенник:	Далла везийла, хьо нохчи вуй?
Джон:	ХӀан-хӀа, со нохчи вац. ХӀара сан паспорт ду.
Таможенник:	Мичара ву хьо?
Джон:	Америкера ву со, американец ву.
Таможенник:	Хьан цӀе хӀун йу?
Джон:	Сан цӀе Джон йу.
Таможенник:	Сан цӀе Шамиль йу. Хьо Америкера дуьйна кхуза веана?
Джон:	Веана. Со студент ву. Со нохчийн мотт Ӏамош ву.
Таможенник:	Дика ду. ХӀара хьан паспорт ду. Марша вогӀийла!
Джон:	Баркалла.

♦♦♦

Tamozhennik:	Vash pasport, pazhaluista.
Djon:	De dikə xyl!
Tamozhenik:	Dal veziil, hwo noxchi vui?
Djon:	haa~-haa~, so noxchi vac. Harə sa~ passport du.
Tamozhenik:	Michar vu hwo?
Djon:	Ameriker vu so, amerikanec vu.
Tamozhenik:	Hwa~ c'e hu~ ju?
Djon:	Sa~ c'e Djon ju.
Tamozhenik:	Sa~ c'e Shamil ju. Hwo Ameriker dyyna quzə veana?
Djon:	Veana. So student vu. So noxchi mott wamosh vu.
Tamozhenik:	Dikə du. Harə hwa~ pasport du. Marsh voghiil!
Djon :	Barkall.

DIALOGUE I: AT THE GROZNY AIRPORT

John, an American tourist, studies Chechen. He has just arrived at Grozny Airport and approaches the customs official.

Customs official:	*(In Russian)* Your passport, please.
John:	*(In Chechen)* Hello!
Customs official:	Hello, are you Chechen?
John:	No, I am not a Chechen. Here is my passport.
Customs official:	Where are you from?
John:	I am from America, I am an American.
Customs official:	What is your name?
John:	My name is John.
Customs official:	My name is Shamil. Why are you here? *(lit. How did you come here?)*
John:	I am a student. I am learning the Chechen language.
Customs official:	OK. Here is your passport. Welcome!
John:	Thank you.

Керла Дешнаш / NEW WORDS

де, денош (д:д) day
дика good
де дика хуьлда! hello!
хьо (хьан) you (your)
со (сан) I (my)
хӀара this
паспорт, паспорташ (д:д) passport
хӀун? what?
нохчи (в:й) Chechen *(noun)*
цӀе, цӀераш (й:й) name
мичара where (from)
американец, американцеш
  (д:д) American
америкера from America

деш doing
студент, студенташ (в:б) student
мотт, меттанаш (б:д) language
доьшуш studying
маршо, маршонаш (й:й) freedom
марша вогӀийла welcome
баркалла thank you
кхуза here
муха how
кхаьчна came *(past tense of "to come")*
хӀан-хӀа no
хӀаъ yes

🎧 2 ДИАЛОГ II

Джон: Хьава! Суьйре дика хуьлда хьан! Муха йу хьо?
Хьава: Далла везийла! Со дика йу. Хьан гӀуллакхаш муха ду?
Джон: Сан гӀуллакхаш дика ду, амма кӀадвелла со.
Хьава: ХӀара сан да ву. Цуьнан цӀе Ӏарби йу.
Джон: Салам Ӏалейкум!
Ӏарби: ВалӀалейкум ассалам. Марша воглийла!

◆◆◆

Djon: Hwava! Syyrie dikə xyld hwa~! Muux ju hwo?
Hwava: Dal veziil! So dikə ju. Hwa~ ghullqsh muux du?
Djon: Sa~ ghullqsh dikə du, amma k'aadvell so.
Hwava: Harə sa~ daa vu. Cyna~ c'e Warbi ju.
Djon: Salam waleikum.
Warbi: Vawaleikum assalam. Marsh voghiil!

DIALOGUE II: Meeting a Friend

John passes through customs, and sees his Chechen friend, Hwava, there to meet him...

John: Hwava! Hello! How are you?

Hwava: Hi! I am good. How are you?

John: I am well, but tired.

Hwava: This is my father. His name is Arbi.

John: Hello!

Arbi: Hello. Welcome!

Керла Дешнаш / New Words

Салам Ӏалейкум! Hello!
ВаӀалейкум ассалам *response to* Салам Ӏалейкум!
гӀуллакх, гӀуллакхаш (д:д) affair (*business*)
амма but
кӀадв.елла / кӀадй.елла tired (*masculine / feminine*)
да, дай (в:б) father, fathers
цуьнан his/her/its

Граматика / Grammar

Noun Classes

One of the most notable features of Chechen grammar is the presence of noun classes. Depending on how one counts, Chechen nouns can be grouped into either four or six noun classes. Only the first class for humans corresponds to gender, as found in more familiar Indo-European languages.

Unfortunately, there is no way to determine the class of a Chechen noun by its appearance. Rather, Chechen noun class is marked by verb and adjective agreement. The verbs that agree in class are a minority (roughly 30 percent); and only a small group of adjectives agree with the nouns they describe. You have already encountered a few of these verbs and adjectives in the above dialogue (кладв.елла / кладйе.лла; ду / йу).

The initial consonant of the Present tense form of the verb '*to be*' (**д.у**) marks a noun's class. Chechen grammarians use the Present tense form of '*to be*' (in Chechen grammar also referred to as a copular verb) to denote the noun classes. We will group Chechen nouns into six classes: two for humans and four for all other nouns. Let's start with the class for humans.

	Human classes (адамийн классаш)	
singular	ву	йу
plural	бу	бу

The human class functions like gender in other European languages. Nouns and pronouns that refer to human male gender are marked with "**ву**"; and nouns and pronouns that refer to human female gender are marked with "**йу**" in the singular.

The male class (**ву**) is used for male pronouns and nouns that are naturally male:

Со ву.	*I am*. (male speaker)
Кlант дика ву.	*The boy is good.*
Ваша дика ву.	*The brother is good.*

бу marks both plural and the third person plural pronoun *they*:

Кlентий дика бу.	*The boys are good.*
Уьш дика бу.	*They are good.*

The female class (**йу**) is used for female pronouns and nouns naturally female:

Со йу.	*I am*. (female speaker)
Йоl дика йу.	*The girl is good.*
Хьо дика йу.	*You* (female) *are good.*

As in the male class, **бу** marks both plural and the third person plural pronoun *they*:

Йоларий дика бу.	*The girls are good.*

Agreement gets a bit more complicated when we look at professions and relationships, as nouns are marked according to the gender of the person referenced:

Иза лор йу.	*She is a doctor.*
Иза лор ву.	*He is a doctor.*
Хlара сан доттагl йу.	*This is my girlfriend.*
Хlара сан доттагl ву.	*This is my friend.*
Хlара сан шич ву.	*This is my* (male) *cousin.*
Хlара сан шич йу.	*This is my* (female) *cousin.*

The following four classes do not correspond to any phonetic or tangible quality (i.e., shape, size, countability, etc.).

	Class III	Class IV	Class V	Class VI
singular	ду	йу	бу	бу
plural	ду	йу	бу	ду

These other four noun classes can be confusing but remember that noun classes don't necessarily describe the noun itself. If this is intimidating, do not worry. Everyone (including Chechens) gets agreement wrong sometimes, and Chechens will absolutely understand you even if you use the wrong noun class!

Class	Singular	Plural	Translation
III	гlуллакх (ду)	гlуллакхаш (ду)	*affair, affairs* (business)
IV	суьйре (йу)	суьйренаш (йу)	*evening, evenings*
V	толам (бу)	толамаш (бу)	*victory, victories*
VI	болх (бу)	белхаш (ду)	*job (or work), jobs*

Note: In this book, all nouns in the vocabulary section and glossary will include the noun's class written as: Class 1 (в:б), Class 2 (й:б), Class 3 (д:д), Class 4 (й:й), Class 5 (б:б), Class 6 (б:д). Memorizing the classes at the beginning will help you as you form sentences later.

Chechen Pronouns

Chechen pronouns have noun classes just like nouns. Which noun class the pronoun will take depends on which noun the pronoun represents. Take a look at this table to see all possible noun classes for pronouns.

English (sing.)	Chechen	English (pl.)	Chechen
I	со ву/йу	*we*	тхо ду (*exclusive*) вай ду (*inclusive*)
you	хьо ву/йу	*you*	шу ду
he/she/it	и / иза ву/йу/бу/ду	*they*	уьш бу/ду/йу

As you can see from the above, Chechen pronouns are slightly different from English. Where English differentiates gender in the third person singular (he/she), Chechen does not.

But Chechen does differentiate the first-person plural *we*. There are two ways to say *we* in Chechen:

Тхо ду   *We are* (exclusive)
Вай ду   *We are* (inclusive)

Which one you choose depends on whether you want to include the listener(s) when saying *we*. If you want to talk about yourself and others (but not the listener), you should use **тхо**. You should use **вай** if you want to include the listener as well. For example:

Тхо болх беш ду.   *We* (excluding you) *are working.*
Вай болх беш ду.   *We* (including you) *are working.*

Тхо туькана доьлхуш ду.   *We are going to the store (but you're not).*
Вай туькана доьлхуш ду.   *We are going to the store (and you're coming).*

This can be confusing at first. One trick for choosing between **тхо** or **вай** is to remember the word for the Chechen and Ingush combined nation: **вайнах**. Вайнах translates to "our people." The term <u>includes</u> both Chechens and Ingush, therefore **вай** must be <u>inclusive</u>.

Luckily, compared to *"we"* saying *"you all"* (plural) in Chechen is quite easy: it's just **шу**, which takes **ду**. If you've studied other languages before, you're probably wondering whether **шу** (2nd person plural) is also the polite form of **хьо** (2nd person singular). The answer is no. You use **хьо** when you're talking to one person, it does not matter if they are a small child or village elder (воккха/йоккха стаг).

Finally, we come to *"they,"* or in Chechen **уьш**. Уьш is a run-of-the-mill pronoun, just like the English *"they."* It takes **бу** when speaking about human beings:

Уьш болх беш **бу**.	***They*** *are working.*
Уьш дика **бу**.	***They*** *are good.*

But now look at these two sentences:

Сан йиша-ваша дика **ду**.	*My siblings are nice (good).*
Сан йиша-ваша дика **бу**.	*My siblings are nice (good).*

What's the difference? None. Both work. Some Chechens may prefer to say **бу** since *"siblings"* could be replaced by *"they."* Others say **ду**, the more common plural form.

The Question Particle -й

You've probably already noticed a difference between **ву/йу/ду** above, and this sentence in the first dialogue:

Далла везийла, хьо нохчи ву**й**?

This suffix **-й** added to the verb makes a statement a question:

Хьо нохчи ву.	*You are Chechen.*
Хьо нохчи **вуй**?	*Are you Chechen?*
Иза лор йу.	*She is a doctor.*
Иза лор **йуй**?	*Is she a doctor?*

This suffix **-й** is not required when a sentence already includes a question word. The following are the most important question words (хаттаран дешнаш) in Chechen:

Х1ун?	What?
Маца?	When?
Мича?/Мичахь?	To where?/Where?
Мила?	Who?
Муха?	How?
Мел?	How much?
Маса?	How many?

Культура / CULTURE

Chechen Greetings

In Chechen culture greetings are an important part of tradition. How you greet someone depends on your relation to that person, and if they are male or female.

Men usually greet each other with "**Assalamu Alaikum.**" More and more women also use the greeting, both with each other and with a man. In informal settings between friends, the Russian *privet* is common. In formal settings you will encounter the following:

I уьйре дика хуьлда хьан!
Good morning! (lit. *May have you a good morning!*)

Де дика хуьлда хьан!
Good afternoon! (lit. *May you have a good day!*)

Суьйре дика хуьлда хьан!
Good evening! (lit. *May have you a good evening!*)

Буьйсе дика хуьлда хьан!
Good night! (lit. *May have you a good night!*)

The response is: "Далла везийла/йезийла/дезийла." You will use "Далла везийла" to respond to a male; "Далла йезийла" to a female; and "Далла дезийла" to many people (males and females).

Упражненеш / EXERCISES

Exercise 1: *Translate the following.*

1. Hello! (*to a man*) _____

2. How are you? (*to a woman*) _____

3. Good evening! _____

4. Good morning! _____

5. Good night! _____

6. Good day! _____

7. Hey! (*informal between friends*) _____

8. Are you Chechen? _____

Respond to the following:

1. Ӏуьйре дика хуьлда хьан! _____

2. Де дика хуьлда хьан! _____

3. Суьйре дика хуьлда хьан! _____

4. Буьйсе дика хуьлда хьан! _____

Exercise 2: *Fill in the blanks with the proper noun class:* ву/йу/бу/ду.

1. Хӏара сан кӏант _____.

2. Хьан цӏе хӏун _____?

3. Хӏара сан да _____.

4. Хьо муха _____? *(female)*

5. Со Американец _____. *(male)*

6. Хьо Американка_____. *(female)*

7. Сан гӏуллакхаш дика _____.

8. Хьо мила _____? *(male)*

Exercise 3: *Fill in the blanks of the dialogue with the phrases you have learned.*

Джон: Хьава! Суьйре дика хуьлда хьан! Муха йу хьо?

Хьава: _____. Хьан гӀуллакхаш муха ду?

Джон: Сан гӀуллакхаш дика ду, амма кӀадвелла.

Хьава: _____. Цуьнан цӀе Ӏарби йу.

Exercise 4: *Translate the following into Chechen using the vocabulary from this lesson.*

1. She is a doctor. _____

2. My brother is a student. _____

3. My friend (*female*) is a good doctor (лор). _____

   _____

4. She is from America._____

5. The doctor (*male*) is from America. _____

6. Where are you (*male*) from? _____

7. The boy is tired. _____

8. She is tired. _____

Exercise 5: *Translate the following into Chechen using the inclusive and exclusive forms of "we"* (вай/тхо), *and the singular and plural forms of "you"* (хьо/шу).

1. We (*but not you*) are Chechen. _____

2. We (*including you*) are Chechen. _____

3. You (*singular*) are American (*male or female*). _____

   _____

4. You all are American. _____

5. You (*singular*) are a doctor, but we (*excluding you*) are students.

_____

6. You all are tired. _____

7. We (*excluding you*) are tired. _____

8. We are Chechen, but you are American. _____

_____

Exercise 6: *Translate the following questions into Chechen using the question particle* -й.

1. Are you Chechen? _____

2. Is she a doctor? _____

3. Are we (*inclusive*) students? _____

4. How are the Americans? _____

5. Are you from America? _____

6. Are we (*exclusive*) teachers? _____

7. Is he a Chechen? _____

8. Are they (уьш) Americans? _____

Exercise 7: *Translate the following paragraph into English.*

Де дика хуьлда! Сан цIе Аслан йу. Со студент ву. Со Америкера ву, амма нохчи ву. Сан да лор ву. Сан нана хьехархо (*teacher*) йу. Уьш нохчий бу. Сан йиша-ваша студенташ бу. Тхо студенташ ду. Хьо нохчи вуй? Хьан йиша-ваша студеташ буй? Хьан да лор вуй? Цуьнан цIе хIун йу? Шу мичара ду?

_____

_____

_____

_____

_____

_____

Exercise 8. *Write a short description of yourself. What is your name? Where are you from? Is there anything else you can say from the words you've learned?*

Корта II: Цахь
Lesson 2: At Home

Knowledge Check: In the following dialogues, underline the nouns and match them with their noun class. Which question words do we already know? What does the -й suffix mean?

Lesson Plan:

- Absolutive case
- Present Progressive tense
- Allative case amd a Locative form (saying "in" or "at")
- Saying "I have," "you have," etc.
- The negative form of д.у "to be"

3   ДИАЛОГ I: Хьаван цӀахь

Хьава: Джон, хӀара сан нана Малика йу.

Джон: Суьйре дика хуьлда хьан, Малика! ХӀун деш ду шу, муха Ӏа шу?

Малика: Марша вогӀийла, Джон! Дика Ӏа тхо-м. Хьо схьа муха кхечира?

Джон: Дика кхечира. Дела реза хуьлда!

Малика: Схьавола, хӀума кхоллар йу вай!

Джон: ХӀаъ!

♦♦♦

Hwava: Djon, harə sa~ naan Malika ju.

Djon: Syyrie dikə xyld hwa~, Malika? Hu~ desh du shu, muux wa shu?

Malika: Maarsh voghiil, Djon! Dikə wa txo-m. Hwo shwa muux qechir?

Djon: Dikə qechir. Deel rez xyld!

Malika: Shwavola, hum qollar ju vai!

Djon: Ha'!

DIALOGUE I: AT HWAVA'S HOME

John is invited to Hwava's home, where he meets the rest of her family.

Hwava: John, this is my mother, Malika.

John: Good evening, Malika! How are you, how are you living?

Malika: Welcome, John! I am fine. How was your trip? *(lit. How did you get here?)*

John: It was ok. *(lit. I got here well.)* Thank you!

Malika: Come in, let's eat!

John: Yes!

Керла Дешнаш / NEW WORDS

нана, наной (й:б) mother
Суьйре дика хуьлда хьан! Good evening!
Хӏун деш ду шу? How are you? (*lit.* What are you doing?)
Муха ӏа шу? How are you living?
Схьавола! Come!
тхо we (*exclusive*)
Хӏум кхоллар йу! Let's eat! (*lit.* We will bite a thing!)
(схьа) кхечира arrived (here)

4   ДИАЛОГ II: Стол тӀехь

Ӏарби:	Хьан да-нана хӀун деш бу, Джон?
Джон:	Дика Ӏаш бу уьш.
Ӏарби:	Маса йиша-ваша ду хьан?
Джон:	Сан цхьаъ йиша йу, цхьаъ ваша ву.
Ӏарби:	Дика ду. Мичахь Ӏаш бу уьш?
Джон:	Сан йиша Санкт-Петербургехь университетехь доьшуш йу. Сан ваша Мериленд штатехь Ӏаш ву. Иза цигахь хьехархо болх беш ву.
Ӏарби:	Уьш нохчийн мотт Ӏамош буй?
Джон:	ХӀан-хӀа. Сан йиша нохчийн мотт Ӏамош яц, амма сан ваша нохчийн мотт Ӏамош ву.

◆◆◆

Warbi:	Hwa~ daa-naan hu~ desh bu, Djon?
Djon:	Dikə wash bu ysh.
Warbi:	Mas jish-vash du hwa~?
Djon:	sa~ chwa' jish ju, chwa' vash vu.
Warbi:	Dikə du. Michahw wash bu ysh?
Djon:	Sa~ jish Sankt-Peterburgehw universitetehw doeshush ju. Sa~ vash Merilend shtatiehw wash vu. Iz cigahw hwexarxo bolx besh vu.
Warbi:	Ysh noxchii~ mott wamosh bui?
Djon:	Ha~ha. Sa~ jish noxchii~ mott wamosh jac, amma sa~ vash noxchii~ mott wamosh vu.

DIALOGUE II: AT THE TABLE

Arbi: What are your parents doing, John?

John: They are fine. (lit. *They are living well.*)

Arbi: How many siblings do you have?

John: I have one sister and one brother.

Arbi: Ok. Where are they living?

John: My sister is studying at St. Petersburg University. My brother is living in Maryland. He is working as a teacher there.

Arbi: Are they learning the Chechen language?

John: No. My sister is not learning Chechen, but my brother is learning Chechen.

Керла Дешнаш / NEW WORDS

да-нана (д) parents (lit. *father-mother*)
йиша, йижарий (й:б) sister
ваша, вежарий (й:б) brother
йиша-ваша (д:б) siblings (lit. *sister-brother*)
цхьаъ one
Іаш living
д.оьшуш studying, reading
Маса? How many?
университет, университеташ (й:й) university
штат, штаташ (й:й) state
цигахь there
хьехархо, хьехархой (в/й:б) teacher
болх б.еш working
Іамош learning

Граматика / Grammar

Absolutive Case

Grammatical case is a way of understanding a noun's relationship to other words in the sentence. Case is often marked as an ending. In English, however, we use strict word order and prepositions (to, with, for, etc.) to help us understand the relationship between a noun and the other parts of the sentence.

We have already met the Absolutive (Nominative) case with words such as мотт, книга, йиша, ваша, etc. This case is *unmarked,* which means that it doesn't have any case endings:

Хlара **книга** йу.
*This is a **book**.*

Кхузахь сан **ваша** ву.
*Here is my **brother**.*

Absolutive Plural

The plural is usually formed by adding the suffix **-ш** or **-аш**. For example:

книга – книга**ш** *(book – books)*
гlуллакх – гlуллакх**аш** *(thing – things)*
паспорт – паспорт**ш** *(passport – passports)*

Many nouns see a vowel shift, the insertion of **-н-**, or both in addition to the suffix **-ш** or **-аш**:

мотт – метта**наш** *(language – languages)*

Several nouns, particularly those that denote a profession or family members, take the ending **-й**:

да – да**й** *(father – fathers)*
нана – нано**й** *(mother – mothers)*
хьехархо – хьехархо**й** *(teacher – teachers)*

And, of course, some nouns are irregular:

Singular	Plural
ча йу (*bear*)	черчий йу (*bears*)
у ду (*board*)	аннаш ду (*boards*)
стаг ву/йу (*person*)	нах бу (*people*)
етт бу (*cow*)	бежнаш ду (*cows*)

As we briefly noted, the switch from singular to plural will often see a vowel shift; and later, we will see that these shifts can also occur when the noun changes cases. This phenomenon is called **ablaut**, and English nouns are not immune: *goose – geese; tooth – teeth; mouse – mice.*

We already provide nouns' plural forms and noun class in the vocabulary section. For now, plural forms should be memorized. With repetition, one can get a sense for when and how vowel shifts will occur.

In the previous lesson, when we introduced noun classes, we showed the singular and plural agreement. Here's the table again:

Class	Singular	Plural	Translation
III	гӀуллакх (ду)	гӀуллакхаш (ду)	*thing, things*
IV	суьйре (йу)	суьйренаш (йу)	*evening, evenings*
V	толам (бу)	толамаш (бу)	*victory, victories*
VI	болх (бу)	белхаш (ду)	*job (work), jobs*

And now, you can perhaps see why we introduced nouns in the New Word lists in the following way: книга, книгаш (й:й).

Using the information given here, how would one say, *here is the book,* or *here are the books*? First you note that книга is Class IV (й:й). Agreement, therefore, will take **йу** in the singular. You can also see that the plural is formed by adding **-ш**, which also takes **йу**. Thus, we can build the following two sentences:

Кхузахь книга **йу**. *Here is a/the book.*

Кхузахь книга**ш** **йу**. *Here are (the) books.*

Present Progressive Tense

In the above dialogues, you have seen several examples of the Present Progressive tense in Chechen.

Иза цигахь хьехархо **болх беш ву**.
*He **is working** there as a teacher. (He works there as a teacher.)*

Хьан да-нана хIун **деш бу**?
*What are your parents **doing**? (How are they?)*

Мичахь **Iаш бу** уьш?
*Where are they **living**? (Where do they live?)*

In Chechen grammar it is very important if a verb is transitive or intransitive. As a refresher: a transitive verb takes a direct object, while an intransitive verb does not—i.e., it only has a subject.

Transitive: I   see   the boy.
              subject verb   direct object

Intransitive: I   walk.
              subject   verb

Chechen distinguishes transitive and intransitive verbs through case and agreement. In the Present Progressive tense, luckily, only agreement is important. Let's start with the transitive verb **Iамо** *"to learn."* In general, the Present Progressive tense is formed with the ending **-ш** plus **ву/ йу/бу/ду** depending on which class the noun belongs to. There are many different patterns for how the verb will change from the infinitive (**Iамо**) to the Present Progressive. But let's start with this example:

Iамо + ш = Iамош
to learn + ш = learning

Now, let's look at the agreement:

Иза нохчийн мотт Iамош **ву**.
***He** is learning the Chechen language.*

Из нохчийн мотт Iамош **йу**.
***She** is learning the Chechen language.*

Уьш нохчийн мотт Іамош **бу**.
They are learning the Chechen language.

As you can see, the copula *"to be"* agrees with the subject. In the first two sentences, the verb is the only marker for gender. In the third example, the copula agrees with *"they."*

Now let's see what happens if a *"baby"* (бер д:д) learns Chechen:

Бер нохчийн мотт Іамош **ду**.
*The **baby** is learning the Chechen language.*

Not every verb is like Іамо. In the dialogue there was another verb that meant *"to study."* Let's take a look again and notice how the participle **йу** agrees with *"sister."*

Сан йиша Санкт-Петербургехь университетехь **доьшуш йу**.
My sister is studying at St. Petersburg University.

Now, let's take a closer look at the verb **д.еша**, *"to study / to read."* First, when we list a verb that takes noun class agreement we put a period after the "д." As mentioned before, not all verbs need to agree in noun class. The Present Progressive form of **д.еша** is **д.оьшуш**, which is formed from the Present tense (we will see this in the next lesson) plus **-ш**. This form is called a gerund, which will come up later in the book. For now, however, let's think of it as part of the Present Progressive tense. Thus, the following forms are possible for *"studying/reading"* in the Present Progressive:

в.оьшуш (an unlikely form)
й.оьшуш
б.оьшуш
д.оьшуш

Here is the tricky part though. The transitive verb must agree with the direct object which will appear in the Absolutive case:

книга йоьшуш   газета доьшуш
reading the book   *reading the newspaper*

The copula, however, agrees with the subject:

Иза книга йоьшуш ву.	*He is reading the book.*
Иза книга йоьшуш йу.	*She is reading the book.*
Вай книга йоьшуш ду.	*We are reading the book.*
Уьш книга йоьшуш бу.	*They are reading the book.*

But what about this sentence?:

Сан йиша Санкт-Петербургехь университетехь **доьшуш йу.**
***My sister** is **studying** at St. Petersburg University.*

"*Studying*" here takes **д** agreement because the default setting for a transitive verb is **д**. That is also why we had the following sentence in the dialogue:

Хьан да-нана хIун деш бу?
What are your parents doing? (How are your parents?)

Here **хIун** "*what*" is unknown, so it takes the default **д.еш**. But for **болх (б)** "*work,*" we get:

Иза хьехархо болх беш ву.
He is working as a teacher. (lit. *He is doing teacher work.*)

Intransitive verbs are simpler, as they will always agree with the subject. Let's take a look at the present continuous form of **лаш** "*to live*":

Со Америкехь лаш ву.
I am living in America.

Иза университетехь лаш йу.
She is living at the university.

Уьш Нохчийчохь лаш бу.
They are living in Chechnya.

Шу гӀалахь лаш ду.
You (all) are living in the city.

Allative Case and a Locative Form

Chechen uses the postposition **-ехь** to show location:

Америк**ехь**	*in America*
Нохчийч**охь**	*in Chechnya*
университет**ехь**	*in university*

As you can see, often where English uses a preposition ("in," "at," etc.), Chechen employs the Locative form. The Locative is built through the Allative case, typically ending in **-е** or **-га**. The Allative describes motion towards an object or place. "**-хь**" describes the location, typically translated as "in" or "at":

университет	университет**е**	университет**ехь**
university	*to the university*	*at the university*

For now, when you are saying you are in a city or country, add the Allative "**-е**" then the Locative form "**-хь**." If the city or country already ends with a vowel, just add "**-хь**."

The Locative form also appears in important question words and adverbs: ци-га-хь "*in*" or "*at*" there:

Мича-хь Iаш бу уьш?
Where-at do they live?

Saying "I have," "you have" etc.

You've seen all the pronouns and their agreements, as well as how to say "*my*" and "*your*." This means you already know how to say, "*I have*" and "*you have*" in Chechen. Let's look at the following sentences:

Со кIант ву. **Сан** ийша **йу**.	*I am a boy. I have a sister.*
Сан пасспорт **ду**.	*I have a passport.*
Хьаван ахча **ду**.	*Hwava has money.*

To say *I have x*, Chechens use the phrase: *my x is/are*. In the first sentence, the speaker is male (as indicated by the **ву**). The speaker says he has a sister, which takes **йу**. Note that the copula "*to be*" agrees not with the subject or speaker, but with the noun that is possessed.

The Negative of д.у "to be"

To recap, here is **д.у** for all noun classes:

	Human classes (адамийн классаш)		Other things (кхийолу хӏуманийн классаш)			
	I	II	III	IV	V	VI
singular	ву	йу	ду	йу	бу	бу
plural	бу	бу	ду	йу	бу	ду

In English we use "*not*" to negate the verb "*to be*." For example:

I am a doctor.   I am *not* a doctor.

In Chechen, the negative form of "*to be*" in the Present tense retains the noun class agreement and replaces -**у** with -**ац**:

Со лор **ву**. *I'm a* (male) *doctor.*
Со лор **вац**. *I'm not a* (male) *doctor.*

	Human classes (адамийн классаш)		Other things (кхийолу хӏуманийн классаш)			
	I	II	III	IV	V	VI
singular	вац	йац	дац	йац	бац	бац
plural	бац	бац	дац	йац	бац	дац

Let's look at some examples:

Иза студент йу. Со студент **вац**. *She is a student. I am not a student.*
Уьш дика **бац**. *They are not good.*
Сан йиша **йац**. *I don't have a sister.*
Хӏара сан паспорт **дац**. *This isn't my passport.*

Культура / Culture

As a Guest in a Chechen Home

Chechen society and culture are still very traditional. Upon entering a house, a guest will typically greet the host who opens the door saying "Ассаламу алайкум" *("Salam aleikum")* if the person is male, and "Де дика хуьлда шун" (*"Good afternoon")* if she is female. Once the guest steps in he may add, "ХӀун деш ду шу?" (*"How are you?"*) which refers to the whole family.

Make sure to always remove your shoes when entering a Chechen household! Chechens are very tidy and will have slippers (кӀархаш) for you to wear. In our dialogue, after a short chat about family, Malika invites John to the dining room. Chechens will always have food prepared for guests. Traditionally, the male host (хӀусамда) will sit at the table and talk, while women usually bring in the dishes such as pie (чепалгаш).

If the guest is the family's relative then the women will often sit at the dinner table as well. The culture of hospitality (хьошалла) is famous throughout the Caucasus. Chechens show a guest respect by inviting them into their personal lives and displaying trust right away.

Упражненеш / Exercises

Exercise 1. *Fill in the blanks using words from word bank.*

нохчийн мотт	цӀе	студент	йу	нана	да	йиша

Сан _____ Джон йу. Со _____ ламош ву.
Со _____ ву.

Хьава студентка _____. Малика цуьнан _____ йу.
ІарбИ Хьаван _____ ву.

Exercise 2. *Translate the following sentences into English.*

1. Со хьехархо ву._____

2. Хьо студент ву._____

3. Хьава йоӏ йу._____

4. Джон кӏант ву._____

5. Ӏарби да ву._____

6. Малика нана йу._____

7. И/иза лор ву._____

8. Тхо туристаш ду._____

Exercise 3. *Read the dialogue below and answer the following two questions in Chechen.*

Ӏарби: Хьан да-нана хӏун деш бу, Джон?

Джон: Дика Ӏаш бу уьш.

Ӏарби: Маса йиша-ваша ду хьан?

Джон: Сан цхьаъ йиша йу, цхьа ваша ву.

How are John's parents doing?

_____

How many siblings does John have?

_____

Exercise 4. *Fill in the blanks using the correct noun class.*

1. Джон турист _____.

2. Хьава студентка_____.

3. Малика лор _____ .

4. Шаӏрани профессор _____.

5. Тхо хьехархой _____.

6. Йижарий кхузахь_____.

7. Йиша-ваша университетехь_____.

8. Уьш йаздархой _____.

Exercise 5. *Translate the following sentences into Chechen.*

1. This is my sister.

   _____

2. This is not my brother.

   _____

3. This is not my mother.

   _____

4. This is my father.

   _____

5. I (*male*) am not at the university.

   _____

6. You (*female*) are at school.

   _____

7. We (*exclusive*) are at the airport.

   _____

8. We (*inclusive*) are at the library.

   _____

Exercise 6: *Translate the following text into English:*

Сан цӏе Скайлер йу. Со Вашингтон штатехь ӏаш йу. Со нохчи йац, амма со нохчийн мотт буьйцуш йу. Со ингалс меттан хьехархо йу. Аса ишколехь хьоьху. Сан дешархой дика бу. Тхан ишкола гӏалахь йу. Сан йиша Нохчичохь ӏаш йу.

   _____

   _____

   _____

_____

_____

_____

Exercise 7: *Write a few sentences using profession words.*

   Example: Сан да хьехархо ву. *(My father is a teacher.)*

Корта III:
Университете вахар
Lesson 3:
Going to University

Knowledge Check: In the dialogues in this lesson, underline the nouns and match them with the noun class. Can you find an example of saying "*to have*"? Which nouns and question words are in the Locative case? Which verbs are in the Present Progressive?

Lesson Plan:
- Genitive case
- Personal Pronouns: Adding the Ergative and Dative
- The Present tense
- Adverbs
- Months of the Year

5 **ДИАЛОГ I: Хьаван цӀахь**

Хьава: Джон, тахана хьо хӀун деш ву?

Джон: Тахана со университете воьдуш ву.

Хьава: Университете хӀунда воьдуш ву хьо?

Джон: ХӀунда аьлча ас нохчийн мотт Ӏамабо, ткъа цигахь нохчийн меттан урокаш йу сан. Аса оьрсийн а, ингалсан а меттанаш дуьйцу, ас нохчийн маттахь доьшу.

Хьава: А-а, оьрсийн мотт а буьйцу ахьа?

Джон: ХӀаъ, суна дика оьрсийн мотт а бийца хаьа, ткъа цӀахь ох ингалсан мотт бен ца буьйцу.

Хьава: Ахь оьрсийн маттахь йаздо?

Джон: ХӀан-ХӀа, аса оьрсийн маттахь ца йаздо.

◆◆◆

Hwava: Djon, taxan hwo hu~ desh vu?

Djon: Taxan so universitete voedsh vu.

Hwava: Universitiete hunda voedsh vu hwo?

Djon: Hunda aelch as noxhiin mott wamobo, tq'a cigahw noxchii~ metta~ uroksh ju sa~. As oersiin mottii, ingalsiin mott byyc, amma as noxchii~ mattahw doesh.

Hwava: A-a, oersiin mott a byycu ahw?

Djon: Ha', suun dik oersiin mott biica a xae'a, tq'a oxa ingalsa~ mott be~ ca byyc ts'ahw.

Hwava: Ahw oersiin mattahw jazdo?

Djon: Ha~-ha, aas oersiin mattahw ca jazdo.

DIALOGUE I: AT HWAVA'S HOUSE

Hwava: John, what are you doing today?

John: Today I am going to the university.

Hwava: Why are you going to the university?

John: Because I learn Chechen and I have Chechen classes over there. I speak Russian and English, but I am studying Chechen.

Hwava: Oh, do you speak Russian as well?

John: Yes. I speak Russian very well, but we (my family) only speak English at home.

Hwava: Do you write in Russian?

John: No, I don't write in Russian.

Керла Дешнаш / NEW WORDS

тахана today
хӏунда why
хӏунда аьлча because (*lit:* to say why)
бен ца only
ткъа and, but
урок, урокаш (й:й) class
оьрсийн мотт (б) Russian
ингалсан мотт (б) English
ца not
д.ан to do **(д.о; д.еш)**
д.еша to read **(д.оьшу; д.оьшуш)**
д.ийца to speak **(д.уьйцу; д.уьйцуш)**
д.аха to go **(д.оьду; д.оьдуш)**
йазд.ан to write **(йазд.о; йазд.еш)**
хаа to know **(хаьа; хууш)**

ДИАЛОГ II: Телефон чухула

Джон:	Алло. Де дика хуьлда хьан, Шалрани!
Шалрани:	Далла везийла, Джон. Муха ду хьан гlуллакхаш?
Джон:	Дика ду. Хьо тахана мичахь ву?
Шалрани:	Со тахана университетехь ву, амма кхана со ишколе воьдуш ву.
Джон:	Со хьо волчу маца ван мегар ду?
Шалрани:	Вторникехь, шолгlачу апрелехь ван йиш йуй хьан?
Джон:	Йиш ю. Со вторникехь хьо волчу университете вогlуш ву.
Шалрани:	Дика ду, вайшиъ библиотекехь гура ву.
Джон:	Дела реза хуьлда. lодика йойла!
Шалрани:	Гура ду вай!

◆◆◆

Djon:	Allo, de dikə xyld hwa~ Shawrani [Shah-rah-nih]!
Shawrani:	Dall veziil Djon. Muux du hwa~ ghullqsh?
Djon:	Dikə du. Hwo taxan michahw vu?
Shawrani:	So taxan universitietehw vu, amma qaan so ishkole voedsh vu.
Djon:	Suo hwo volch maac va~ megar du?
Shawrani:	Vtornikehw, sholghachu aprelehw va~ jiish jui hwa~?
Djon:	Jiish Ju. So vtornikiehw hwo volch universiiete voghush vu.
Shawrani:	Dikə du, vaishi' bibliotekiehw guur vu.
Djon:	Del rez xyld. Wadik joil!
Shawrani:	Guur du vai!

DIALOGUE II: ON THE PHONE

John calls a professor.

John: Hello. Good afternoon, Sharani!

Sharani: Hello, John. How are you? (*lit:* How are your things?)

John: Good. Where are you today?

Sharani: I am at the university today, but tomorrow I am going to school.

John: When can I visit you?

Sharani: Can you come on Tuesday, April 2?

John: Yes, I can. On Tuesday I am coming to you at the university.

Sharani: Ok, we will meet at the library.

John: Thank you. Goodbye!

Sharani: See you!

Керла Дешнаш / NEW WORDS

кхана tomorrow

хьо волчу to you (*to a male*)

хьо йолчу to you (*to a female*)

мегар ду *similar to* дика ду; Okay

йиш (й) opportunity; possibility

вайшиъ (в/й) "the two of us" (*inclusive*) (*exclusive is* тхойшиъ)

Ӏодика йойла! Goodbye!

Гура ду вай! See you!

Маца? When?

вторникехь on Tuesday

шолгӀачу апрелехь the second of April

д.ан to do (д.о; д.еш); to come (д.огӀу; догӀуш)

ган to see (го; гуш)

Граматика / GRAMMAR

Genitive Case

To recap, we have already seen the Absolutive case with words such as мотт, книга, йиша, ваша, etc. This case is unmarked, which here means there's no ending. This is their default form:

Хӏара **книга** йу.   Кхузахь сан **ваша** ву,
This is a **book**.   Here is my **brother**.

We have also met the Genitive case through personal pronouns: сан, хьан, цуьнан, etc. The Genitive class shows possession, often marked in English by "-s" or "of," as well as the relationship between two nouns. In Chechen the Genitive case is most often marked by **-ан, -нан, -ин**, or **-чун**. Compare these sentences:

Студентан книга.
The **student's** book.

Джон **кӏант** ву.   **Кӏентан** машен цигахь йу.
John is a **boy**.   The **boy's** car is there.

When we were looking at plural forms in the Absolutive case, we mentioned that ablaut (vowel change) also occurs when the noun changes cases. These ablaut shifts should be memorized.

Absolutive: ваша (*son*)   цӏа (*house*)
Genitive: вешан (*of the son*)   цӏенан (*of the house*)

The Chechen linguist A.G. Matsiev has classified Chechen nouns into four declensions; in other words, four patterns of case endings. The linguist Johanna Nichols has described up to fifteen declensions. We will go further into declensions in later lessons, yet it's important to introduce Matsiev's system early.

We've already met nouns in the first, third, and fourth declensions. We will add a second declension noun, гота *"plow,"* as an example. Note that the genitive for first declension nouns, with or without ablaut, is **-ан**. Second declension nouns add an **-н-** or **-р-** before the **-ан**. The vowel in third declension nouns is **-и-** rather than -a-, and in fourth declension nouns, which are often professions, a **-ч-** appears.

You can see we've also added a first declension noun with ablaut shift. Nichols' system, with more declensions, is to a certain extent the result of sorting nouns by ablaut shift and *extension* (the -н-, -р-, -ч- consonants we discussed).

	First Declension	First Declension Ablaut *(no extension)*	Second Declension	Third Declension	Fourth Declension
Abs. Sing.	студент *(student)*	мотт *(language)*	гота *(plow)*	йиша *(sister)*	хьехархо *(teacher)*
Gen. Sing.	студентан	меттан	готанан	йишин	хьехархочун
Abs. Pl.	студенташ	меттанаш	готанаш	йижарий	хьехархой
Gen. Pl.	студентийн	меттанийн	готанийн	йижарийн	хьехархойн

More on Personal Pronouns: Adding the Ergative and Dative

Here comes one of the trickier parts of Chechen for English speakers. Follow the pronoun in the next sentences. How does it change?

Аса/Ас нохчийн мотт lамабо.
I study Chechen.

Оьрсийн мотт а буьйцу **ахь**?
*Do **you** speak Russian?*

Суна дика оьрсийн мотт бийца а хаьа.
I know how to speak Russian well. (lit. *I know to speak Russian well.*)

But:

Со нохчийн мотт буьйцуш ву.
I am speaking Chechen.

So why are there three ways to say "*I*" and "*you*" in Chechen (and for that matter, all other personal pronouns)? Again, Chechen syntax—the process by which words form sentences—is based on the verb. We'd argue that this is the most important obstacle for learning Chechen. If you get this, you get the language. Therefore, we want you to get the basic concepts early. Don't worry if you make mistakes. Let's compare:

Со ишколе воьду.	**Аса/Ас книгаш** йоьшу.
I go to school.	*I read books.*

As we said earlier, Chechen grammar focuses on the *relation* between verb, noun class, and agreement. Not word order. In the above examples, "*go*" is *intransitive*. Hence, the subject "*I*" takes the Absolutive case, and the verb agrees with the subject. In other words, if the verb is intransitive, "*I*" is Absolutive.

Now look at the second example. The verb "*read*" is *transitive*. Thus, the direct object takes the Absolutive case, while the subject takes the Ergative case. The verb agrees with the direct object in the Absolutive case, not the Ergative case. In other words, if the verb is transitive, "*I*" is Ergative.

This is simply another way of marking the relation between subject and object! Instead of changing the case of the direct object, we change the case of the subject. It is also not uncommon: up to 25 percent of the world's languages mark subjecthood through ergativity. It is, however, confusing for speakers of non-ergative languages, especially when noun class agreement is involved. We will give you lots of opportunity to practice.

Just one more thing we need to add quickly, so that our discussion of subjecthood can be relatively complete. It's not enough that we change the subject depending on the in/transitive nature of the verb. When verbs express feeling, or a sense, the subject is often in the *Dative case*. For example:

Суна хаьа.	**Суна** хазахета.
I know.	*I like.*

Notice how the Chechen for the English pronoun "*I*" looks different from both its Absolutive form, **Со**, and its Ergative form, **Аса**. This is another grammatical case, the Dative case, whose function we will explain in detail later.

Below are the personal pronouns in the Absolutive, Ergative, Genitive, and Dative cases:

	I	you	he/she/it	we (*exc.*)	we (*incl.*)	you (*pl.*)	they
Abs.	со	хьо	иза/и	тхо	вай	шу	уьш
Erg.	ас/аса	ахь/ахьа	цо	ох/оха	вай	аш/аша	цара
Gen.	сан	хьан	цуънан	тхан	вайн	шун	церан
Dat.	суна	хьуна	цунна	тхуна	вайна	шуна	царна

Аса, ахьа, оха, аша are used in poetry with "a" at the end. Using them without "a" is correct in any other type of writing except poetry.

The Present Tense

Chechen, like English, has multiple ways to express the Present tense. We have already seen the Present Progressive tense, which—for the most part—can be translated into English with its own Present Progressive tense:

Тахана со университете **воьдуш ву.**
*Today I **am going** to the university.*

As we noted in Lesson 2, the Present Progressive is a gerund that takes the suffix **-ш**.

The Present tense is formed with the Present tense root of the verb plus **-a** or **-y.** The **-y** ending occurs if the preceding syllable contains the vowels -о, -оь, -у, -уь, -ю, -юь. Any other vowel stems will take **-a.** This, unfortunately, is not the tricky part. What is tricky is memorizing the patterns for ablaut change. This ablaut change is fairly similar to what are termed strong verbs in English. Any learner of German will be familiar with this concept as well. Here are some examples of strong verbs in English:

I find vs. *I found*   *I grind* vs. *I ground*   *I give* vs. *I gave*

Chechen verbs are similar to English strong verbs. The verb stems will often change to indicate the tense. How these vowels shift falls into general patterns along the lines of "*find, found.*" We will dig deeper into these patterns in coming lessons, but let's look first at the verbs we know. Remember "д." marks the fact that the verb agrees with a noun's class.

Pattern	Infinitive	Present	Gerund
ий → уьй	д.ийца *(to speak)*	д.уьйцу *(speaks)*	д.уьйцуш *(speaking)*
е → оь	д.еша *(to read/study)*	д.оьшу *(reads/studies)*	д.оьшуш *(reading/studying)*
а → аь	хаа *(to know something)*	хаьа *(knows)*	хууш *(knowing)* [irregular]
а → о	ган *(to see)*	го *(sees)*	гуш *(seeing)* [irregular]

Of course, it wouldn't be Chechen without irregular verbs. There are not many irregular verbs in Chechen, but the ones that do exist occur all the time.

Infinitive	English	Present	Gerund
д.аха	to go	д.оьду	д.оьдуш
д.ан	to do; to make	д.о	д.еш

The verb "д.ан" is important because it helps create new verbs. English has many ways to turn a noun into a verb, for instance: *memory – memorize; problem – problematize; music – make music*. Like the last example, Chechen takes a noun and adds "*to do; to make*" to form a verb. We've already seen:

йазд.ан *to write* (йазд.о; йазд.еш)

This is a combination of the root **йаз** borrowed from Turkic (i.e., Turkish yazmak, *to write*), plus **д.ан**. *To write* declines the same way as *to make*. Getting this verb down pat now will save you lots of time later.

Transitive verbs that mark noun class must agree with the object, not the subject. Thus, the following Present tense forms are possible for йазд.ан (йазд.о; йазд.еш):

Ас **йаздо** кехат.   Ас **йазйо** книга.   Ас **йазбо** мотт.
I **write** *the letter.*   *I* **write** *the book.*   *I* **write** *the language.*

Йуххедехкина Дешнаш / EXTRA VOCABULARY

Adverbs

The adverbs below often trigger the Present tense. Some of these words will also trigger a separate verb form that implies habitual or repeated action (the Iterative), but don't worry about that for now.

наггахь sometimes
сих-сиха often
даиманна, массо а хенахь always
цкъа а ца never
наг-наггахь from time to time
хlора дийнахь every day
хlора кlиранахь every week
хlора баттахь every month
хlора шарахь every year
оршот дийнахь (понедельникехь) on Monday
lуьйранна in the morning
делкъана in the afternoon
суьйранна in the evening

Культура / CULTURE

Months of the Year / Шеран Батташ

Chechens most often use the Russian months of the year (note that months are not capitalized in Russian and Chechen):

январь (б:д)	January	июль (б:д)	July
февраль (б:д)	February	августе (б:д)	August
март (б:д)	March	сентябрь (б:д)	September
апрел (б:д)	April	октябрь (б:д)	October
май (б:д)	May	ноябрь (б:д)	November
июнь (б:д)	June	декабрь (б:д)	December

However, there are older Chechen names for the months that go back to a time when Chechens practiced paganism. These names were abandoned once Chechens converted to Christianity, followed by Islam:

English Translation	Pre-Islamic Months	Chechen Version (Current)	Russian Version
January	нажи-бутт	кхолламан бутт	январь
February	чиллан-бутт	чиллин бутт	февраль
March	биэкарг-бутт	бекарг бутт	март
April	тушоли-бутт	оханан бутт	апрель
May	сели-бутт	хІутосург бутт	май
June	мангал-бутт	асаран бутт	июнь
July	маьтсел-бутт	мангалан бутт	июль
August	эгиш-бутт	хаьттан бутт	август
September	тав-бутт	товбецан бутт	сентябрь
October	ардари-бутт	эсаран бутт	октябрь
November	эрха-бутт	лаьхьанан бутт	ноябрь
December	огІой-бутт	гІуран бутт	декабрь

Упражненеш / Exercises

Exercise 1. *Fill in the blanks using words from box.*

хӀора дийнахь	цкъа а ца	сих-сиха	наггахь
Ӏуьйранна	даимана	массо а хенахь	

1. _____ со университете йоьду.
2. Ас оьрсийн мотт _____ Ӏамабо.
3. Ахь _____ нохчийн мотт буьйцу.
4. Хьан доьзало _____ ингалсан мотт буьйцу.
5. Ахь оьрсийн маттахь _____ ца йаздо?
6. Джонна _____ нохчийн мотт буьйцу.

Exercise 2. *Make the following verbs negative.*

1. Воьду (*go*) _____
2. Олу (*speak*) _____
3. Туху (*hit*) _____
4. Оьцу (*buy/take*) _____
5. Молу (*drink*) _____
6. Хаьа (*know*) _____
7. Го (*see*) _____
8. Доьшу (*read*) _____

Exercise 3. *Write the following sentences using pronouns in parentheses in Ergative case.*

1. (со) _____ нохчийн мотт буьйцу.
2. (хьо) _____ нохчийн мотт ца буьйцу.
3. (тхо) _____ оьрсийн маттахь йаздо.
4. (шу) _____ оьрсийн маттахь ца йаздо.

5. (и/иза) _____книгаш йоьшу.

6. (вай) _____иза ца молу.

7. (Уьш) _____иза ца доьшу.

8. (вай) _____книгаш ца йазйо.

Exercise 4. *Translate the following sentences into Chechen.*

1. I go to university every day.

_____

2. Sometimes I speak Chechen.

_____

3. Hwava reads every day.

_____

4. Sharani works at university.

_____

5. We (*exclusive*) don't read Chechen books every year.

_____

6. John goes to Chechnya every year.

_____

7. Malika reads every week.

_____

8. Warbi speaks Russian every day.

_____

Exercise 5. *Read the following text and respond to the comprehension questions:*

Сан цIе Шалрани йу. Со университетехь профессор ву. Сан доттагI Джон со волчу вогIу хIора баттахь. Оха дуккха а книжкаш йоьшу. Джон нохчийн мотт Iамош ву.

1. Цуьнан цӀе хӀун йу?

_____

2. ШаӀрани мила ву?

_____

3. Цуьнан доттагӀ мила ву?

_____

Exercise 6. _Sort the modern Chechen names of months into each season section on the chart below:_

Кхолламан	ХӀутосург	Товбецан
Чиллин	Асаран	Эсаран
Бекарг	Мангалан	Лаьхьанан
Оханан	Хаьттан	ГӀуран

Ӏа ду (_winter_)	БӀаьсте йу (_Spring_)	Аьхке йу (_Summer_)	Гуьйре йу (_Autumn_)

Exercise 7. _Translate the following sentences into English:_

1. Кхолламан баттахь арахь ло догӀу.

_____

2. ГӀуран баттахь Ӏа хуьлу.

_____

3. Эсаран бутт хаза бу.

_____

Exercise 8. *Fill in the blanks in the following dialogue.*

Джон: Алло, _____ хьан Шаlрани!

Шаlрани: Далла везийла, Джон. Муха _____?

Джон: _____. Хьо тахана мичахь ву?

Шаlрани: Со _____университетехь ву, амма кхана со ишколе воьдуш ву.

Джон: Со хьо волчу маца ван мегар ду?

Шаlрани: Вторникехь, _____ван йиш йуй хьан?

Джон: Йиш ю. Со вторникехь хьо волчу университете воглуш ву.

Шаlрани: Дика ду, _____ гура ву.

Джон: Дела _____. lодика йойла!

Шаlрани: Гура _____!

Корта IV:
Университетехь
Lesson 4:
At the University

Knowledge Check: In the below dialogues underline the pronouns and state whether they are in the absolutive, genitive, or dative cases. Look at the verbs, are they intransitive or transitive? Why is this important? From now on, the Chechen versions of the dialogue will only be in Cyrillic. Listen carefully to the audio to hear how spoken Chechen differs from the literary standard.

Lesson Plan:
- Ergative and Dative case
- Future tenses
- More on irregular verbs
- Days of the week
- Cardinal numbers 1 to 20
- Ordinal numbers 1st to 20th
- Telling time

ДИАЛОГ I: Университетехь

Шаӏрани: Ассалам Алейкум, Джон.

Джон: Ваалейкум ассалам, Шаӏрани. Муха ву хьо?

Шаӏрани: Со-м дика ву, ткъа хьо?

Джон: Со а ву дика! Сан лекцин расписани йуй хьоьгахь?

Шаӏрани: Йу, хьан кӏиранахь кхо лекци хир йу.

Джон: Вайна лекцехь хӏун оьшур йу?

Шаӏрани: Студенташна тептар а оьшур ду, къолам а оьшур бу.

Джон: Студенташа компьютер лелайой класс чохь?

Шаӏрани: Хӏаъ, дешархоша компьютерш а ноутбукш а лелайо.

Джон: Маца хир йу вайн хьалхара лекци?

Шаӏрани: Хӏокху кӏиранахь оршот дийнахь, ӏуьйранна бархӏ даьлча хир йу вайн хьалхара лекци.

Джон: Дика ду со хӏора оршот дийнахь вогӏур ву хьан лекци.

ДИАЛОГ II: Библиотекехь

Джон: Суьйре дика хуьлда. Нохчийн литература мичахь йу шун?

Библиотекарь: Далла везийла. Иза лоьмар кхоъ йолчу ишкап уллехь йу.

Джон: Дика ду, со кхана йухавогӏур ву кхоъ даьлча.

Библиотекарь: Тхо дӏакъевлина ду йеарийн дийнахь. Хьо пӏераскан дийнахь вагӏахь дика хир ду.

Джон: Маса даьлча пӏераскан дийнахь схьайеллало библиотека?

Библиотекарь: Исс-ах даьлча схьайеллало, амма итт сахьт дала пхийтта минот йисича вагӏахь диках хир ду.

Джон: Ткъа кӏиран дийнахь болх бой аш?

Библиотекарь: Хӏан-хӏа, ца бо.

Джон: Мегш ду. Дела реза хуьлда! Со пӏераскан дийнахь схьавогӏур ву.

DIALOGUE I: AT THE UNIVERISTY

Sharani: Hello, John.

John: Hello, Sharani. How are you?

Sharani: I'm well. And you?

John: I'm also well! Do you have my lecture schedule on you?

Sharani: Yes, in your week there will be three lectures.

John: What will we need in the lecture?

Sharani: Students will need a notebook and pen.

John: Do students use a computer in class?

Sharani: Yes, students use computers and laptops.

John: When will our first lecture be?

Sharani: This week our first lecture will be on Monday at eight in the morning.

John: OK. I will go to your lecture this Monday.

DIALOGUE II: AT THE LIBRARY

John: Good morning. Where is your Chechen literature (section)?

Librarian: Welcome. It is near shelf number three.

John: Ok, I will come back tomorrow at three o'clock.

Librarian: We are closed on Thursday. If you come on Friday, it will be good.

John: At what time does the library open on Friday?

Librarian: It opens at 9:30, but if you come at 9:45 it will be better.

John: And do you work on Sunday?

Librarian: No, we don't.

John: OK, be well. I will come on Friday.

Керла Дешнаш / New Words I

лекци, лекцеш (й:й) lecture
расписани, расписанеш (й:й) schedule
тептар, тептарш (д:д) copybook, notebook
компьютер, компьютерш (й:й) computer
ноутбук, ноутбукш (й:й) laptop
класс чохь in the classroom
хьоьгахь on you
къолам, къоламаш (б:д) pencil
хьалхара first
хӀокху кӀиранахь *lit.* in this week
библиотека, библиотекаш (й:й) library
оьшур will need **(эша; оьшу; оьшуш)**
хир will be **(хила; д.у)**
в.огӀур will go **(д.аха; д.огӀу; д.огӀуш)**
лелад.о to use (something); to wear (clothes); to take care of
    (лелад.ан; лелад.о; лелад.еш)

Керла Дешнаш / New Words II

со-м as for me (-**м** *adds emphasis*)
литература, литератураш (й:й) literature
лоьмар, лоьмарш (й:й) number
лоьмар кхоъ йолчу *lit.* "to number three being"
ишкап, ишкапш (й:й) closet; shelf, bookshelf
уллехь near, close, next to
Маса даьлча? At what time?
дӀакъьевлина closed
д.агӀахь if you (*pl.*) come
исс-ах даьлча 9:30
-ах half
сахьт, сахьтш (д:д) hour; clock, watch
диках better
йухавогӀур will come back **(йухад.аха; йухад.оьду; йухад.оьдуш)**
схьавогӀур will come here **(схьад.аха; схьад.оьду; схьад.оьдуш)**
схьад.еллало to open **(схьад.еллад.ала; схьад.еллало;**
                        схьад.еллалуш)

Граматика / Grammar

Ergative and Dative Case

In the previous lesson, we learned the Genitive case for nouns and about vowel shift, or ablaut, which occurs frequently to the roots of Chechen nouns. We also learned in the previous lesson the Ergative and Dative cases for personal pronouns. Here they are again:

	I	**you**	**he/she/it**	**we** *(exc.)*	**we** *(incl.)*	**you** *(pl.)*	**they**
Abs.	со	хьо	иза/и	тхо	вай	шу	уьш
Erg.	аса	ахьа	цо	оха	вай	аша	цара
Gen.	сан	хьан	цуънан	тхан	вайн	шун	церан
Dat.	суна	хьуна	цунна	тхуна	вайна	шуна	царна

Let's take a look at the 3rd person singular, **иза/и**, and its final syllable:

Ergative: ц-о   **Dative: цун-на**

These endings become the case endings for Chechen nouns in the singular.

	First Declension	**First Declension Ablaut**	**Second Declension**	**Third Declension**	**Fourth Declension**
Abs. Sing.	студент *(student)*	мотт *(language)*	гота *(plow)*	йиша *(sister)*	хьехархо *(teacher)*
Erg. Sing.	студенто	матто	готано	йишас	хьехархочо
Dat. Sing.	студентана	меттана	готана	йишина	хьехархочуна

Notice, however, that the ergative singular for йиша *"sister"* is **йишас**. This is because the ergative singular for humans ends in either **-a** or **-ac**.

	First Declension	First Declension Ablaut	Second Declension	Third Declension	Fourth Declension
Abs.	хьава	джон	да	ваша	йиша
Erg.	хьавас	джона	дас	вашас	йишас
Dat.	хьавана	джонна	дена	вешина	йишина

Now let's look at the 3rd person plural, **уьш** *(they)*, and its final syllable:

> **Ergative:** цар-**а** *(they)*
> **Dative:** цар-**на** *(to them)*

We can add these suffixes onto the Absolutive plural of the nouns below to get the Ergative and Dative plurals. Note that while the -ш disappears in the Absolutive case for fourth declension nouns, it returns in the Ergative and Dative plural. The same occurs for йиша, though other third declension nouns have regular plurals (i.e., мача (мачин) - мачаш "*shoe*").

	First Declension	First Declension Ablaut	Second Declension	Third Declension	Fourth Declension
Abs. Pl.	студенташ *(students)*	меттанаш *(languages)*	готанаш *(plows)*	йижарий *(sisters)*	хьехархой *(teachers)*
Erg. Pl.	студенташа	меттанаша	готанаша	йижарша	хьехархоша
Dat. Pl.	студенашна	меттанашна	готанашна	йижаршна	хьехархошна

Like the Ergative personal pronouns, the Ergative case is used when the noun is the subject of a transitive verb:

Студент**о** книгаш йоьшу.
The student is reading (the) books.

Вежар**ша** нохчийн мотт буьцу.
The brothers speak the Chechen language.

Note, again, that the "й" in "йоьшу" and the "б" in "буьцу" agree with книгаш and мотт respectively.

The Dative case in Chechen serves two important purposes. First, as an indirect object. As a reminder, the indirect object is often the person or thing that is receiving an object. For example, in the sentence: "I give the book to the student," "student" is the indirect object and "the book" the direct object of the verb "to give."

Let's look at that same sentence in Chechen: "Аса студентана книга ло." First, as you can see, the pronoun "Аса" *(I)* is in the Ergative case. The direct object (книга) of the Present tense form of "*to give*" is unmarked (Absolutive case), while the indirect object (студент) is in the Dative case.

The Dative case in Chechen can also function as the subject of a verb. Remember the verb from Lesson 3, хазахета? Хазахета "*to like*," is a compound word:

хаза (*pretty, beautiful, pleasing*) plus **хета** (*to seem*)

The subject of хазахета (the person or thing "liking" something) takes the Dative case:

Стеденташна книга хазахета.
The students like the book.
(lit. *"The book seems pleasing to the students."*)

In this construction, хазахета is not too different from similar ways to say "*I like*" in some well-known Indo-European languages—Spanish *me gusta,* for example. But Chechen takes this a step further. **Хета** is a verb that conveys a perception or a sense. And in Chechen the Dative as subject is also used for more literal senses, take for example **го** "*to see*":

Дена кӀант го.
The father sees the boy.

The father is the subject of the Present tense form of **го** "*to see*." **КӀант** "*the boy*" is in the Absolutive case. Keeping this in mind, how would you translate the following sentence: "Со хьуна гой?"? If you answered, *"Do you see me?"* you're on the right track!

Future Tenses

There are two Future tenses in Chechen: the Future Possible tense and the Future Real tense.

Future Possible Tense

The Future Possible tense is less common than the Future Real tense. However, since the Future Real tense is formed from the Future Possible tense, we will introduce this tense first.

The Future Possible tense is formed by adding -**p** to a verb's Present tense form. For example, in Lesson 3 we learned the following verbs:

д.еша (д.оьшу; д.оьшуш) *to read/study*
д.ийца   (д.уьйцу; д.уьйцуш) *to speak*

The Future Possible form of *"to read"* is: д.еша → д.оьшу → **д.оьшур**:

Цо доьшу. *He reads. / He studies.*

Цо доьшу**р**. *He will (may) study.*

Compare how доьшур must agree in the Future Possible tense with the object of *"read"* or *"studied"*:

Цо книга йоьшу**р**.
He will (may) be reading a (the) book.

Цо нохчийн мотт lамо**р**.
He will be studying Chechen.

The Future Possible form of *"to speak"* is: д.ийца → д.уьйцу → **д.уьйцур**:

Оха дуьйцу. *We speak.*

Оха нохчийн мотт буьйцу**р**. *We will possibly speak Chechen.*

The intransitive verb д.аха *"to go"* is irregular: д.аха → д.оьду → **гlур**:

Со воьду. *I go.*

Со гlу**р**. *I will (may) go. / I will possibly go.*

The Future Possible tense conveys an *incomplete* action. Whether an action is complete or incomplete is reflected in a verb's *aspect*. *Perfective* is the term for aspect that reflects a completed action, while *imperfective* reflects an incomplete action. Compare, for example, in English:

I went home. (perfect)
I was going home. (imperfect)

The Future Possible tense in Chechen is used when the speaker does not know if the action will be completed or does not expect the action to be completed:

Ас книга язйер. (**Note:** "д.ер" is the future tense form of "д.ан.")
I will (may) write a book. / I will possibly write a book.

Future Real Tense

The Future Real tense form reflects the speaker's belief that the action will be completed (*perfect*). It is formed by adding the particle **д.у** to the Future Possible tense. Let's look at another irregular verb similar to д.аха "*to go*"— "*to come*" д.ан → д.огӀу → д.огӀур:

Уьш богӀу**р**.
They will (may) come. Or: *They will possibly come.*

Уьш богӀу**р бу**.
They will come.

Хьо йогӀу**р**.
You (female) will possibly come.

Хьо йогӀу**р йу**.
You (female) will come.

Note how the particle **д.у** agrees with the subject of the intransitive verb д.ан. Now, let's look at the formation of the Future tense for transitive verbs. (Note that we already saw this example sentence above for the Future Possible tense.):

Ас книга йазйе**р**.
I will (may) write a book. Or: *I will possibly write a book.*

The "й" in "йер" agrees, of course, with книга. "Аса" could either be a male or a female speaker. Of the tenses we have learned so far, the class agreement of the subject for transitive verbs is only reflected in the Present Progressive tense:

Ас книга йазйо.
I write the book. (Present tense)

Со книга йазйеш ву.
I am writing the book. (Present Progressive tense)

Ас книга йазйер.
I may write the book. (Future Possible tense)

Аса книга йазйир йу.
I will write the book. (Future Real tense)

You may have expected: Аса книга йазйер ву. Or: Со книга йазйер ву. But neither of these forms are possible in Chechen. The particle д.у can only agree with the Absolutive case. Because the Future tense is derived from the Future Possible tense, and requires the Ergative, д.у must agree with the object.

More on Irregular Verbs

Below are the irregular verbs we have met in Chechen thus far with their present and future forms. Дан and ган could be considered a pair of regular verbs following the same pattern, but since their gerunds are irregular, we will consider them irregular verbs.

English	Infinitive	Present	Present Progressive	Future Possible	Future
to do / *to make*	д.ан	д.о	д.еш д.у	д.ер	д.ийр д.у
to see	ган	го	гуш д.у	гур	гур д.у
to go	д.аха	д.оьду	д.оьдуш д.у	д.оґур	д.оґур д.у
to come	д.ан	д.оґу	д.оґуш д.у	д.оґур	д.оґур д.у
to give	д.ала	ло	луш д.у	лур	лур д.у
to be	хила	д.у	–	хир	хир д.у

Irregular verbs need to be memorized, and it is especially important for the learner to gain a firm grasp of **д.ан** "*to do*" and **д.ала** "*to give.*" As we will see in the coming lessons, many common verbs are formed from a noun or adjective plus д.ан or д.ала. We have already encountered one in йаздан "*to write.*"

Days of the Week

As you saw from the dialogue, to say "on Monday, on Wednesday, etc." you must take the day of the week and add the Chechen word for "*day,*" **де**, in the Locative. The day can either take the Genitive case or stand alone.

Nominative	Locative	Translation
оршот	оршот дийнахь	*on Monday*
шинара	шинара дийнахь	*on Tuesday*
кхаара	кхаарийн дийнахь	*on Wednesday*
еара / йеара	еарийн / йеарийн дийнахь	*on Thursday*
пlераска	пlераска дийнахь	*on Friday*
шот	шота дийнахь	*on Saturday*
кlиранде	кlирана дийнахь	*on Sunday*

Cardinal Numbers 1 to 20

Below are the cardinal numbers one through twenty. Chechen speakers will use both Chechen and Russian equivalents.

Number	Chechen	Russian
1	цхьаъ	один
2	шиъ	два
3	кхоъ	три
4	д.иъ	четыре
5	пхиъ	пять
6	йалх	шесть

7	ворхӏ	семь
8	бархӏ	восемь
9	исс	девять
10	итт	десять
11	цхьайтта	одинадцать
12	шийтта	двенадцать
13	кхойтта	тринадцать
14	д.ейтта	четырнадцать
15	пхийтта	пятнадцать
16	йалхитта	шестнадцать
17	вуьрхӏитта	семнадцать
18	берхӏитта	восемнадцать
19	ткъайоьсна	девятнадцать
20	ткъа	двадцать

The numbers 4 and 14 must agree with the class of the noun they describe:

йиъ йоӏ *four girls*   виъ стаг *four boys*

бейтта болх *fourteen jobs*

The Chechen noun stays in the singular when followed by a number.

Ordinal Numbers 1st – 20th

Number	Chechen Ordinal	Number	Chechen Ordinal
1st	хьалхара	11th	цхьайтталгӏа
2nd	шолгӏа	12th	шийтталгӏа
3rd	кхоалгӏа	13th	кхойтталгӏа
4th	д.оьалгӏа	14th	д.ейтталгӏа
5th	пхоьалгӏа	15th	пхийтталгӏа

6th	йалхалгӀа	16th	йалхитталгӀа
7th	ворхӀалгӀа	17th	вуьрхӀитталгӀа
8th	бархӀалгӀа	18th	берхӀитталгӀа
9th	уьссалгӀа	19th	ткъайоьснalgӀa
10th	уьтталгӀа	20th	ткъалгӀа

Telling Time

There are two ways to ask what time it is in Chechen:

Вайна маса даьлла?   *What time is it?*
Вайна маса сахьт даьлла? *What time is it?*

"Вайна маса даьлла?" literally means "*to us how much has finished?*"
"Вайна маса сахьт даьлла" literally translates to "*to us how many hours have finished.*"

To say "*it's one o'clock; two o'clock,*" etc. just take the number and add **сахьт даьлла**:

ХӀинца бархӀ **сахьт даьлла**.
It's now eight o'clock.

ХӀинца ши **сахьт д.аьлла**.
It's now two o'clock. (Note that дейтта agrees with сахьт ду.)

To say it's half past the hour, add **-ах** "*half*" to the number:

ХӀинца шийтта-**ах** даьлла.
It's twelve-thirty (12:30) now.

ХӀинца кхоъ-**ах** даьлла.
It's three-thirty (3:30).

The form "**кхоъ-ах даьлла**" is used when you are naming the time. But when you are stating the time when an action is occurring, then **даьлча** is used:

Хӏинца кхо сахьт **даьлла**, амма библиотека **кхоъ-ах даьлча** схьайеллало.
It is three o'clock right now, but the library opens at three-thirty.

To say a certain amount of minutes *before* the hour, use **йаьлча х долу**. "йаьлча х долу" translates to something like "*minutes before the x hour strikes*":

Вайна пхийтта минот **йаьлча** <u>пхиъ</u> **долу**.
It's fifteen minutes before <u>five</u> (4:45).

Вайна ткъе пхи минот **йаьлча** <u>йалх</u> **долу**.
It's twenty-five minutes before <u>six</u> (5:35).

There is another construction to say *before* the hour, which we also saw in the dialogue. It uses the infinitive form of **долу** and **д.иса** (*to be left*):

Амма итт сахьт **дала** пхийтта минот йисича вагӏахь диках хир ду.
*But if you come at fifteen minute **before** ten (9:45) it is better.*

To say a certain number of minutes past the hour Chechen uses ordinal numbers in the substantive case (which we have not encountered yet). Since the ordinal number is an adjective, it will also change while declined. We will discuss declined adjectives later, but for now notice that the form is **-алгӏачух**. Let's look at an example:

Вайна пхи минот кхо**алгӏачух** йаьлла.
It's five after third (2:05).

Here, Chechen literally says "*five minutes after the third.*" Note that once you've passed two o'clock, you're now in the *third* not the *second* hour.

Вайна итт минот пхи**алгӏачух** йаьлла.
It's 4:10. (Lit. "ten minutes finished of the fifth")

To say, "in the morning/afternoon/evening/night," Chechen uses the Dative case:

Ас **ӏуьйранна** исс-ах даьлча йаахӏума йуу.
***In the morning**, at nine-thirty (9:30), I eat.*

Со **дийнахь** пхиъ даьлча цӀа воьду.
At five o'clock (5:00) **in the afternoon** *I go home.*

Ас **суьйранна** итт даьлча книга йоьшу.
At ten o'clock (10:00) **in the evening** *I read a book.*

Со **буьйсанна** шийтта даьлча дӀайуьжу.
At twelve o'clock (12:00) **at night** *I go to sleep.*

Note: **дӀад.ижа (дӀад.уьжу, дӀад.уьжуш д.у)** *to sleep*

Культура / CULTURE

Borrowing of Russian Words

The majority of vocabulary related to school and study is borrowed from Russian. Many Chechen linguists are often concerned about the scale of borrowing from Russian and try to create new Chechen terms to supplant Russian loanwords. Chechen speakers for the most part have not adopted these new terms.

Of course, borrowing words is a natural process for any language. English is famously a language with a significant portion of loanwords from French. Long before Russian influence Chechen borrowed many words from Turkic and Arabic. Several days of the week (оршот, пӀераска, кӀиранде) are borrowed from Georgian. This is not to take away from Chechens' concerns. Indeed, Chechens will frequently switch back and forth from Russian, also a natural linguistic process, but one that raises serious worries about the future status of the language.

Chechens will use Russian for counting money and quoting prices. This is a function of the education system, both in the Soviet Union and today, when all subjects were taught in Russian except for one course on Chechen language and literature. So, Chechens may well be both perplexed and impressed if a foreigner says "оршот" instead of "понедельник"!

Йуххедехкина Дешнаш
NEW WORDS: SCHOOL RELATED

ручка, ручкаш (й:й) pen
кехат, кехатш (д:д) paper
кӏайн у, кӏайн аннаш (д:д) whiteboard
мел, мелш (б:д) chalk
портфель, портфельш (б:д) backpack
папка, папкаш (б:д) binder
гӏант, гӏентш (д:д) chair
парта, парташ (й:й) desk
стёрка, стёркаш (й:й) eraser
глобус, глобусш (й:й) globe
латтсурт, латтсуьрташ (д:д) map
сурт, суьрташ (д:д) picture, photo
кружка, кружкаш (й:й) mug, cup
куьзганаш (д) glasses
бой, бойнаш (й:й) curtains
стогар, стогарш (б:д) lamp

Упражненеш / EXERCISES

Exercise 1. *Translate the following sentences into English.*

1. Сан кхана лекци йу.

_____

2. Со кхана библиотеке гӏур ву.

_____

3. Оршот дийнахь Джон библиотекехь хир ву.

_____

4. Йеарийн дийнахь Шаӏранис лекци лура йу.

_____

5. Кхолламан баттахь университет схьайоьллур йу.

_____

6. Сан класс чохь компьютер хир йу.

_____

Exercise 2. _Write the following times using numbers._

1. Вайна ши сахьт даьлла. _____

2. Вайна итт даьлла. _____

3. Вайна сахьт даьлла. _____

4. Пхийтта минот йаьлча шиъ долу. _____

5. Ткъе пхи минот йаьлча сахьт долу. _____

6. Вайна кхо сахьт даьлла. _____

7. Вайна пхоьалгІачух йалх минот йаьлла. _____

8. Вайна доьалгІачух ворхІ минот йаьлла. _____

Exercise 3. _Write the times below in Chechen._

1. 5:00 _____

2. 6:00 _____

3. 7:30 _____

4. 8:15 _____

5. 9:30 _____

6. 10:10 _____

7. 11:05 _____

8. 12:55 _____

Exercise 4. *Read about a librarian's daily routine below. Answer the questions after the text. The clues for answers are in the text.*

Библиотекарь хІора Іуьйранна йалх даьлча схьалагІотту (gets up). Цо йаахІума ворхІ даьлча йуу, тІаккха бархІ даьлча автобус тІехь балха (to work) йоьду. Библиотека исс-ах даьлча схьайеллало. Суьйранна пхиъ даьлча библиотекарь цІа йоьду. ЦІахь йалх-ах даьлча библиотекаро йаахІума йуу.

1. Библиотекарь маса даьлча схьалагІотту?

   _____

2. Цо йаахІума маса даьлча йуу?

   _____

3. Иза автобус тІехь маса даьлча балха йоду?

   _____

4. Библиотека маса даьлча схьайеллало?

   _____

5. Библиотекарь суьйранна маса даьлча цІа йоду?

   _____

Exercise 5. *Translate the following Future tense phrases into English.*

1. Со вогІур ву._____

2. Со йогІур йу._____

3. Уьш богІур бу._____

4. Шу догІур ду._____

5. Цо доьшур ду._____

6. Вай йаздийр ду._____

7. Ахь нохчийн мотт буьйцур бу._____

Exercise 6. *Read the table with ordinal numbers in this lesson and fill in the blanks. English translations will help you.*

1. Со_____ бер ду сан доьзаллехь.
   I am the third child in my family.

2. Малика Iарбин_____зуд йу.
   Malika is Arbi's first wife.

3. Хьава_____бер ду.
   Hwava is the second child.

4. Джон _____турист ву.
   John is the fifth tourist.

Exercise 7. *Think of your daily routine. Create sentences using the time and sequence words.*

_____

_____

_____

_____

_____

_____

_____

Корта V: Сени чохь
Lesson 5: In the University Hallway

Knowledge Check: What is the difference between the Future Real and Future Possible tenses? Review the Ergative and Dative cases. When is the Ergative case used? If the verb agrees in noun class, will it agree with the Absolutive or Ergative case?

Lesson Plan:
- Family Members
- Recent Past tense
- Observed Past tense
- Imperatives: making commands
- Instrumental case

9 **ДИАЛОГ I: Студентийн Вовшахкхетар**

Джон: Де дика хуьлда хьан. Сан цӀе Джон йу, со керла студент ву.

Ваха: Далла везийла, марша вогӀийла!

Джон: Хьан цӀе хӀун йу? Хьо мила ву?

Ваха: Сан цӀе Ваха йу, со хьан накъост хир ву кху семестрехь.

Джон: Хьоьца хир вуй со аудитори чохь?

Ваха: Хьо соьца хир ву даиманна а, ас хьуна гӀо дийр ду. Хьо дуккха хан йуй Нохчичохь волу?

Джон: Йац, Со цхьа кӀира хьалха веара кхуза.

Ваха: Хьаьнца веара хьо?

Джон: Со суо веара. Суна хазачу меттигашка воьдуш хазахета.

Ваха: Хьавана гирий хьо?

Джон: Гира, Хьава а, цуьнан да-нана а гира суна.

Ваха: Ва, Джон, хьажал хьо! Баккъала нохчийн цӀа чу вахи хьо?

Джон: ХӀаъ, цига а ваха, нохчийн мотт а бийци, чай а мели, чӀепалгаш а дии!

Ваха: Муха хийтира хьуна? Даар мерза дарий йа дацара?

Джон: Суна хазахийтира, даар мерза дара.

Ваха: Хьо маца веара Нохчийчу, погода муха йара Соьлжа-ГӀалахь?

Джон: Со кхуза Оршот дийнахь веара. Погода? ХенахӀоттам бохий ахь?

Ваха: Хьажахь! Мел дика Ӏеми хьуна нохчийн мотт!

Джон: ХенахӀоттам Нохчийчохь инзаре дика бара. ЧӀогӀа шийла йа йовха а йацара, догӀа а ца догӀура.

Ваха: Мегар ду. Аудитори чохь гура ду вай, Борз!

DIALOGUE I: MEETING ANOTHER STUDENT

John: Hello. My name is John, I am a new student.

Vaxa: Hello, welcome!

John: What is your name? Who are you?

Vaxa: My name is Vaxa, I will be your partner this semester.

John: Will I be with you in the auditorium?

Vaxa: You will always be with me, and I will help you. Have you been in Chechnya for a long time?

John: No, I came here one week ago.

Vaxa: Did you come with someone?

John: No, I came alone. I like going to beautiful places.

Vaxa: Have you met Hwava?

John: Yes, I met Hwava and her parents.

Vaxa: Wow, John. listen to you (*lit.* you said)! You went to a real Chechen home?

John: Yes. I went there, spoke Chechen, drank tea, and ate ch'epalgash!

Vaxa: How did you like it? Was the food delicious or not?

John: I liked it, it was tasty.

Vaxa: When you came to Chechnya, how was the weather in Grozny?

John: I came here on Monday. Weather *(in Russian)*? Are you talking about the weather *(in Chechen)*?

Vaxa: Oh, look how well you learned Chechen!

John: The weather was very good. It was not very cold or hot, and it was not raining.

Vaxa: Good. See you in the auditorium, *Borz*!

¹⁰ ДИАЛОГ II: Класс чохь

Профессор: Де дика хуьлду шун!

Студенташ: Далла везийла, марша вогӏийла, профессор.

Профессор: Сан цӏе Шаӏрани йу. Со шуна нохчийн мотт хьоьхуш профессор ву. Шуьгахь тептарш, къоламаш йа ручкаш йуй?

Студент 1:   Тхуна хӏокху лекцехь книгаш оьший?

Профессор: Оьшу. "Нохчийн меттан бакъонаш" дешаран книга оьшу шуна. Ткъа хӏинца шайн цӏерш у тӏехь дӏайазйе.

Студент 1:   Сан цӏе Мурад йу. Мел мичахь бу?

Студент 2:   Мел парти тӏехь бу.

Студент 1:   Ас ма-аллара, сан цӏе Мурад йу, сан фамили Хамстаханов йу. Со цӏера Котар-Йуьртар ву. Сан доьзалехь бархӏ стаг ву. Далла хастам болуш, сан воккхах волу ваша а, сан жимах волу шича а соьца Соьлжа-Гӏалахь ӏаш бу.

Профессор: Дела реза хуьлда, Мурад. Охьахаа. Джон, схьаволахьа кхузахь хьайн цӏе йазйехьа. Мурада санна хьайх лаьцна дийцахьа.

Джон классан хьалха дӏахӏуттту.

Де дика хуьлда шун дешархой! Сан цӏе Джон йу, со керла дешархо ву. Со цӏера Америкера ву. Ас дика университет чекхйаьккхира Америкехь, тӏаккха со библиотеке болх бан вахара. Цул тӏаьхьа, суна дешаран книжка карийра, и дешаран книжка нохчийн маттахь йара, иштта волавелира со нохчийн мотт ӏамабан. Сан доьзал жима бу, сан цхьа йиша а йу, цхьа ваша а ву. Сан да а, сан воккхахволу ваша а чӏогӏа лекха бу, амма сан йиший наний лоха бу. Ткъа со царна йуккъехь ву: башха лекха вац, йа лоха а вац. Сан денаний, дедай къена бу, пенсехь бу, амма сан да-наний болх беш ду.

DIALOGUE II: IN THE CLASSROOM

Professor: Hello, everyone!

Students: Hello. Welcome, professor.

Professor: My name is Shawrani. I am the professor teaching you all Chechen. Do you have your notebooks, pens, and pencils?

Student 1: Do we need any books in this class?

Professor: Yes. You need the textbook "Conversations in the Chechen Language." And now write each of your names on the blackboard.

Student 1: My name is Murad. Where is the chalk?

Student 2: The chalk is on the desk.

Student 1: As I was saying, my name is Murad, my last name is Xamstaxanov. I am from Kotar-Yurt. In my family there are eight people. Thanks to God, my older brother and younger cousin live with me in Grozny.

Professor: Welcome, Murad. Sit down. John, come up and write your name. Like Murad, tell [us] about yourself.

John stands in front of the class.

Hello, students! My name is John, I am a new student. I am from America. I graduated from university in America, then went to work in a library. After that, I found a book, which was about the Chechen language, and I began to study Chechen. My family is small, I have one sister and one brother. My father and older brother are very tall, but my sister and mother are short. So, I'm in the middle of them: neither tall nor short. My grandmother and grandfather are old, in retirement, but my parents work.

Керла Дешнаш I / NEW WORDS I

керла new
накъост, накъостий (в/й:б) peer, friend, assistant, partner
аудитори, аудитореш (й:й) auditorium
аудитори чохь in the auditorium
семестр, семестрш (й:й) semester
хlокху семестрехь in this semester
гlо (д:д) help, assistance
д.уккха much, a lot
хан, хенаш (й:й) time
хьалха before, ago
со-суо; хьо-хьуо by myself; by yourself
даар, даарш (д) food
мерза delicious, tasty
хенахlоттам; погода (й) weather
меттиг, меттигаш (й:й) place
хазачу меттигашка to beautiful places
инзаре very
чlогlа very
шийла cold
д.овха hot
Догlа догlу. It's raining.
Догlа догlура. It used to rain.
баккъала real
Хьажахь! Look!
мел how
мегар ду OK (*lit.* it's possible)
борз, берзалой (й:й); Борз (ву) wolf; term of endearment for men

Керла Хандешнаш / NEW VERBS

гlо дан to help (д.о; д.еш; д.и)
д.ан to come (д.огlу; д.еа)
ган to see, to meet (го; гуш; ги)
д.аа to eat (д.уу; д.ууш; д.ии)
ала to say (олу; олуш; эли)
хьажа to look (хьожу; хьожуш; хьаьжи)

Керла Дешнаш II / New Words II

хьоьхуш teaching
профессор, профессорш (в:б) professor
бакъо, бакъонаш (й:й) rule, law; policy; rights
ДӀайазйе! Write!
парти тӀехь on the desk
фамили, фамилеш (й:й) last name
Далла хастам бу Thanks to God. (*Alhamdulillah*.)
д.оккхах д.олу the oldest
жимах д.олу the youngest
шича, шичой (в,й:б) cousin
ас ма-аллара as I said
Мурада санна like Murad
дешархо, дешархой (в:б) student, pupil, learner
мел, мелаш (б:д) chalk
парта, парташ (й:й) desk
у, аннаш (д:д) blackboard; board
дешаран книга, книгаш (й:й) textbook
папка, папкаш (б:д) folder
закладка (й:й) bookmark
тӀоьрмиг (б:д) backpack, bag

Керла Хандешнаш / New Verbs

хьеха to teach (**хьоьху; хьийхи**)
дӀайазд.ан to write down (**дӀайзд.о; дӀайазд.и**)
охьахаа to sit down (**охьахуу; охьахии**)
д.олад.ала to begin something (**д.олад.о; д.олад.и**)
д.олад.ала to begin (*intransitive*) (**д.олало; д.олад.ели**)
дӀахӀотта to stand up (**дӀахӀутту; дӀахӀоьтти**)

Йуххедехкина дешнаш / Family members

нана, наной (й:б) mother
да, дай (в;б) father
йоl, йоlарий (й:б) daughter
кlант, кlентий (в:б) son
ваша, вежарий (в:б) brother
йиша, йижарий (й:б) sister
вешин кlант, вешин кlентий (в:б) nephew (*brother's son*)
йишин кlант, йишин кlентий (в:б) nephew (*sister's son*)
вешин кlент-кlант, вешин кlент-кlентий (в:б) brother's grandson
йишин кlент-кlант, йишин кlент-кlентий (в;б) sister's grandson
вешин йоьl-йоl, вешин йоьl-йоlрий (й:б) brother's granddaughter
йишин йоьl-йоl, йишин йоьl-йоlрий (й:б) sister's granddaughter
шича, шичой (й/в:б) cousin
ненваша, ненвежарий (в:б) uncle (*from mother's side*)
деваша, девежарий (в:б) uncle (*from father's side*)
ненйиша, неннижарий (й:б) aunt (*from mother's side*)
дейиша, дейижарий (й:б) aunt (*from father's side*)
ненана, ненананой (й:б) grandmother (*mother's mother*)
денана, денаной (й:б) grandmother (*father's mother*)
ненда, ненадай (в:б) grandfather (*mother's father*)
деда, дедай (в:б) grandfather (*father's father*)
кlент-кlант, йишин кlент-кlентий (в;б) grandson
йоьl-йоl, вешин йоьl-йоlрий (й:б) granddaughter

Adjectives describing people

лекха tall
лоха short
къена old
къона young
жима small
д.оккха big
хаза beautiful
ирча ugly
хьекъале smart
lовдал stupid
вон bad
дика good

самукъане funny
оьгlазе gloomy, sad
малойолуш lazy
къинхьегаме hardworking
къинхетаме kind, charitable
догlаьржа mean
майра brave
стешха cowardly
комаьрша generous
сутар greedy

Граматика / GRAMMAR

Past Tenses

In Lesson 4 we learned the Future Real tense and Future Possible tense in Chechen. Now, we will learn two new tenses: Recent Past tense and Observed Past tense, both for describing actions that occurred in the past.

Recent Past Tense

Let's first take a look at the following line in the dialogue:

> Джон: Хlаъ, цига а ваха нохчийн мотт а бийци, чай а мели, чlепалгаш а дии!
> *John: Yes, I went there, spoke Chechen, drank tea, and ate ch'epalgash!*

The forms в.агли, б.ийци, мели, and д.ии are all in the *Recent Past tense*. The *recent past*, as its name suggests, describes events that *just* happened. The tense is most often formed through vowel shift, so the Recent Past stems must be memorized. In Lesson 3 we introduced ablaut patterns for the Infinitive and Present tense. Let's now add the Recent Past.

Pattern	Infinitive	Present	Recent Past
ий → уьй	д.ийца (to speak)	д.уьйцу (speaks)	д.ийци (just spoke)
е → оь	д.еша (to read / to study)	д.оьшу (reads / studies)	д.ийши (just studied)
а → аь	хаа (to know)	хаьа (knows)	хии (just knew, learned)
а → о	ган (to see)	го (sees)	ги (saw)

Now let's look at two more verbs:

Pattern	Infinitive	Present	Recent Past
a → o	мала *(to drink)*	молу *(drinks)*	мели *(just drank)*
a → o	ала *(to say)*	олу *(says)*	эли *(just said)*

Notice that the two verbs above follow the same pattern: a → o → e. This is because мала and ала belong to the same *conjugation*. Verbs that follow the same pattern when changing tense, aspect, or mood belong to the same conjugation.

Chechen, according to the linguist Johanna Nichols, has around thirty-four conjugations. Many of these conjugations, however, feature only a few verbs. We will begin introducing you to the different conjugations. Here are a few we've met, classified according to Nichols' *Chechen English Dictionary*.

Conjugation	Infinitive	Present	Recent Past
XXVI	д.ийца *(to speak)*	д.уьйцу *(speaks)*	д.ийци *(spoke)*
XX	д.еша *(to read/study)*	д.оьшу *(reads/studies)*	д.ийши *(studied)*
VIII	хаа *(to know)*	хаьа *(knows)*	хии *(knew)*
XXX	ган *(to see)*	го *(sees)*	ги *(saw)*
V	мала *(to drink)*	молу *(drinks)*	мели *(drank)*

In addition to the thirty-four conjugations, Chechen has many irregular verbs that do not follow a pattern. Here is the Recent Past form for the irregular verbs you have already encountered:

	Infinitive	Present	Present Progressive	Future Possible	Recent Past
to do / to make	д.ан	д.о	д.еш д.у	д.ер	д.и
to go	д.аха	д.оьду	д.оьдуш д.у	д.оɼуp	д.ахи
to come	д.ан	д.оɼy	д.оɼyш	д.оɼуp	д.еа
to give	д.ала	ло	луш д.у	лур	д.ели
to be	хила	д.у	–	хир	хили

Note: As we continue to introduce new verb forms, we will show the patterns behind each conjugation.

Observed Past Tense

The Observed Past tense, or as other grammars describe it, the *Witnessed Past*, describes actions that the speaker has witnessed or experienced. It is formed from the Recent Past tense by adding **-pa** to the Recent Past form. We saw the following examples in the dialogue:

Ас дика университет чекхйаьккхи**ра** Америкехь.
I graduated from a good university in America.

Тlаккха со библиотеке болх бан ваха**ра**.
Afterwards, I went to the library to work.

Since the speaker experienced the events himself, he uses the Observed Past Tense. Let's take a look at a few more examples:

Regular Verbs				
Conjugation	Infinitive	Present	Recent Past	Observed Past
XXVI	д.ийца (*to tell*)	д.уьйцу	д.ийци	д.ийцира
XX	д.еша (*to read/ study*)	д.оьшу	д.ийши	д.ийшира

VIII	хаа (*to know*)	хаьа	хии	хиира
V	мала (*to drink*)	молу	мели	мелира

Irregular Verbs			
Infinitive	**Present**	**Recent Past**	**Observed Past**
д.ан (*to do*)	д.о	д.и	д.ира
ган (*to see*)	го	ги	гина
д.аха (*to go* pl.)	д.оьду	д.аха	д.ахара
д.ан (*to bring*)	д.оьгӏу	д.еа	д.еара
д.ала (*to give*)	ло	д.ели	д.елира
хила (*to become*)	хуьлу	хили	хилира

Imperatives: Making Commands

The Imperative in Chechen corresponds to commands in English. English commands like "*Read!*" and "*Please read!*" have separate forms in Chechen. To form a basic command, simply use the infinitive form of the verb:

 Хьажа! *Look!*

The suffix **-л** adds firmness to the command:

 Хьажал! *You must look!*

To form polite versions of the Imperative, we need to think about aspect, that is, whether we want an action to be completed or not. When an action is ongoing, we say the aspect is imperfective. When an action is completed, it is perfective. Thus, we can also build the following forms:

Хьажахь!
Please be watching! / Please watch! (to one person)

Хьажалахь.
Please watch. (to one person)

Хьажийш.
Please be watching. / Please watch. (to two or more people)

Хьажалаш.
Please watch. (to two or more people)

To form a negative command, use *ма*, not *ца*:

Ма хьажалахь!
Please don't watch!

NOUNS: INSTRUMENTAL CASE

Note the following two sentences:

Со Джон**ца** цӀа вахара.
*I went home **with** John.*

Со кьоламаш**ца** йазйеш йу.
*I am writing **with** pencils.*

The Instrumental case in Chechen (**-ца**) is used to convey *with whom* or *with what* an action is occurring. It can also be used to describe the means by which an action is occurring:

Цо шур кружка**ца** мелира.
*He drank the milk **with a cup**. (*lit: *by means of a cup)*

Forming the Instrumental case is fairly straightforward. All four declensions add the suffix **-ца**. In the chart below, note that in the second declension the **-н-** extension stays, as expected. The third declension retains the vowel **-и**. Note **-чу** becomes a diphthong **-чуь** in the fourth declension. In the second column, the first declension with an ablaut example, note the appearance of the vowel **-а-**. The vowel corrects for what would otherwise be three consonants in a row (double тт plus ц), which would be awkward to pronounce:

	First Declension	First Declension Ablaut	Second Declension	Third Declension	Fourth Declension
Abs. Sing.	студент (*student*)	мотт (*language*)	гота (*plow*)	йиша (*sister*)	хьехархо (*teacher*)
Instr. Sing.	студентца	маттаца	готанца	йишица	хьехархочуьнца

The Instrumental plural is fairly regular. In the first, second, and third declensions, simply add the suffix **-ца** to the Absolute plural. For the fourth declension, add **-шца** to the Absolute singular:

	First Declension	First Declension Ablaut	Second Declension	Third Declension	Fourth Declension
Abs. Pl.	студенташ	меттанаш	готанаш	йижарий	хьехархой
Instr. Pl.	студенташца	меттанашца	готанашца	йижаршца	хьехархошш

Note, for the third declension йижарий - йижаршца is slightly irregular. So let's take a quick look at another third declension noun, мач-а "*shoe*":

мач-а *shoe*   мача-ш *shoes*
мач-и-ца *with the shoe*   мача-ш-ца *with the shoes*

The vowels for personal pronouns in the Instrumental case become diphthongs, except in the first person plural inclusive form:

	I	you	he/she/it	we (exc.)	we (incl.)	you (pl.)	they
Abs.	со	хьо	иза/и	тхо	вай	шу	уьш
Erg.	ас/аса	ахь/ахьа	цо	ох/оха	вай	аш/аша	цара
Gen.	сан	хьан	цуьнан	тхан	вайн	шун	церан
Dat.	суна	хьуна	цунна	тхуна	вайна	шуна	царна
Instr.	соьца	хьоьца	цуьнца	тхоьца	вайца	шуьца	цаьрца

Упражненеш / EXERCISES

Exercise 1. *Read John's monologue and rewrite it as a female.*

Де дика хуьлда шун дешархой! Сан цӏе Джон йу, со керла дешархо ву. Со цӏера Америкера ву. Сан ткъе йалх шо ду. Ас нохчийн мотт, оьрсийн мотт а, ингалс мотт а буьйцу. Суна меттанаш хазахета. Ас дика университет чекхйаьлккхира Америкехь, тӏаккха со библиотеке болх бан вахара. Йуха ас жимма хьехархойн болх бира. Цул тӏаьхьа, суна керла дешар карийра, и дешар нохчийн маттахь дара, ишттa волавелира со нохчийн мотт ӏамабан. Йуха со Нохчийчу веара сайн дикка нохчийн мотт ӏамабан.

_____

_____

_____

_____

_____

_____

_____

_____

_____

_____

Exercise 2. *Translate the following sentences into Chechen, using the Recent Past tense.*

1. I drank water. _____

2. You helped. _____

3. They ate chepalgash. _____

4. We (*inc.*) said "thank you." _____

5. She read a book. _____

6. He saw a computer. _____

7. Liza knew the time. _____

8. Beshto went to the library. _____

Exercise 3. *Translate these sentences from English to Chechen using the Observed Past tense.*

1. Malika saw the auditorium.

_____

2. The students drank hot tea.

_____

3. The brothers went to their house.

_____

4. We (*excl.*) bought milk.

_____

5. They were at home.

_____

6. You saw him at the university.

_____

7. The teacher spoke to the students.

_____

8. You (*pl.*) wrote a letter.

_____

Exercise 4. *Fill in the blanks using the correct case for each noun given in parentheses.*

1. (Студенташ)_____ишколе вахара.

2. Хьо нохчийн (мотт)_____доьшуш ву.

3. Ваха шен (да)_____гIалайукъеЪ (*town center*) веара.

4. Цара (вежарий)_____пикник йо аьхка хIора шарахь.

Exercise 5. *Translate the sentences from Exercise 4 into English.*

1. _____

2. _____

3. _____

4. _____

Exercise 6. *Write the imperfective and perfective "polite" Imperative forms for both the singular and plural of the following verbs.*

1. Мала _____

2. Хьажа _____

3. Дийца _____

4. Ца дийца _____

5. Ала _____

6. ДIахIотта _____

7. Охьахаа _____

8. Тилла _____

Exercise 7. *Fill in the blanks using nouns in the Instrumental case and translate into English.*

1. Хьо хьаьнца Iаш ву? Со сайн _____Iаш ву.

_____

2. Хьо университете хьаьнца воьду? Со университете _____воьду.

_____

3. Хьо балха стенца воьду? Со балха_____ воьду.

_____

4. Хьо кафе хьаьнца воьду? Со кафе_____воьду.

_____

5. Ахь чай стенца молу? Ас чай_____молу.

_____

Exercise 8: *Translate the following sentences into Chechen using Instrumental case.*

1. I drink tea with sugar.

_____

2. We go to work (with) a car.

_____

3. She wants tea with sugar.

_____

4. I go to market with my mother.

_____

5. He studies Chechen by (with) a book.

_____

Корта VI: Базарахь
Lesson 6: At the Market

Knowledge Check: In this lesson's dialogues, highlight each verb and mark its tense.

Lesson Plan:
- The Substantive and Comparative cases
- Case review with declensions
- Pronouns
- Modal verbs
- Preverbs
- Numbers 21 to 10,000

ДИАЛОГ I

Джона, Хьава, Малика а туькана баха хьокъехь къамел деш бу.

Джон: Суна шур а, хасстоьмаш а, жижиг оьшу.

Малика: Муьлха хасстоьмаш оьшу хьуна?

Джон: Со картолш а, хохаш а, помидорш а, копаст а эца воллу.

Хьава: Джон, хьуна хохаш мерзахета?

Джон: ХIаъ, суна хохаш деза.

Хьава: Муьлха тайпа жижиг эца лаьа хьуна?

Джон: Котаман а, бежанан жижиг оьшу суна.

Хьава: Дика ду, хьуна маца ваха лаьа туькана йа базар?

Джон: Кхана дахалур ду аьлла хетий хьуна вай?

Хьава: ХIаъ, вай беркат базар гIур ду аьлла хета суна.

Малика: Хьо йаахIума йан воллу?

Джон: Со чIепалгаш датта гIерта. Хала дуй и?

Малика: Ва-а нана ма йала хьан! Атта дац дера!

Хьава: Джон, хьуна дам а, кIалд, йеттшура а йеза хьуна.

Джон: Аш гIо дийр дуй суна кхана?

Хьава: Дера дийр ду!

DIALOGUE I: AT THE MARKET

John, Hwava, and Malika discuss going to the store.

John: I need milk, vegetables, and meat.

Malika: Which vegetables do you need?

John: I'm planning to buy potatoes, onions, tomatoes, and cabbage.

Hwava: John, do you like onions? (Lit. *Do you like the taste of onions?*)

John: Yes, I love onions.

Hwava: Which type of meat do you want to buy?

John: I want (*lit.* need) to buy chicken and beef.

Hwava: Ok, when do you want to go to the store or market?

John: Do you think that we can go tomorrow?

Hwava: Yes, I think we'll go to Berkat market.

Malika: Are you going to cook something?

John: I'll try to bake ch'epalgash. Is it difficult?

Malika: Bless you! It's not easy!

Hwava: John, you need flour, cottage cheese, and kefir.

John: Will you help me tomorrow?

Hwava: We will!

12 ДИАЛОГ II

Маликий Джоний Беркат базара схьакхочу. Уьш арахула лела, тlаккха базар чубоьлху. Йохкархочун тlебоьлху уьш. Стол тlехь тайп-тайпана жижиг ду.

Малика:	Мах дика хуьлда хьан!
Йохкархо:	Дела реза хуьлда! Шуна хlун жижиг деза?
Джон:	Суна цхьа котам еза.
Йохкархо:	Хьуна йоккха йа жима котам еза?
Джон:	Жиманиг лохьа суна.
Йохкархо:	Хlа, схьалаца. Кхин хlумма а оьший шуна?
Малика:	Хlаъ, оха цхьа кийла бежанан жижиг оьцур ду.
Йохкархо:	Схьалаца. Малика, хьан доьзал муха бу? Хьан могшалла муха йу?
Малика:	Уьш дика бу. Сан могшалла дика йу. Хьан мах муха дlабоьду?
Йохкархо:	Ахча даккха хала ду. Аьхка корта ца кхихкича-lай йай кхехкар бац.
Малика:	Иза-м бакъ ду! Гур ду вай.

Маликий Джоний кхечу йохкархочун уллехь соцу.

Джон:	Мах дика хуьлда хьан! Помидоран хlун мах бу?
Йохкархо:	Кийланах шийтта туьма доьху.
Малика:	Ахча дац соьгахь.
Джон:	Хlумма дац, суна оьцуш ма йу хlорш, ас дlалур ду ахча. Картолах хlун доьху?
Йохкархо:	Картолан мах шовзткъе итт сом бу.
Малика:	Йеза йу. Шовзткъе пхи соьмах цхьа кийла схьалой ахь?
Йохкархо:	Дика ду. Хохаш дезий шуна?
Джон:	Деза. Хlун доьху?

DIALOGUE II: AT THE STALL

Malika and John arrive at Berkat Bazar. They walk around Berkat, then enter. They approach a vendor. On the table are different types of meat.

Malika: May the price be good!

Vendor: Hello! Do you need meat?

John: I need one chicken.

Vendor: Do you need a large or small chicken?

John: Give me the small one.

Vendor: Sure, here you go. Do you need anything else?

Malika: Yes, we will buy one kilo of beef.

Vendor: Here you go. Malika, how is your family? How's your health?

Malika: They are well. My health is good. How is business? [*Lit.*: How are your prices going?]

Vendor: Making money is tough. If in the summer your head doesn't boil, then your pot won't boil in winter.

Malika: That's true! See you!

Malika and John stop at the other vendor's table.

John: Good afternoon! What is the price for tomatoes?

Vendor: One kilogram is 120 rubles.

Malika: I don't have money on me.

John: It's okay, we are buying it for me, I will pay. How much are potatoes?

Vendor: Potatoes are 210 rubles per kilogram.

Malika: It's expensive. Do you give one kilogram for 205?

Vendor: Okay. Do you want onions?

John: Yes. How much?

Йохкархо: кхузткъе.

Джон: Дорах ду, ас ши кийла оьцу. Копаст йуй хьогахь? Суна ца го.

Йохкархо: Йу. Цуьнан мах цхьа бӀе доьзткъе бу.

Джон: Мегар ду. Массо хӀуманех хӀун долу?

Йохкархо: (дагардеш): Сто двадцать плюс двести пять, плюс сто восемьдесят, плюс сто двадцать Шестьсот двадцать пять рублей.

Джон: Йалх бӀе ткъе пхи сом?

Йохкархо: (воьлуш) хьуна нохчийн маттахь нохчола дика дагардан хаьа?

Малика: Вайн массаралла диках!

Джон: ХӀан-хӀа, аш сол исбаьхьа буьйцу нохчийн мотт.

Vendor: 60

John: It's cheap. I'll buy 2 kilos. Do you have cabbage? I don't see it.

Vendor: Yes. Its price is 180 (rubles).

John: Okay. How much for everything?

Vendor: (*calculating*) 120 plus 205 plus 180 plus 120. (*In Russian*) 625 rubles.

John: 625 rubles?

Vendor: (*laughing*) You know how to count in Chechen better than a Chechen?

Malika: Better than all of us!

John: No, you speak the Chechen more beautifully than I.

Керла Дешнаш / New Words I

шур, шуреш (й:й) milk
туька, туьканаш (й:й) store
хасстом, хасстоьмаш (б:д) vegetable
жижиг, жижигаш (д:д) meat
картол, картолш (й:й) potato
хох, хохаш (б:д) onion
помидор, помидорш (й:й) tomato
копаст, копастш (й:й) cabbage
котаман жижиг (д) chicken (*meat*)
бежанан жижиг (д) beef
хала difficult
атта easy
кхана tomorrow
дам (д) flour
дера of course, definitely
кӀалд, кӀалдш (й:й) cottage cheese
йеттшура (й) kefir
Беркат базар, базарш (й:й) *open farm market in Grozny*

Керла Хандешнаш / New Verbs I

гӀорта to try, to attempt (to do) **(гӀерта, гӀоьрти)**
къамел дан to talk, to discuss **(къамел до, къамел ди)**
эца to buy; to take **(оьцу, ийци)**
д.оллу planning to
мерзахета to like (*taste*) **(мерзахета, мерзахийти)**
д.ахало to be able to go **(д.ахало; д.ахад.аьлли)**
дахалур ду аьлла that (we) can go
йаахӀума йан to cook **(йаахӀума йо; йаахӀума йи)**
д.атта to bake **(д.отту; д.етти)**

Керла Дешнаш II / New Words II

мах, мехаш (б:д) price
кийла, кийланаш (й:й) kilogram
йохкархо, йохкархой (в/й:б) seller
могшалла, могшаллонаш (й:й) health
хох, хохаш (б:д) onion
жиманиг the small one
исбаьхьа very beautiful, amazing
копаст (й:й) cabbage
д.орах cheap
д.еза expensive; heavy
Иза-м бакъ ду! This is right!, That's true!

Керла Хандешнаш / New Verbs

арахула лела to walk around **(арахула лела; арахула лели)**
ахча даккха to earn money **(ахча доккху; ахча даьккхи)**
дӏадӏаха to go up **(дӏадӏ.оьду; дӏадӏ.ахи)**
кхехка to boil **(кхехка; кхихки)**
д.охка to sell **(д.ухку; доьхки)**
дагард.ан to count **(дагард.о; дагард.и)**
д.ела to laugh, to smile **(д.оьлу; д.ийли)**
д.ала *here:* to cost **(д.олу; д.ели)**
схьалаца to catch; to hold **(схьалоцу; схьалеци)**

Граматика / Grammar

The Substantive Case

The Substantive case denotes, as the Chechen linguist A.G. Matsiev noted, "the material from which an object is made, or the whole from which a part has been detached." In this sense, the Substantive expresses the essence of a noun. The Substantive case can be a bit tricky at first, as there is no one way to translate it into English. Where Chechen uses the Substantive case, English often reverts to prepositions such as *for, in,* or *per.*

One common use of the Substantive case is for saying the price of an object and its weight. We read the following in the dialogue above:

Шовзткъе пхи соьмах цхьа кийла схьалой ахь?
Do you give one kilogram for 205?

The Substantive ending -**ax** expresses the inherent value of one kilo, *for* 205 rubles.

Массо а хlуман**ах** хlун долу?
How much for everything? (Lit. *Of all the thing(s) what finishes?*)

"Массо а хlуманах" (*everything*) is describing the essence of "*what.*"

Кийлан**ах** шийтта туьма доьху.
It costs 120 (rubles) per kilo.

Here, the Substantive denotes a measurement, which can be translated into English as *per.*

For the first and second declensions, the Substantive singular takes -**ax**; the fourth declension takes -**чух**:

	First Declension	First Declension Ablaut	Second Declension	Third Declension	Fourth Declension
Abs. Sing.	студент (*student*)	мотт (*language*)	гота (*plow*)	мача (*shoe*)	хьехархо (*teacher*)
Subst. Sing.	студент**ах**	матт**ах**	готан**ах**	мач**ах**	хьехархо**чух**

The first through third declensions take **-ex** in the Substantive plural—not **-ашех***! The fourth declension takes **-йх**.

	First Declension	First Declension Ablaut	Second Declension	Third Declension	Fourth Declension
Abs. Pl.	студенташ (*students*)	меттанаш (*languages*)	готанаш (*plows*)	мачаш (*shoes*)	хьехархой (*teachers*)
Subst. Pl.	студент**ех**	меттан**ех**	готан**ех**	мач**ех**	хьехархо**йх**

The Comparative Case

The Comparative case is used, as its name suggests, to compare nouns. We saw the Comparative case in the dialogues above:

Йохкархо (воьлуш): Хьуна нохчийн маттахь нохчол дика
дагардан хаьа?
*Seller (laughing): You know how to count in Chechen better than a
Chechen?*

Малика: Вайн массаралла диках!
Malika: Better than all of us!

The Comparative case is particularly important for comparative statements, i.e., "A is more X than B." In Chechen, a comparative statement consists of an adjective or adverb and two nouns. In the construction, "A is more X than B," noun B will take the Comparative case. Let's take a look at other sentences:

Джон кlантал воккха ву.   Хьава Джонал кlадйелла йу.
John is older than the boy.   *Hwava is more tired than John.*

Pronouns also take the Comparative case:

Хьо сол хазах йу.
You are prettier than me.

The first and second declensions take **-ал** in the singular. The third declension takes **-ил** and the fourth declension takes **-чул**:

	First Declension	First Declension Ablaut	Second Declension	Third Declension	Fourth Declension
Abs. Sing.	студент (*student*)	мотт (*language*)	гота (*plow*)	мача (*shoe*)	хьехархо (*teacher*)
Comp. Sing.	студент**ал**	матт**ал**	готан**ал**	мач**ил**	хьехархо**чул**

The first through third declensions take **-ел** in the plural. The fourth declension takes **-йл** in the plural.

	First Declension	First Declension Ablaut	Second Declension	Third Declension	Fourth Declension
Abs. Pl.	студенташ (*students*)	меттанаш (*languages*)	готанаш (*plows*)	мачаш (*shoes*)	хьехархой (*teachers*)
Comp. Pl.	студент**ел**	меттан**ел**	готан**ел**	мач**ел**	хьехархой**л**

Note: To make an adjective comparative (good – better) or superlative (good – best), Chechen adds suffixes to the adjectives. For the comparative degree, add **-x**. For the superlative, **уггар** "*most*" comes before the adjective:

Хlара студент сол дика**х** ву.
This student is better than me.

Хlара студент дика**х** ву.
This student is better.

Хlара студент **уггар** дика ву.
This student is the best.

Chechen Cases: Declensions

You have now encountered each of the eight main cases in Chechen. Let's review, looking at each declension.

First Declension, No Ablaut		
	Singular	*Plural*
Abs.	студент (*student*)	студенташ
Gen.	студентан	студентийн
Dat.	студентана	студенташна
Erg.	студента	студенташа
Instr.	студентаца	студенташца
Subst.	студентах	студентех
Comp.	студентал	студентел
All. / Loc.	студентига / студентигахь	студенташка / студенташкахь

There is only one form here we have yet to meet: the Locative plural. As we learned in Lesson 2, the Allative case expresses the direction to something. It forms the basis for other endings which express direction or location.

Absolutive	**Allative**	**Locative**
университет	университ-е	университет-е-**хь**
university	*to the university*	*at the university*

Absolutive	**Allative**	**Locative**
университеташ	университеташка	университеташка**хь**
universities	*to the universities*	*at the universities*

In the dialogues, we saw several pronouns in the Locative, which is a useful way of saying whether something is "on you." These forms are built from the Allative case of the personal pronoun, plus -**хь**.

Ахча дац соьга**хь**.
I don't have money on me.

Копаст йуй хьоьгахь?
Do you have cabbage? (Lit. *At you is there cabbage?*)

Now, let's take a look at the first declension noun with ablaut:

First Declension with Ablaut		
	Singular	*Plural*
Abs.	мотт (*language*)	меттанаш
Gen.	меттан	меттанийн
Dat.	меттана	меттанашна
Erg.	матто	меттанаша
Instr.	маттаца	меттанашца
Subst.	маттах	меттанех
Comp.	маттал	меттанел
All. / Loc.	матте / маттахь	меттанашка / меттанашкахь

The first declension with ablaut, no extension—in Nichols' system, the third declension—features many nouns whose ablaut descends "from ancient Nakh-Dagestani alternations."[9] Some nouns, like мотт and борз see two vowel shifts in different cases, i.e., "e" in the genitive and dative; "a" in the other oblique cases. Others, like ca "*soul*" have only one vowel shift in all oblique cases (all cases other than the Absolutive).

First Declension with Ablaut		
	Singular	*Plural*
Nom.	ca (*soul*)	синош
Gen.	син	синойн
Dat.	сина	синошна

[9] See: Nichols, Johanna, and A. D Vagapov. *Chechen-English and English-Chechen Dictionary*. London: Routledge Curzon, 2004.

Erg.	сино	синоша
Instr.	сица	синашца
Subst.	сих	сийх
Comp.	сил	сийл
All. / Loc.	сига / сигахь	синошка / синошкахь

Second declension nouns feature extension, usually **-н-** or **-р-**. They can feature no ablaut or ablaut:

Second Declension: N Extension, No Ablaut		
	Singular	*Plural*
Abs.	гота (*plow*)	готанаш
Gen.	готанан	готанийн
Dat.	готана	готанашна
Erg.	готано	готанаша
Instru.	готанца	готанашца
Subst.	готанах	готанех
Comp.	готанал	готанел
All. / Loc.	готане / готанехь	готанашка / готанашкахь

Second Declension: N Extension, Ablaut		
	Singular	*Plural*
Abs.	цIено (*house*)	цIенош
Gen.	цIийнан	цIенойн
Dat.	цIенна	цIеношна
Erg.	цIийно	цIеноша

Instr.	цӏийнаца	цӏеношца
Subst.	цӏийнах	цӏенех
Comp.	цӏийнал	цӏенел
All. / Loc.	цӏийне / цӏийнехь	цӏеношка / цӏеношкахь

The **-p-** extension also features no ablaut and ablaut forms. Here we decline цӏе *"name" and* цӏе *"fire."* Note the difference as each word declines:

Second Declension: R Extension, No Ablaut		
	Singular	*Plural*
Abs.	цӏе (*name*)	цӏерш
Gen.	цӏеран	цӏерийн
Dat.	цӏерана	цӏерашна
Erg.	цӏеро	цӏераша
Instr.	цӏерца	цӏерашца
Subst.	цӏерах	цӏерех
Comp.	цӏерал	цӏерел
All. / Loc.	цӏере / цӏерехь	цӏерашка / цӏерашкахь

Second Declension: R Extension, Ablaut		
	Singular	*Plural*
Abs.	цӏе (*fire*)	цӏерш
Gen.	цӏеран	цӏарийн
Dat.	цӏарна	цӏарашна
Erg.	цӏаро	цӏараша
Instr.	цӏарца	цӏарашца

Subst.	цӀарах	цӀарех
Comp.	цӀарал	цӀарел
All. / Loc.	цӀаре / цӀарехь	цӀарашка / цӀарашкахь

The third declension features the vowel -и- in the Genitive. Nichols labels this an "i extension." We have seen мача (*shoe*) already:

Third Declension		
	Singular	*Plural*
Abs.	мача	мачаш
Gen.	мачин	мачийн
Dat.	мачина	мачашна
Erg.	мачо	мачаша
Instr.	мачица	мачашца
Subst.	мачих	мачех
Comp.	мачил	мачел
All. / Loc.	мачига / мачигахь	мачашка / мачашкахь

The third declension also features nouns that take ablaut. For example, йиша / ваша "*sister / brother*":

Third Declension, Ablaut		
	Singular	*Plural*
Abs.	йиша / ваша	йижарий / вежарий
Gen.	йишин / вешин	йижарийн / вежарийн
Dat.	йишина / вешина	йижаршна / вежаршна
Erg.	йишас / вешас	йижарша / вежарша
Instr.	йишица / вешица	йижаршца / вежаршца
Subst.	йишах / вешах	йижарех / вежарех

Comp.	йишал / вешал	йижарел / вежарел
All. / Loc.	йишига / вешига	йижаршка / вежаршка

Finally, here is the fourth declension fully declined. Nichols labels this declension the "-chu- extension." The fourth declension is primarily for professions and terms for people:

Fourth Declension		
	Singular	*Plural*
Abs.	хьехархо (*teacher*)	хьехархой (*teachers*)
Gen.	хьехархочун	хьехархойн
Dat.	хьехархочунна	хьехархошна
Erg.	хьехархочо	хьехархоша
Instr.	хьехархочуьнца	хьехархошца
Subst.	хьехархочух	хьехархойх
Comp.	хьехархочул	хьехархойл
All. / Loc.	хьехархочуьнга / хьехархочуьнгахь	хьехархошка / хьехархошкахь

The word for a "Chechen person," нохчо, is also a fourth declension noun:

Fourth Declension		
	Singular	*Plural*
Abs.	нохчо	нохчий
Gen.	нохчочуьн	нохчийн
Dat.	нохчочунна	нохчашна
Erg.	нохчочо	нохчаша
Instr.	нохчочуьнца	нохчашца

Subst.	нохчочух	нохчех
Comp.	нохчочул	нохчойл
All. / Loc.	нохчочуьнга / нохчочуьнгахь	нохчашка / нохчашкахь

Chechen Cases: Pronouns

Here are the personal pronouns declined in all eight cases:

	I	you	he/she/it	we (exc.)	we (incl.)	you (pl.)	they
Nom.	со	хьо	иза/и	тхо	вай	шу	уьш
Gen.	сан	хьан	цуьнан	тхан	вайн	шун	церан
Dat.	суна	хьуна	цунна	тхуна	вайна	шуна	царна
Erg.	аса/ас	ахьа/ахь	цо	оха/ох	вай	аша/аш	цара
Instr.	соьца	хьоьца	цуьнца	тхоьца	вайца	шуьца	цаьрца
Subst.	сох	хьох	цунах	тхох	вайх	шух	царах
Comp.	сол	хьол	цул	тхол	вайл	шул	царел
All. / Loc.	соьга / соьгахь	хьоьга / хьоьгахь	цуьнга / цуьнгахь	тхоьга / тхоьгахь	вайга / вайгахь	шуьга / шуьгахь	цаьрга / цаьргахь

Modal Verbs

Modal verbs are verbs that express need, desire, ability, etc. In English, *must, can, should, need,* and *want,* are all examples of modal verbs. Modal verbs in English are followed by the infinitive (eg., I want *to learn*; He needs *to study*). We have already met several modal verbs in Chechen. Here they are again:

Infinitive	Present	Future possible	Recent past	English Translation
лаа	лаьа	луур	лии	*want*
хаа	хаьа	хуур	хии	*know*

хета	хета	хетар	хийти	*seem*
эша	оьшу	оьшур	ийши	*need*
д.еза	д.еза	д.езар	д.ийзи	*love, need*

The subject of a Chechen modal verb is typically in the Dative case, while the object is in the Absolutive case:

Цунна иза хаьа.   Беранна шура оьшу.
He knows it.   *The baby needs milk.*

Chechen modal verbs often take the infinitive:

Суна Iама **лаьа**.
I want to learn.

The verb д.еза must agree with noun class. Depending on context, it can either mean *"love"* or *"need"*:

йолана помидорш **йеза**.
The girl loves tomatoes. / The girl needs tomatoes.

If the infinitive following деза is intransitive, then деза (and, potentially, the infinitive) will agree with the subject:

Со в.аха **в.еза**.
I (male) need to go.

However, to express the need *to do* something (as opposed to the need *of* something), the subject will appear in the Genitive case. Compare the two sentences:

Сан в.аха **в.еза**.   Суна помидорш **йеза**.
I need to go. / I have to go.   *I need tomatoes.*

If the verb in the infinitive has, or could potentially have, two objects, the subject of the modal will appear in the Ergative case. This is to avoid the ambiguity of two datives:

Цунна компьютер **оьшу**.   Цо суна компьютер эца **йеза**.
He needs a computer.   *He needs to buy me a computer.*

As in English, хета *"like"* can be both a modal verb and a verb that takes an object. Several compounds can be built from хета:

Compound	Example	Meaning
хазахета	Суна и торт **хазахета**. *I like this cake.*	Like the shape or how it looks (visually). Used for only the visual quality.
дикахета	Суна и торт **дикахета**. *I like this cake.*	Like the quality (inside). Used for anything that can have a good quality, even humans.
мерзахета	Суна и торт **мерзахета**. *I like this cake.*	Like the taste. Only used for edible things.

Preverbs

We've seen a few examples now of verbs we know with certain prefixes attached. These prefixes, which we will call preverbs, add extra meaning to a basic verb. They can convey direction, repetition, or take on a new meaning (think of how simple prepositions can change the semantics of a verb: "to throw" vs. "to throw up").

Preverbs often resemble postpositions, which will come up in a few future lessons. For speakers of Russian, preverbs function in a similar way to *prefixes*, though they do not necessarily carry the same sense of aspect.

In the affirmative, the preverb is attached to the verb. In the negative, however, **ца** comes in between the preverb and verb:

Preverb	Present affirmative	Present negative
дла (*away from*)	длакхуссу (*throw away*)	дла ца кхуссу (lit. *away no throw*)
тle (*onto*)	тlекхуссу (*throw onto*)	тle ца кхуссу (lit. *onto no throw*)
схьала (*up*)	схьалакхуссу (*throw up**)	хьала ца кхуссу (lit. *up no throw*)

кӏела (*under*)	кӏелакхуссу (*throw under*)	кӏела ца кхуссу (lit. *under no throw*)
охьа (*down*)	охьакхуссу (*throw down*)	охьа ца кхуссу (lit. *down no throw*)
схьа (*to*)	схьакхуссу (*throw to*)	схьа ца кхуссу (lit. *to no throw*)

*Not "*vomit*," which is леттад.ан.

Chechen Numbers 21 to 10,000

The Chechen number system is vigesimal, based on the number ткъа (*20)*. Here are the numbers 21 – 40:

21	ткъе цхьаъ	31	ткъе цхьайтта
22	ткъе шиъ	32	ткъе шийтта
23	ткъе кхоъ	33	ткъе кхойтта
24	ткъе д.иъ	34	ткъе д.ейтта
25	ткъе пхиъ	35	ткъе пхийтта
26	ткъе йалх	36	ткъе йалхитта
27	ткъе ворхӏ	37	ткъе вуьрхӏитта
28	ткъе바рхӏ	38	ткъе берхӏитта
29	ткъе исс	39	ткъе ткъайоьсна
30	ткъе итт	40	шовзткъа

The numbers 40, 60, and 80 can be translated literally as "two twenties," "three twenties," "four twenties." Number building, like 226 below, is straightforward:

40	шовзткъа	80	д.езткъа
50	шовзткъе итт	90	д.езткъе итт
60	кхузткъа	100	бӏе
70	кхузткъе итт	226	ши бӏе ткъе йалх

The word for "thousand" is **эзар**:

1000	цхьаъ эзар	6000	йалх эзар
2000	шиъ эзар	7000	ворх1 эзар
3000	кхоъ эзар	8000	барх1 эзар
4000	д.иъ эзар	9000	исс эзар
5000	пхиъ эзар	10000	итт эзар

Культура / Culture

Expressions

Chechens love to sprinkle phrases into their speech. An example of one is "**Ва-а нана ма йала хьан!**" This literally means "*May your mother not die!*" It is used to express care, love, and pity.

There is an opposite expression "**Нана йала хьан!**" which is typically used when a speaker is disappointed about something or doesn't like an idea. It literally means "*May your mother die.*" This is not necessarily directed to the listener, it can be directed at an idea the speaker hates, for example. We would suggest only using this phrase with good friends, in informal settings first!

Упражненеш / Exercises

Exercise 1. *Fill in the table using the Substantive and Comparative cases. Then, mark which declension the noun belongs to.*

English	Absolutive	Substantive	Comparative	Declension
language	мотт	маттах		
		дех		
brothers				
			книгел	
		йишах		
	хьехархой			

Exercise 2. *Translate the following sentences into Chechen using the Comparative case or comparative adjectives.*

1. John is better than the boy.

   _____

2. These tomatoes are more expensive than the potatoes.

   _____

3. Hwava is more tired than me.

   _____

4. My teacher is the smartest.

   _____

5. My apartment is bigger than your house.

   _____

Exercise 3. *Match the Chechen phrases with the English translations:*

1. Хьавана чорп дикахета   a. We (*incl.*) like cabbage.
2. Iарбина квартира дикахете   b. Arbi likes the apartment.
3. Суна помидорш дикахета   c. Malika likes the meat.
4. Вайна копаст дикахета   d. We like lovzar.
5. Маликина жижиг мерзахета   e. I like tomatoes.
6. Тхуна ловзар хазахета   f. Hwava likes soup.

Exercise 4. *Answer the following questions in complete sentences.*

1. Хьоьгахь копаст йуй?

   _____

2. Хьоьгахь ахча дуй?

   _____

3. Цуьнгахь книжка йуй?

   _____

4. Туьканахь жижиг дуй?

_____

5. Базарахь помидорш йуй?

_____

6. Беркатехь картолш йуй?

_____

7. Шугахь шура йуй?

_____

8. Цаьргахь чӀепалгаш дуй?

_____

Exercise 5. _Fill in the blanks with nouns. Use any nouns from this lesson and nouns that mean food where you encounter_ **мерзахета.**

1. Суна _____ дикахета, амма _____ дика ца хета.

2. Суна _____ мерзахета, амма _____ мерза ца хета.

3. Суна _____ хазахета, амма _____ хаза ца хета.

4. Суна _____ дикахета.

5. Суна _____хазхахета.

Exercise 6. _Write these numbers in numerical form._

1. Шовзткъа _____
2. Шовзткъе итт _____
3. Ткъе итт _____
4. Ткъе бехӀитта _____
5. Дезткъа _____

Exercise 7. *Use the preverb grammar table from this lesson to translate the following.*

   1. Дlакхуссу   _____

   2. Схьакхуссу   _____

   3. Охьакхуссу   _____

   4. Кlелакхуссу   _____

   4. Схьалакхуссу   _____

   6. Тlекхуссу   _____

Exercise 8. *Complete this short dialogue using the sentence starters.*

Али: Жижигах хlун доьху?

Хаважи: Жижигах _____ сом доьху.

Али: Хьаьжкlех хlун доьху?

Хаважи: Хьаьжкlех _____ сом доьху.

Али: _____ хlун доьху?

Хаважи: _____ сом доьху.

Али: _____?

Хаважи: _____.

Корта VII: Туьканахь
Lesson 7: At the Store

Knowledge Check: In the dialogues in this lesson, underline the nouns and mark their case and declension. Can you point out the modal verbs in the dialogues?

Lesson Plan:
- The Present Perfect tense
- Verbs: The Real Conditional mood
- Declining question words
- Forming nouns from verbs and adjectives
- Syntax: Some clausal constructions
- More on adjectives
- Preposition "about"

ДИАЛОГ I

Джонний Вахий концелярски туькана воьдуш ву. Цаьрна университетан хӀуманаш эца лаьа. Уьш туькана чубоьлху.

Ваха: Хьуна концелярски хӀуманаш хӀунда йеза?

Джон: Суна керла концелярски хӀуманаш йеза, хӀунда аьлча сан хӀуманаш Америкехь йу. Тептаршка хьожий вай?

Ваха: Дика ду, муьлха тептарш эца лаьа хьуна?

Джон: Суна сайна тайп-тайпана басахь тептарш оьшийла хаьа. Тайп-тайпана урокаш Ӏамочу хенахь ас хӀора урокана шен тептар леладо.

Йохкархо: Гӏо оьший шуна?

Джон: Оьшу. Шуьгахь тайп-тайпана басахь тептарш дуй?

Йохкархо: Ду. Тхоьгахь Ӏаьржа, кӀайн, цӀен, сийна, можа, баьццара тептарш ду.

Джон: Ма дика ду! Уьш даккхий ду йа кегий ду?

Йохкархо: Бехка ма билла, тхоьгахь хӀора барамехь шаболу бос бац. ЦӀениг доккха ду, Ӏаьржаниг жима ду, ткъа кӀайн тептарш кегий ду и кхин дӀа а.

Джон: Со даккхийчу тептаршка хьожур ву.

Йохкархо: Кхузахь ду хьуна уьш.

Джон: Ас цӀениг а, сийнаниг а, можаниг а оьцур ду. Къоламаш мичахь ду?

Йохкархо: ДӀогахь стол тӀехь ду.

Ваха: Суна схьакарийна уьш!

Джон: Гуттар а дика ду-кх и! Ваха, хьо кийча вуй?

Ваха: Кийча ву. ДӀавоьдий вайшиъ?

DIALOGUE I: At the Store

John and Vaxa are going to the school supply store. They want to buy school supplies. They enter the store.

Vaxa: Why do you need to buy school supplies?

John: I need new school supplies because my things are in America. Shall we look at the notebooks?

Vaxa: Ok. Which notebooks do you want to buy?

John: I know that I need notebooks in different colors. While taking different classes, I give each class its own notebook.

Salesperson: Do you need help?

John: Yes. Do you have notebooks in different colors?

Salesperson: Yes, we do. We have black, white, red, blue, yellow, and green notebooks.

John: Oh great! Are they big or small?

Salesperson: Unfortunately, in each size we don't have every color. The red one is big, the black one is small, and the white ones are small, etc.

John: I'll look at the big notebooks.

Salesperson: Here they are [for you].

John: I'll buy the red one, the blue one, and the yellow one. Where are the pens?

Salesperson: Over there on the table.

Vaxa: I've found them!

John: Excellent! Vaxa, are you ready?

Vaxa: Ready. Shall we leave?

¹⁴ ДИАЛОГ II

Джон а Ваха а книгийн туькана боьлху.

Ваха: Кхуза хӏунда даьхкина вай?

Джон: Со нохчийн меттан курс Ӏамош велахь, суна нохчийн литературан книгаш оьшур йу.

Ваха: Вай Дела, башха самукъане хӏума-м дац хӏара!

Джон: И хӏунда боху ахь? Дера ду-кх хӏара-м самукъане хӏума.

Ваха: Ахь книгаш лоьхучу хенахь со кхузахь хиана Ӏийр ву.

Джон: Дика ду, садаӏа хьайна.

Джон книган тӏе а хьоьжуш, лаьтташ ву.

Йохкархо: Хьо стенга хьожуш ву? А-а, дӏогарчуьнга хьоьжуш ву! И книга Нохчийчоьнан историех а экономиках а лаьцна йу.

Джон: Оьшуш (важный) тема йу хӏара. Суна традиционни нохчийн культура Ӏамош хазахета, шуьгахь нохчаллах а, нохчийн литературех а лаьцна книгаш йуй?

Йохкархо: Йу дера! Суна хазахета хьуна нохчийн мотт Ӏамабан лаарна. Нохчийн литературин моӏла хӏара бу.

Джон: Баркалла, со литература йеша воллу амма иза вуно хала йу. Хьоьгахь нохчийн филологин книгаш йуй?

Йохкархо: Цхьа ши-кхоъ йу. Хӏорш йу хьуна.

Джон: Баркалла, ас ерриге схьаоьцу, ахча мичахь дӏадалан деза?

Йохкархо: Баркалла, ас хьуна совгӏатна хӏара нохчийн историн книга луш йу. Со хӏокху книган автор ву.

Джон: Дала саӏла йойла хьан книга! Ас хазахетарца йоьшур йу.

DIALOGUE II: AT THE BOOKSTORE

John and Vaxa enter a bookstore.

Vaxa: Why have we come here?

John: If I am studying a Chechen course, I will need books on Chechen literature.

Vaxa: Oh my god, not something very fun!

John: Why do you say that? It is something fun.

Vaxa: While you look for books, I'll be seated here.

John: Okay, enjoy yourself.

John is standing and looking at a book.

Salesman: What are you looking for? Oh, you're looking at that one. That book is about Chechen history and economics.

John: This is an important topic. I like to study traditional Chechen culture. Do you have books on *noxchalla* and Chechen literature?

Salesman: Of course, we have! I like that you want to learn the Chechen language. This is the row for Chechen literature.

John: Thank you. I want to read Chechen literature, but it is very difficult. Do you have books on Chechen philology?

Salesman: Some two or three. Here you are.

John: Thank you, I'll take it all, where should I pay?

Salesman: Thank you, I'm giving you this book of Chechen history as a present. I am the author of this book.

John: May God reward you for your book! I will read it with pleasure.

Керла Дешнаш I / NEW WORDS I

концелярски хӀуманаш (й) school supplies
керла new
хӀунда аьлча because
муьлха which
сайна to myself
тайп-тайпана different
бос, беснаш (б:д) color
хан, хенаш (й:й) time
хӀора every
гӀо (д) help
ӏаьржа black
кӏайн white
цӏен red
сийна blue
можа yellow
баьццара green
доккха / даккхий large (*sing.*) / large (*pl.*)
жима / кегий small (*sing.*) / small (*pl.*)
бехк ма била excuse me; don't blame me
барам, барамаш (б:д) size
шадолу each
къолам, къоламаш (б:д) pen
кхин дӏа а et cetera, and so on
дӏогахь over there
Гуттар а дика ду-кх! Excellent!
кийча ready
тептар, тептарш (д:д) notebook

Керла Хандешнаш I / NEW VERBS I

д.еза to need; to love (**д.еза; д.ийзи; д.езна**)
хьажа to look, to watch (**хьожу; хьаьжи; хьаьжна**)
эца to buy; to take (**оьцу; ийци; эцна**)
лаа to want (**лаьа; лии; лиъна**)
эша to must; to need (**оьшу; ийши; эшна**)
ӏама to study, to learn (**ӏема; ӏеми; ӏаьмма**)

лелад.ан to take care of; to use; to wear (лелад.о; лелад.и;
   лелад.ина)
схьакард.ан to find (схьакард.о; схьакард.и; схьакард.ина)

Керла Дешнаш II / New Words II

Вай Дела! Oh my god!
башха not very, not too
самукъане fun
Нохчийчоь (й) Chechnya
истори, истореш (й:й) history
экономика (й) economy
нохчалла (й) noxchalla *(traditional Chechen code of conduct)*
моГла, моГланаш (б:д) row
оьшуш тема, теманаш (й:й) important topic
филологи (й) philology
цхьа *here:* some
ерригге all
совГлат, совГлаташ (д:д) present
саГла, саГланаш (д:д) alms

Керла Хандешнаш II / New Verbs II

д.аха to go *(pl.)* (д.оьлху; д.ахи; д.ахана)
д.ахка to come *(pl.)* (д.оГГу; д.аьхки; д.аьхкина)
баха to tell; to speak (боху; бехи; баьхна)
лаха to look for (лоху; лехи; лехна)
хаа to sit (хаьа; хии; хиина)
lан to remain, to stay (lа; lи; lийна)
саДала to relax, to enjoy oneself (саДоlу; саДоьlи; саДоьlна)
латта to stand (лаьтта; лаьтти; лаьттина)
схьаэца to buy up; to take up (схьаоьцу; схьаийци; схьаэцна)
дlад.алан to give (away) (дlало; дlад.ели; дlад.елла)
ахча (дlа)далан to pay (ахча дlало; ахча дlадели; ахча дlаделла)

Граматика / Grammar

Present Perfect Tense

The Present Perfect tense in Chechen corresponds to the English Perfect tense, e.g. "I eat" vs. "I have eaten." The Present Perfect describes the *present* state of an action having been completed. Compare, for example, the difference in English between "I ate cereal" and "I have eaten cereal." The former describes a specific action, the latter the state of being a person who has experienced eating cereal. In the dialogues, we saw a few examples of the Present Perfect:

Суна схьакарийна уьш!　　Кхуза хӏунда даьхкина вай?
I have found them!　　*Why have we come here?*

The Present Perfect is formed by adding the suffix **-на** or **-ина** to the Perfect stem of the verb. Some verb roots don't take a suffix, but rather double the consonant at the end of their stem. If a verb ends in -д, -л, -т, or -тӏ the consonant is doubled followed by **-а**. (Effectively, the н in -на disappears.) Here are a few examples:

Infinitive	Present Perfect	English Translation
эца	эц**на**	*have bought*
д.еша	д.еш**на**	*have read*
д.ийца	д.ийц**ина**	*have told*
ала	аь**лла**	*have said*
д.ала	д.е**лла**	*have given*
хета	хе**тта**	*have seemed*

The Present Perfect tense, along with the Infinitive, Present tense, and Recent Past tense, form the *principal parts* of the Chechen verb. That is, the Infinitive and these three tenses will give you the stems from which you can build other verb tenses. Let's take a look at the verb хьажа "*to watch*." We have to know the infinitive of the verb, хьажа, in order to build sentences with modal verbs:

Суна телевизоре **хьажа** лаьа.
I want to watch television.

With the Present tense stem, хьожу, we can form the Present tense, the Present Continuous tense, the Potential Future tense, and the Real Future tense:

Со телевизоре **хьожу**.
*I **watch** television.*

Со телевизоре **хьожуш** ву.
*I **am watching** television.*

Со телевизоре **хьожур**.
*I **may watch** television.*

Со телевизоре **хьожур** ву.
*I **will watch** television.*

With the Recent Past stem, we can form the Recent Past tense and the Obvious Past tense:

Со телевизоре **хьаьжи**.
*I **just watched** television.*

Со телевизоре **хьаьжира**.
*I **watched** television.*

And finally, with the Present Perfect stem we can form the Present Perfect tense:

Со телевизоре **хьаьжна**.
*I **have watched** television.*

Note: It is important to memorize each principal part of the Chechen verb, which is why in this lesson and all the lessons going forward we list them with every new verb. For instance:

Баха *to tell; to speak* (**боху; бехи; баьхна**)

Verbs: the Real Conditional Mood

As in English, in Chechen there are different types of "if" statements. Their construction and tense differ depending on whether the speaker believes an action is likely to happen (Real Condition) or unlikely to happen (Unreal Condition). In the above dialogues, we saw the following sentence:

Со нохчийн меттан курс Іамош велахь, суна нохчийн
    литературан книгаш оьшур йу.
If I am studying a Chechen course, I will need books on Chechen literature.

As we can see, this "if" statement reflects a real condition. If x occurs, y will occur. To form the mood, we use the Present Progressive form of the verb plus **д.елахь**. As you can probably guess, д.елахь agrees with the subject:

Иза университете йоьдуш **йелахь**, цо массо хӀума Іамадийр ду.
If she goes to university, she will learn everything.

To put the "if" statement in the Present tense, add **-хь** to the Infinitive form of the verb:

Ас нохчийн мотт Іамаба**хь**, суна нохчийн литературан книгаш
    оьшур йу.
If I study Chechen, I will need books of Chechen literature.

Declining Question Words

In the dialogue we saw the following:

Хьо стенга хьожуш ву?
What are you looking for?

"Стенга" is the Locative form of хӀун, "*what.*" The question words "*what,*" "*who,*" "*how much,*" and "*how many*" are given here fully declined:

	What?	Who?	How much?	How many?
Abs.	хІун	мила	мел	маса
Gen.	стенан	хьенан	меланнан	масаннан
Dat.	стенна	хьанна	меланна	масанна
Erg.	сте	хьа	меламма	масамма
Instr.	стенца	хьаьнца	меланца	масанца
Subst.	стенах	хьанах	меланнах	масаннах
Comp.	стенал	хьанал	меланнал	масаннал
Loc.	стенга	хьаьнга	меланга	масанга

Forming Nouns from Verbs and Adjectives

We saw in the dialogue the following sentence:

Ас хазахетарца йоьшур йу.
I will read it with pleasure.

As you may have noticed, the Chechen word for *"pleasure,"* хазахетар, is derived from the verb хазахета, *"to like."* Indeed, by adding the suffix **-p** to the infinitive form of the verb you can make virtually any verb a noun:

хаа (*to know*)   хаа**р** (*knowledge*)
деша (*to read*)   деша**р** (*reading*)

The grammatical term for this form is "masdar," and it functions like a gerund. Masdar forms take (б:б) and are first declension nouns with no ablaut.

хазахетар (*pleasure*)		
	Singular	*Plural*
Absolutive	хазахетар	хазахетараш
Genitive	хазахетаран	хазахетарийн
Dative	хазахетарна	хазахетаршна

Ergative	хазахетаро	хазахетарша
Instrumental	хазахетарца	хазахетаршца
Substantive	хазахетарах	хазахетарех
Comparative	хазахетарал	хазахетарел
Locative	хазахетаре	хазахетаршка

We saw a complicated sentence involving a declined masdar in the dialogues:

Суна хазахета хьуна нохчийн мотт Іамабан **лаарна**.
I like that you want to learn the Chechen language.

Here, лаар, "*wanting*," takes the Dative case, as it is the subject of хазахета "*to like*".

The suffix **-лла** turns an adjective into a noun:

хаза (*beautiful*)   хазалла (*beauty*)
Нохчийн (*Chechen*)   Нохчалла (*Checheness, Chechen code of conduct*)

These nouns belong to the third declension take (й:й):

хазалла (*beauty*)		
	Singular	*Plural*
Absolutive	хазалла	хазаллаш
Genitive	хазаллин	хазаллийн
Dative	хазаллина	хазаллашна
Ergative	хазалло	хазаллаша
Instrumental	хазаллица	хазаллашца
Substantive	хазаллах	хазаллех
Comparative	хазаллал	хазаллел
Locative	хазалле	хазаллашка

SYNTAX

Syntax is the arrangement of words and phrases to form grammatical sentences in a language. Up until now, the syntax in the dialogues has mostly consisted of short, declarative statements and questions. Now, we will start introducing more advanced ways to go into detail when speaking Chechen.

Saying "Why"

In Dialogue I in this lesson, John said:

> Суна керла концелярски хӀуманаш йеза, **хӀунда аьлча** сан хӀуманаш Америкехь йу.
> *I need new school supplies because my things are in America.*

"**хӀунда аьлча**" functions similarly to "*because*" in Chechen. Like English, it can follow the clause being modified and answers the question хӀунда?, "*why?*" Аьлча is derived from the verb ала, "*to say*," which will be covered later.

Saying "While"

Chechen uses a special construction **-чу хенахь** to describe an action occurring simultaneously with another action. To construct a "*while*" clause, add **-чу** to the present tense of the verb followed by **хенахь**, which is simply the Locative form of хан, "*time*." (Technically, this is a participle, which describes хан and declined in the Locative. We will cover participles later.)

> Тайп-тайпана урокаш ламо**чу хенахь** ас хӀора урокана шен тептар леладо.
> *While taking different classes, I give each class its own notebook.*

Subordinate Clauses

In Chechen there are many ways to introduce a Subordinate clause (a clause that is subordinate to the main clause, often rendered in English as "that x"). Chechen forms Subordinate clauses differently than English. Most notably, the verb in the Subordinate clause comes *before* the main clause. The first type of construction we will look at is with the verbs **хаьа** "*to know*" and **лаьа** "*to want*".

If you want to say, "*I know that x*," you need the verb хаьа. The verb in the Subordinate clause is then formed from the Present tense. Remove -у and add -**ийла**: оьшу → оьш- → оьш**ийла**:

Суна сайна тайп-тайпана басахь а барамехь а тептарш
оьшийла хаьа.
I know that I need my notebooks in different colors and sizes.
Literally: *I know my needing of notebooks in different colors and sizes.*

We've seen лаьа "*to want*" before. For example, in the Dialogue in Lesson 6:

Муьлха тайпа жижиг эца **лаьа** хьуна?
What kind of meat do you **want** *to buy?*

When the subject of "*to want*" and the implied subject of the action "эца" are the same, then Chechen uses the Infinitive. When they are different, however, Chechen needs to use a different construction:

Суна ахьа жижиг оьцийла **лаьа**. / Ахьа жижиг оьцийла **лаьа** суна.
I **want** *you to buy meat.*

Цунна со ишколе воьдийла **лаьа**.
He **wants** *me to go to school.* (Lit. *He wants that I go to school.*)

Saying "we two," "you two," etc.

It is typical in colloquial Chechen to add -**шиъ** to pronouns if there are two individuals involved in the action. This is also possible in English, of course, e.g.: "*You two, go over there!*" The -**шиъ** pronouns take the same noun class as their non-шиъ counterparts.

Вайшиъ	We two (*you and me*)
Тхойшиъ	We two (*me and someone else*)
Шушиъ	You two (*you and someone else*)
Уьшшиъ	They two (*someone and someone*)

MORE ON ADJECTIVES

Declining Adjectives with Nouns

In the sentence below we see *"notebooks"* in the Locative plural. Notice what happens to the adjective даккхий *"big"*:

Со **даккхийчу** тептаршка хьожур ву.
*I will look at the **big** notebooks.*

Here the adjective *"big"* describes a noun, *"notebook."* An adjective that describes a noun in the sentence is a dependent adjective. Dependent adjectives must be declined along with nouns. Luckily, they only have one other form in the Oblique cases; that is, the cases other than the Absolutive. For an example, let's decline хаза цла *"the beautiful house"* in all cases:

хаза цла *"the beautiful house/houses"*		
	Singular	*Plural*
Absolutive	хаза цла	хаза цленош
Genitive	хазачу цлийнан	хазачу цленойн
Dative	хазачу цленна	хазачу цленошна
Ergative	хазачу цлийно	хазачу цленоша
Instrumental	хазачу цлийнаца	хазачу цленошца
Substantive	хазачу цлийнах	хазачу цленех
Comparative	хазачу цлийнал	хазачу цленел

Free Adjectives

Free adjectives, or independent adjectives, are adjectives that can stand alone as a noun. They are formed by adding **-ниг** or **-иг** to an adjective. Following are some examples:

Dependent	Free	English Translation
цӏен	цӏениг	*the red one*
кӏайн	кӏайниг	*the white one*
ӏаьржа	ӏаьржаниг	*the black one*
можа	можаниг	*the yellow one*
баьццара	баьццарниг	*the green one*
боьмаша	боьмашниг	*the brown one*
сийна	сийнаниг	*the dark blue one*
цӏехо-можа	цӏехо-можаниг	*the orange one*

Free adjectives decline like fourth declension nouns in the singular. Plural forms should be memorized.

можаниг *"the yellow one"*		
	Singular	*Plural*
Absolutive	можаниг	можанаш
Genitive	можачун	можачеран
Dative	можачунна	можачарна
Ergative	можачо	можачара
Instrumental	можачуьнца	можачаьрца
Substantive	можачух	можачарах
Comparative	можачул	можачарал
Locative	можачуьнга	можачаьрга

Some Particular Adjectives

As we have seen, there are several adjectives that must agree with the noun class of the nouns they describe. Luckily, they are relatively few. They should, however, be memorized. The Chechen linguist A.G. Matsiev gives us the following:

big	доккха / воккха / йоккха / боккха
heavy	деза / веза / беза / йеза
short	доца / воца / йоца / боца
dry	декъа / йекъа / бекъа / векъа
fat	дерстан / верстан / йерстан / берстан
naked	дерзина / верзина / берзина / йерзина
warm	довха / вовха / йовха / бовха
rotten	дехка / вехка / йехка / бехка
long	деха / веха / йеха / беха
cheap	дораха / йараха / вораха / бораха
light	дайн / вайн / йайн / байн
empty	даьсса / ваьсса / баьсса / йаьсса
full	дуьзна / вуьзна / буьзна / йуьзна
gaunt	декъана / векъана / йекъана / бекъана
dense	дуькъа / вуькъа / йуькъа / буькъа
thin/narrow	дуткъа / вуьткъа / йуьткъа / буьткъа

A very few adjectives, like the first one above, доккха *"big,"* also have plural forms:

Со **воккха** ву.   Уьш **баккхий** бу.
I am big (a big person).   *They are big.*

Thus, доккха (*big*) has four forms in the singular (доккха / йоккха / боккха / воккха) and three forms in the plural (даккхий / йаккхий / баккхий) since there is no plural form for in в-.

доккха / йоккха / боккха / воккха	даккхий / йаккхий / баккхий
жима *small* (sing.)	кегий *small* (pl.)

Prepositions: Saying "about" (-лаьцна)

The preposition "*about*" takes the Substantive case in Chechen:

Суна цунах **лаьцна** хlумма а ца хаьа.
*I don't know anything **about** him/her/it.*

Уьш сох **лаьцна** дуьйцуш бу.
*They are talking **about** me.*

Шу экономиках **лаьцна** книга йазйеш дуй.
*Are you all writing a book **about** economics?*

Хьо стенах **лаьцна** ойла йеш ву?
*What are you thinking **about**?*

Упражненеш / EXERCISES

Exercise 1. *Match colors with translations.*

1. цlен   a. white
2. лаьржа   b. red
3. кlайн   c. black

Exercise 2. *Use the adjectives in parentheses to complete the sentences. Noun class at the end will help you to figure out the adjective's form.*

1. Цициган (доккха)_____муцlар йу.

2. Оьпин (доца) _____лергаш ду.

3. Дехкан (деха)_____цlога ду.

4. Сан жlала (дерстан)_____ду.

5. Вон стаг (даьсса)_____ стаг ву.

6. Шура (дораха)_____йу.

7. Бер (дерзина)_____ду.

8. Жима йоl (дерзина)_____йу.

Exercise 3. *Write the free adjective form for the following. Decline the first two as dependent adjectives in the singular and plural. Decline the last two in the singular and plural.*

1. хаза _____

2. дика _____

3. оьзда _____

4. эсала _____

5. деха _____

6. доца _____

7. мерза _____

Exercise 4. *Fill in the blanks using words from word bank.*

лаьцна	баккхий	можа	тхойшиъ	цlениг

1. Суна цунах_____хlумма а ца хаьа.

2. Хьан _____коч йуй? _____йац хьан?

3. _____йуьртахь ву.

4. Сан когаш _____бу.

Exercise 5. *Translate the following sentences into English.*

1. Хlора баттахь баккхий нах арабовлу.

_____

2. Сан даккхий бlаьргаш ду.

_____

3. Хьан кегий цергаш йу.

_____

4. Вайн цициг декъана дуй?

_____

5. Хьан мар (nose) жима буй?

_____

Exercise 6. *Translate the following weather related sentences.*

1. Today, it's sunny. _____

2. Today, is the 11th of May. _____

3. Today, it's warm. _____

4. Yesterday, it rained. _____

5. Yesterday was a cold day. _____

6. Tomorrow, the weather will be like today. _____

_____

Exercise 7. *Match the Russian location names with their Chechen names.* Names of towns in Chechen: Since the control of the USSR, the names of towns in Chechnya have been "Russified." The majority of Chechens use Russian town names, and sometimes they do not know the original Chechen names. For this exercise you will use the Chechen town's names, but we suggest you learn both for your future conversations.

Грозный	Курчалой-гӀала / Куьшалойл
Аргун	Гуьмсе
Гудермес	Орга-ГӀала / Устрада ГӀала
Шали	Невр / Новр-гӀала
Урус-Мартан	Хьалха-Марта / МартантӀе
Курчалой	Соьлжа-ГӀала
Ачхой-Мартан	IашхойМарта / ТӀаьхьа-Марта / ТӀехьа-Марта
Наур	Шела

Exercise 8. *Describe the weather in your area. You have the option to discuss the weather for today, yesterday, or tomorrow. Alternatively, you can provide details about a specific time of year or the typical weather patterns in your location.*

Корта VIII:
Квартира арендовать йар

Lesson 8:
Renting an Apartment

Knowledge Check: In the Dialogues in this lesson, highlight verbs in the Present Perfect tense. Which adjectives in the dialogues agree with noun class?

Lesson Plan:
- Other uses of Perfect tense
- Plural verbs
- Word building with verbs
- Postpositions
- "Where" clauses

 **ДИАЛОГ I**

Джон агенствон офис чоьхьаволу, цунна агент го офис чохь.
Джона шен керла квартира (петар) харжа сацам бина.

Джон: Де дика хуьлда хьан. Муха ду хьан гӀуллакхаш?

Агент: Диканца дукха вехийла. Марша вогӀийла! Хьуна хӀун оьшура?

Джон: Суна квартира арендовать йан лаьа.

Агент: Дика ду, оха хьуна масийтта тайпа гойтур йу. Муьлха мах беза хьуна?

Джон: Суна баттахь ткъа эзар сом мах хилча мега.

Агент: Тхан хьуна хьахо кхо петар йу. Оцу квартирашна чуйогӀу кухнеш а, залш а.

Джон: Мегар ду, суна коьртаниг и квартира университетан уллехь хилар ду.

Агент: ХӀумма дац, тхан шайолу квартираш автобусан остановка йолчехь йу.

Джон: Автобусш сих-сиха совций оцу соцунгӀехь?

Агент: ХӀаъ, уьш даиманна а йоьлху цига, со балха хӀора Ӏуьйранна автобусца богӀу.

Джон: Маца йиш хира йу вайн оцу квартирашка хьажа?

Агент: Кхана хьовсур ду вай.

Джон: Дика ду, кхана гур ду вай.

DIALOGUE I: RENTING AN APARTMENT 1

John enters the office and sees the agent in the office. John has decided to choose a new apartment.

John: Hello. How are you?

Agent: May [you] live long [with] wellness. Welcome! How can I help? [What did you need?]

John: I want to rent an apartment.

Agent: Ok, we will [show you] different types. What price do you want?

John: For me, 20,000 rubles per month is possible.

Agent: We have three apartments [for you]. These apartments include kitchens and hallways.

John: Good, it will also be important that the apartment is close to the university.

Agent: No problem, all our apartments are close to a bus station.

John: Do buses often stop at this (bus) stop?

Agent: Yes, they are always going there. I come by bus almost every day.

John: When will we be able to look at those apartments?

Agent: We will look tomorrow.

John: Ok, see you tomorrow.

ДИАЛОГ II

Ӏуьйранна Джон а агент а вовшахкхета хьалхарчу квартиран хьалха.

Агент: Привет, Джон!

Джон: Дела реза хуьлда сан гӀуллакхе хьажарна.

Агент: ХӀумма дац, Дела реза массарна а хуьлда! Вайшиъ хӀинца хьалхара квартире хьожур ву. ХӀара квартира Мамсурова урамехь йу, гӀалан юккъехь уггаре хазачу меттехь. Вай гӀишлон арахь лаьтташ ду.

Джон: И хаза здани йу! Маса квартира йу оцу гӀишлон?

Агент: Ткъа квартира бен йац. Зданин тӀехьа ткъе бархӀалгӀа маршрутка а соцу. Кхузара маршруткан соцунгӀа йолчу подъезд чухула воьду.

Джон: Ма дика ду и! Вало, квартире бӀаьрг тохий вай?

Джоний агентий квартиран чоьхьаволу. Джона агентига хаттарш до, агента хаттаршна жоьпаш ло.

Агент: Хьуна ма-гарра хӀокху квартиран цхьа дӀавуьжун чоь йу, мебельца уже кечйина йу.

Джон: Маца йоьттина йу хӀара гӀишло? Муьлхачу шарахь йина хӀара?

Агент: Советан Ӏедал долчу хенахь ремонт йина хӀокху чохь.

Джон: Баккъала бохий ахь?

Агент: ХӀан-хӀа, аса забар йо. Кхузара мел долу цӀено тӀамал тӀаьхьа доьттина ду.

Джон: Суна цара доьттина керла цӀенош хазахета. Кухни яахӀума йан дика йу. Схьагарехь, дӀавуьжу чоь чохь шифоньер а, боккха маьнга а бу.

Агент: ХӀаъ, шайолу хӀума йу хӀокху квартирехь. Кхузахь интернет а, ӀаьнтӀаьхь йовхо а, довха хи а хуьлу.

Джон: Ахь селхана соьга ткъа эзар сом мах бу аьлла. Нийса дуй и?

DIALOGUE II: RENTING AN APARTMENT 2

In the morning John and the agent meet in front of the first apartment.

Agent: Hello, John!

John: Thank you for taking care of this matter.

Agent: No problem, may God reward everyone! We will now look at the first apartment. This apartment is on Mamsurov Street, in the middle of a beautiful part of the city. We're standing outside the building now.

John: It's a beautiful building! How many apartments are in the building?

Agent: Only twenty apartments. The bus number twenty-nine stops behind the apartment. From here to the bus stop you go through the building entrance.

John: Excellent! Shall we look at the apartment?

John and the agent enter the apartment. John asks the agent questions, and the agent answers.

Agent: As you can see, this apartment has one bedroom set with furniture.

John: When was this building built? In which years was it built?

Agent: The interior was renovated during Soviet times.

John: For real?

Agent: No, I'm joking. All buildings here are built after the war.

John: I like the new houses they built. The kitchen is great for cooking. I see in the bedroom there is a closet and a big bed.

Agent: Yes, everything is in this apartment. There is internet, heating, and hot water.

John: You told me yesterday this was 20,000 rubles. Is this correct?

Агент: Аьшпаш бац уьш!

Джон: Дика ду, цара мах схьалабоккхур буй?

Агент: Хlара квартира цхьана стеган йу, цо цкъа а мах схьала ца баьккхина. Контрактан мах схьала ца болу. Инфляцин бахьана мах схьалабалахь шо даьлча, хlара квартира йолу накъостаца барт бан мегар ду ахь.

Джон: Дика ду, суна кхузахь lен лаьа. Ас хlара квартира схьаоьцу. Хlара парглат а, цlена а, тийна а меттиг йу. Цулла совнах, суна мах цхьана шарахь хийца ца луш хазахета.

Агент: Хlаъ, квартиран кlелахь а, тlехулахь а lаш бераш дац. Ас хьуна контракт тахана тlаьхьо дlайоуьйтур йу. Куьг йаздиначул тlаьхьа кlира даьлча, хьо квартиран чуван мегар ду.

Джон: Баркалла хьуна, хьо вевзина хазахета. Контракт схьакхачаре хьоьжур ву со, чехкка йуха йохьийтур ду.

Agent: Not a lie!

John: Ok, will they raise the price?

Agent: This apartment belongs to a man who has never raised the
        price. In the contract the price cannot rise. If the rate of
        inflation rises in two years, you can negotiate the price.

John: Ok, I want to stay here. I'll take the apartment. This place is
        quiet and comfortable. Moreover, I like the fact that the price
        doesn't rise.

Agent: Yes, above and below there are no kids. I will send you the
        contract later today. One week after having signed, you can
        move into the apartment.

John: Thank you. It was nice to meet you. I will wait for the contract
        to send it back to you.

Керла Дешнаш I / NEW WORDS I

агенствон офис, офисаш (й:й) agency office
квартира, квартираш (й:й) apartment
петар, петарш (й:й) apartment
Диканца дуккха д.ехийла May you live long and well
масийтта few
тайпа different, type of
мах, мехш (б:д) price
кухни, кухнеш (й:й) kitchen
зал, залш (й:й) living room
коьрта important
уллехь near, close, beside, next to
автобус, автобусаш (й:й) bus
остановка, остановкаш (й:й) bus stop
соцунгӀа, соцунгӀаш (й:й) bus stop
д.олчу where
болх, белхаш (б:д) work, job

Керла Хандешнаш / NEW VERBS

чоьхьад.ала to come in (**чоьхад.олу, чоьхьад.ели, чоьхьад.аьлла**)
харжа to choose (**хоржу, хаьржи, хаьржина**)
чуд.ан to include (**чуд.огӀу, чуд.ели, чуд.аьлла**)
сацам бан to decide (**сацам бо, сацам би, сацам бина**)
арендовать д.ан to rent (**арендовать д.о, арендовать д.и, арендовать д.ина**)
гайта to show (**гойту, гайти, гайтина**)
хьахо to advise, to recommend (**хьоьху, хьийхи, хьийхина**)
саца to stop (*pl.*) (**совцу, севци, севцина**)
д.аха to go (*pl.*) (**д.оьлху, д.ахи, д.ахна**)
хьажа to look (*pl.*) (**хьовсу, хьевси, хьевсина**)

Керла Дешнаш II / NEW WORDS II

хьалхара first
хьалха in front
урам, урамаш (б:д) street
гӀала, гӀаланаш (й:й) city, town

йуккъехь in the middle
уггаре the most
гӀишло, гӀишлош (й:й) building; tower
здани, зданеш (й:й) building
тӀехьа behind
арахь outside
подъезд, подъездаш (й:й) building entrance
чухула through
д.ало let's go
хаттар, хаттарш (д:д) question
жоп, жоьпаш (д:д) answer
хьуна ма-гарра as you see
дӀавуьжу чоь, чоьнаш (й:й) bedroom
мебель, мебельш (й:й) furniture
советан Ӏедал, Ӏедалш (д:д) Soviet government time
тӀом, тӀемаш (б:д) war
схьагарехь as seen
маьнга, маьнгеш (б:д) bed
ишкап/шкаф, ишкапш (й:й) kitchen cabinet
шифоньер, шифоньерш (й:й) wardrobe, closet
гӀуткха, гӀуткхаш (д:д) drawer
куьзг, куьзганаш (д:д) mirror
сени/прихожи, прихожеш (й:й) hall
куз/палс, кузанаш (б:б) carpet
кор, кораш (д:д) window
хи, хиш (д:д) water
интернет, интернетш (й:й) internet
шело, шелонаш (й:й) cold (*n.*)
йовхо, йовхонаш (й:й) heat (*n.*)
батарейка, батарейкаш (й:й) *European-style heating installations*
нел, неларш (й:й) door
диван, диванш (й;й) sofa
стол, стоьлш (й;й) table
гӀант, гӀентш (д;д) chair
хьешан чоь, чоьнш (й;й) guest room
лами, ламеш (б;д) stair
аьшпаш/пуьтш (б) (*only pl.*) lies (a lie)
цунна тӀе in addition

контракт, контарктш (д:д) contract
накъост, накъостий (в/й:б) companion
паргlат comfortable, relaxed
цlена clean
тийна quiet
чехкха fast
кlелахь under, underneath
тlехулахь above, on top
таьхьо later
цкъа а never, not once

Керла Хандешнаш / NEW VERBS

вовшахкхета to meet, to get together (**вовшахкхета, вовшахкхийти, вовшахкхетта**)
латта to stand (**лаьтта, лаьтти, лаьттина**)
бlаьрг тоха to take a look (**бlаьрг туху, бlаьрг туьйхи, бlаьрг тоьхна**)
хаттар дан to ask (**хаттар до, хаттар ди, хаттар дина**)
жоп дала to answer (**жоп ло, жоп дели, жоп делла**)
д.отта to build (**д.утту, д.оьтти, д.оьттина**)
кечд.ан to prepare; to decorate (**кечд.о, кечд.и, кечд.ина**)
забар йан to joke (**забар йо, забар йи, забар йина**)
хила to be (*continuous*), to become (**хуьлу, хили, хилла**)
схьалад.аккха to raise, to take up (**схьалад.оккху, схаьалад.аьккхи, схьаладаьккхина**)
схьалад.ала to rise, to go up (**схьаладолу, схьаладели, схьаладаьлла**)
барт бан to agree (**барт бо, барт би, барт бина**)
lен to stay, to remain (**lа, lи, lийна**)
дlад.аита to send (with someone) (**дlадоуьту, дlадаити, дlадаитна**)
дахьийта to send (**дохьуьйту, дахьийти, дахьийтна**)
куьгйаздан to sign (**куьгйаздо, куьгйазди, куьгйаздина**)
чуд.ан to come in (**чуд.оlу, чуд.еи, чуд.еира**)
д.овза to meet; to recognize (**д.евзу, д.евзи, Д.евзина**)
схьакхача to arrive (**схьакхочу, схьакхечи, схьакхаьчна**)

Граматика / GRAMMAR

Other Uses of the Present Perfect Tense

In the last lesson we met the Present Perfect tense. The Present Perfect tense is used to express the present state of an action that has been completed, as in:

Цо йоьттина хlара гlишло.
He has built this building.

The Present Perfect form of the verb can also function as an adjective. Another term for a verb that functions as an adjective is a participle. We saw in the dialogue:

Маца йоьттина йу хlара гlишло?
When was this building built?

Here, the Present Perfect form, combined with the Present tense of *"to be,"* functions like the passive voice in English:

Хlара гlишло 2021 шарахь йоьттина йу.
This building was built in 2021.

The Present Perfect form is very useful for certain types of clauses in Chechen. For example, we saw in the dialogue:

Куьг **йаздиначул тlаьхьа** кlира даьлча, хьо квартиран чуван мегар ду.
*One week **after having signed**, you can move into the apartment.*

Here, we take the Present Perfect form of куьг йаздан *"to sign,"* куьг йаздина, and add the suffix -**чул** plus the postposition **тlаьхьа**, *"after."* As you may have thought, the suffix -**чул** is the same suffix from the Comparative case. In fact, what we are seeing is the declined form of the Past Participle, in the Comparative case. When the Present Perfect comes before the noun, it functions as a Past Participle, which we will cover later.

Суна **цара доьттина цlенош** хазахета.
*I like the **houses which they built**.*

Plural Verbs

So far, we have only encountered the singular form of verbs. Many Chechen verbs, however, have both a singular and plural form. Whether the verb takes the singular or plural form depends on the number of the noun in the Absolutive case. Thus, intransitive verbs agree with the subject, transitive verbs agree with the object. Compare, for example, the following sentences from the dialogue:

Автобусш сих-сиха **совций** цу соцунгӀа йолчехь?
Do buses often stop at this (bus) stop?

Зданин тӀехьа ткъе бархлалгӀа маршрутка а **соцу**.
*And marshrutka no.28 (*lit. the 28th marshrutka) **stops** in front of
    the building.*

As we can see, **совци** is the plural form of **соцу**. Хьажа also has a plural stem, which we saw in the dialogue.

Маца йиш хира йу вайн оцу квартирашка **хьажа**?
*When will we be able to **look** at those apartments?*

Кхана хьовсур ду вай.
*We **will look** tomorrow.*

Let's look at the conjugation of **хьажа** *"to look"* and **саца** *"to stop"* in the tenses we know:

	хьажа *to look*	
	Singular	*Plural*
Infinitive	хьажа	хьовса
Present	хьожу	хьовсу
Present cont.	хьожуш ду	хьовсуш ду
Recent past	хьаьжи	хьевси
Observed past	хьаьжира	хьаьвсира

Present perfect	хьаьжна	хьаьвсина
Potential future	хьожур	хьовсур
Real future	хьожур ду	хьовсур ду

	саца *to stop*	
	Singular	*Plural*
Infinitive	саца	совца
Present	соцу	совцу
Present cont.	соцуш ду	совцуш ду
Recent past	сеци	севци
Observed past	сецира	севцира
Present perfect	сецна	севцна
Potential future	соцур	совцур
Real future	соцур ду	совцур ду

Generally speaking, the ablaut shifts in singular and plural forms of the verb will mirror each other throughout the conjugations:

хьожу → хьаьжи
хьовсу → хьаьвси

If you can remember the root forms for the singular and plural, then apply the ablaut shifts from the singular and you are more than likely on the right track for conjugating the plural. Right now, however, what's most important is that you can recognize plural forms when you see or hear them.

There are a few verbs that take irregular singular and plural forms. Some of these have yet to be introduced in a dialogue, but it's important to learn them now. Matsiev lists the following:

Singular	Plural	Translation
хьажа	хьовса	*to look*
саца	совца	*to stop* (intransitive)
д.ада	д.овда	*to run*
д.илла	д.ахка	*to put*
д.ала	д.овла	*to finish*
д.ан	д.ахка	*to come*

Word Building with Verbs

Note the following sentences:

Хӏара квартира цхьана стеган йу, цо цкъа а мах схьала ца баькккхина. Контрактан мах схьала ца болу.
This apartment belongs to a man, who has never raised the price. The price of the contract does not rise.

Chechen often creates new verbs through compound words, combining an adjective or noun with important verbs like дан "*to do/make*"; даккха "*to get/take*"; дала "*to give*"; дала "*to finish/end*"; etc. These foundational verbs create hundreds of compounds. They can also be very confusing, so we will detail them below.

дан "*to do/make*"

Дан "*to do/make*" creates many compounds in Chechen. It is conjugated as follows with compounds йазйан "*to write*" and дагардан "*to count*":

	Sing.	Pl.	Compound	Compound
Infinitive	д.ан	–	йазйан	дагардан
Present	д.о	–	йазйо	дагардо
Present cont.	д.еш д.у	–	йазйеш д.у	дагардеш д.у
Recent past	д.и	–	йазйи	дагарди
Observed past	д.ира	–	йазйира	дагардира

Present perfect	д.ина	–	йазйина	дагардина
Potential future	д.ер	–	йазйер	дагардер
Real future	д.ер д.у	–	йазйер д.у	дагардер ду

Дан [dƏ] "*to do/make*" should not be confused with дан [dɑ:] "*to come/arrive*," which as we saw above, also has a plural form. In texts the meanings of these two words are derived from context, and in speaking it is clear which one is which. The pronunciation of «а» in дан "*to do/make*" is very short, almost like no sound, just like schwa at the end. The pronunciation of «а» in дан "*to come/arrive*" is long, same sound as "a" in British English "art."

	Sing.	Pl.	Compound	Compound
Infinitive	д.ан	д.ахка	дагадан	охьадахка
Present	д.огӏу	д.огӏу	дагадогӏу	охьадогӏу
Present cont.	д.огӏуш д.у	д.огӏуш д.у	дагадогӏуш д.у	охьадогӏуш д.у
Recent past	д.еи	д.аьхки	дагадеи	охьадеи
Observed past	д.еара	д.аьхкира	дагадеара	охьадеара
Present perfect	д.еана	д.аьхкина	дагадеана	охьадеана
Potential future	д.огӏур	д.огӏур	дагадогӏур	охьадогӏур
Real future	д.огӏур д.у	д.огӏур д.у	дагадогӏур д.у	охьадогӏур д.у

даккха "*to get/take*"

Like дан "*to do/make*," д.аккха "*to get/take*" (as well as "*to earn*" and "*to spend*") is particularly productive. It is a transitive verb and is conjugated below in the singular and plural with the compounds **схьалабаккха** "*to raise*" (agreeing with max), and **инзарбаха** "*to surprise*" (agreeing with нах "*people*").

	Singular	Plural	Compound	Compound
Infinitive	д.аккха	д.аха	схьалабаккха	инзарбаха
Present	д.оккху	д.оху	схьалабоккху	инзарбоху
Present cont.	д.оккхуш д.у	д.охуш д.у	схьалабоккхуш д.у	инзарбохуш д.у
Recent past	д.аьккхи	д.ехи	схьалабаьккхи	инзарбехи
Observed past	д.аьккхира	д.ехира	схьалабаьккхира	инзарбехира
Present perfect	д.аьккхина	д.аьхна	схьалабаьккхина	инзарбаьхна
Potential future	д.оккхур	д.охур	схьалабоккхур	инзарбохур
Real future	д.оккхур д.у	д.охур д.у	схьалабоккхур д.у	инзарбохур д.у

Дала, дала, or дала?

Дала as an infinitive can mean either "*to give*," "*to finish/end*," or "*to die*." However, these important verbs all have different conjugations.

дала "*to give*": We have already encountered дала "*to give*." The verb frequently appears in intransitive compounds, lending a sense of change, development, or growth. It is conjugated below along with the compounds **кӏадвала** "*to get tired* (agreeing with a male)," which we encountered all the way back in the first lesson, and **д.охд.ала** "*to get warm*." Note, both the adjective and verb agree in noun class in this instance (e.g., квартира йу).

дала "*to give*"

	Singular	Plural	Compound	Compound
Infinitive	д.ала	–	кӏадвала	йохйала
Present	ло	–	кӏадло	йохло
Present cont.	луш д.у	–	кӏадлуш ву	йохлуш йу

Recent past	д.ели	–	кӀадвели	йохйели
Obvious past	д.елира	–	кӀадвелира	йохйелира
Present perfect	д.елла	–	кӀадвелла	йохйелла
Potential future	лур	–	кӀадлур	йохлур
Real future	лур д.у	–	кӀадлур ву	йохлур йу

Often, дан and дала form transitive and intransitive pairs:

Ас квартира йохйо.   Квартира бӀаьста йохло.
I heat the apartment.   *The apartment warms up in the spring.*

дала "to finish/end": Дала "to finish/end" is also highly productive. It is conjugated below with the compound дала "to rise" (agreeing with мехаш) and **айкхдала** "to become known."

дала "to finish/end"

	Singular	Plural	Compound	Compound
Infinitive	д.ала	д.овла	схьалабовла	айкхдала
Present	д.олу	д.овлу	схьалабовлу	айкхдолу
Present cont.	д.олуш д.у	д.овлуш д.у	схьалабовлуш бу	айкхдолуш ду
Recent past	д.ели	д.евли	схьалабевли	айкхдели
Observed past	д.елира	д.евлира	схьалабевлира	айкхделира
Present perfect	д.аьлла	д.евлла	схьалабевлла	айкхдаьлла
Potential future	д.аьр	д.евр	схьалабевр	айкхдаьр
Real future	д.ер д.у	д.евр д.у	схьалабевр бу	айкхдер ду

Like дан/дала, даккха/дала often come in transitive/intransitive pairs in compounds:

Цо **цкъа** а мах **схьала ца баьккхина**. Мах **схьала ца болу.**
*He has **never raised** the price. The price **doesn't rise**.*

Neither of the two forms above, however, should be confused with **дала**, "to die," whose conjugation at first can appear similar to "to give." Where the forms are the same, context and case ("to die" is intransitive, "to give" transitive) should make it clear.

дала *"to die / to give"*

	to die	*to give*
Infinitive	д.ала	д.ала
Present	ле	ло
Present cont.	леш д.у	луш д.у
Recent past	д.ели	д.ели
Obvious past	д.елира	д.елира
Present perfect	д.елла	д.елла
Potential future	лер	лур
Real future	лийр д.у	лур д.у

Postpositions

Unlike English prepositions, which come before the noun, Chechen employs *postpositions*. Like in English, postpositions describe the relation of a noun to its surroundings. Postpositions can take several Locative forms denoting motion towards, away from, through, etc. Thus far, we have learned the Allative case (-e), which denotes movement towards an object, as well as the Locative ending for static positions (-хь). We have also encountered some examples of another Locative ending (-pa), which denotes motion away from an object. For example:

Мичара йу хьо?   Со Америкера йу.
Where are you from?   *I am from America.*

We have already introduced some postpositions, which we have given as set phrases in the new word sections. Below are the most important postpositions in the Locative. The noun stays in the Absolutive case, followed by the postposition. These postpositions should be memorized.

Postposition (Locative)	Translation
тӀехь	*on*
кӀелахь	*under*
бухахь	*underneath*
йуххехь/йистехь/уллехь	*next to, near, close*
тӀехьа	*behind*
хьалха	*in front*
йуккъехь / йуккъехь	*between*
тӀехулахь	*above*
чохь	*inside*
чуьра	*from inside*
арахь	*outside*

Syntax

"Where" Clauses

Like for other subordinate clauses that provide more detail to the main clause (when, why, etc.), Chechen has a special construction for describing location. In the dialogue we saw: Тхан шайолу квартираш автобусан остановка йолчехь йу. This could translate roughly to: *All our apartments are where there's a bus stop.* Or, *All our apartments are by a bus stop.* The construction can also be used in the simple Locative (motion towards):

Кхузара маршруткан соцунгӀа **йолчу** подъезд чухула воьду.
*From here (you) go through the entry **to where** the bus stop is.*

Упражненеш / EXERCISES

Exercise 1. *Create new verbs using the prefixes given in the box and write translations.*

тlе	хьала	охьа	кlела	дlа

1. кхосса _____

2. эца _____

3. д.аха _____

4. д.аккха _____

Exercise 2. *Translate the following sentences into English with postpositions.*

1. Яаахlума кухни чохь йу.

   _____

2. Малика диттана кlелахь йу.

   _____

3. lарби гlанта тlехь ву.

   _____

4. Джон суна уллехь ву.

   _____

5. Батарейкаш коран кlелахь йу.

   _____

6. Кор маьнга йистехь ду.

   _____

7. Сурт маьнга тlехулахь ду.

   _____

8. Квартира шолгlа гlат тlехь йу.

   _____

Exercise 3. *Match the singular verb with its plural.*

1. Хьажа	a. Довда
2. Дада	b. Хьовса
3. Дала	c. Совца
4. Саца	d. Довла

Exercise 4. *Fill in the blanks in this dialogue using the words in the box.*

гӏалан юккъехь	дела реза хуьлда	соцунгӏа	квартира

Джон: _____ сан гӏуллакхе хьажарна.

Агент: Хӏумма дац, Дела реза массарна а хуьлда. Вайшиъ хӏинца хьалхара квартире хьожур ву. Хӏара квартира Мамсурова урамехь йу,_____ уггаре хазачу меттехь. Вай гӏишлон арахь лаьтташ ду.

Джон: И хаза здани йу! Маса_____ йу оцу гӏишлон?

Агент: Ткъе квартира бен йац. Зданин тӏехьа ткъе бархӏалгӏа маршрутка а соцу. Кхузара маршруткан _____ йолчу подъезд чухула воьду.

Exercise 5. *Answer questions about family members.*

1. Хьан ден цӏе хӏун йу?

_____

2. Хьан ден мас шо ду?

_____

3. Хьан да хӏун болх беш ву?

_____

4. Хьан ненан цӏе хӏун йу?

_____

5. Хьан ненан мас шо ду?

_____

6. Хьан нана мила йу?

_____

7. Хьан йижарий вежарий дуй?

_____

8. Хьан мас йиша-ваша ду?

_____

9. Церан цӀерш хӀун йу?

_____

Exercise 6. *Translate the following sentences into Chechen.*

1. I have a cat. _____

2. I have three dogs._____

3. We have four cows._____

4. They have eight goats._____

5. You have two brothers._____

6. I have five sisters._____

7. He has four chickens._____

8. She is nine years old._____

Exercise 7. *Fill in the blanks with the words in the box.*

хӀора дийнахь	даимана	хӀора кӀиранахь	хӀора баттахь
сих-сиха	хӀора шарахь	наггахь	наг-наггахь

1. Со университете _____ йоьду.

2. Со базар _____ йоьду.

3. Тхо кино хьожу _____.

4. Аса _____ сайн цӀеран болх хуьйцу.

5. Аса сайн доттагӀчунна _____ гӀо до.

Exercise 8. *Write a few sentences using new vocabulary from this lesson.*

_____

_____

_____

_____

_____

_____

Корта IX: Зудайалочахь
Lesson 9: At the Wedding

Knowledge Check: Look for compound verbs in the dialogues in this lesson and give each principal part.

Lesson Plan:
- Iterative aspect of verbs
- Causative verbs
- Possessive pronouns
- Reflexive pronouns
- The present gerund
- Declining demonstrative pronouns

ДИАЛОГ I

Хьаван доьзалло Джон шайн шичан зудйалочига кхойкху, цигахь Джонна нохчийн мукъамаш а нохчийн хелхар а Iема. Оцу тевнехь Джонна Хьаван ден аг1ор гергара нах го. Шен гергара нах бевзуьйтуш, зудайалош верг Джонига вистахуьулу.

Джон: Дала декъала дойла шушиъ, Дала барт цхьаъ бойла. Со кхайкхарна Дела реза хуьлда хьуна!

Мохьмад: Джон, хьуна а хуьлда Дела реза, тхо лара а лерина кхуза варна а баркалла. Сайн ненана а, ненада а, деда а бовзийта лаьа суна хьуна. Сан шичо т1евуьгур ву хьо цаьрна.

Шича: Вало Джон, уьш д1огахь стол йистехь Iаш бу.

Джон: Де дика хуьлда шун, сан ц1е Джон йу, со Мохьмадан доттаг1 ву.

Абу-Солт: Далла везийла Джон, сан ц1е Абу-Солт йу. Мохьмад сан к1ента к1ант ву. Х1орш Мохьмадан ненана а, ненда а бу: Юнус а, цуьнан х1усамнана Кемса.

Джон: Шу девзина хазахета.

Абу-Солт: Нохчийн ловзаргехь цкъа а хиллий хьо?

Джон: Ца хилла. Х1ара сан дуьххьара нохчийн зудайалор ду.

Абу-Солт: Хьуна нохчийн г1иллакхаш хаьий?

Джон: Ас г1иллакхаш книжкаш т1ера Iамийна, амма баккхийчу нахера уьш Iамийча дика хир ду аьлла хета суна.

Абу-Солт: Дика ду. Ас хьуна нохчийн г1иллакх-оьздангалла хьоьхур ду.

DIALOGUE I: AT THE WEDDING

*Hwava's family invites John to their cousin's wedding. There John
learns Chechen music and dances. At the party, John sees the relatives
of Hwava's father's side. The fiancé, Mohwmad, introduces his
relatives and talks to John.*

John: God bless you both, may you live happily ever after.
Thank you for inviting me!

Mohwmad: John, thank you too for coming with respect. I want to
introduce you to my [maternal] grandmother, [maternal]
grandfather, and [paternal] grandfather. My cousin will
take you to them.

Cousin: Let's go, John, they are sitting over there next to the table.

John: Good afternoon, my name is John. I am Mohwmad's
friend.

Abu-Solt: Good afternoon, John. My name is Abu-Solt. Mohwmad
is my grandson. These are Mohwmad's maternal
grandmother and maternal grandfather: Yunus and his wife
Kemsa.

John: Nice meeting you.

Abu-Solt: Have you ever been to a Chechen party?

John: No, I haven't. This is my first Chechen wedding.

Abu-Solt: Do you know the Chechen customs?

John: I've learned Chechen customs from books, but I think it
will be better if I learn them from elders.

Abu-Solt: Ok. I will teach you the Chechen customs.

ДИАЛОГ II

Абу-Солта Джонига нохчийн къомах лаьцна дуьйцу.

Олуш ду-кх, нохчийн къам Нухь пайхамарх схьадаьлла ду. Дукха зама хьалха нохчашан шайн дин дара. Тlаккха цхьа эзар пхи бlе шерашкахь нохчаша бусулба дин тlеэца буьйлабелира. Цул тlаьхьа цхьа эзар бархl бlе шерашкахь Оьрсийн Импери нохчийн латташ схьадаха долийра. Оцу шерашкахь нохчийн къам Имам Шамильца оьрсашна дуьхьал летара. Оьрсаша Нохчичоь схьа а йаьккхина, нохчийн латташ Оьрсийн Империн дозанан дакъа хилира. Советан lедал долучу хенахь, Сталина нохчаша цlерабаьхнера Юкъара Азе. Со-суо Казахстанехь вина ву. Сталин веллачу хенахь, Казахстанехь кхойтта шо даьккхинчул тlаьхьа нохчийн къам Даймахке цlадирзира. Нохчийн къоман дуккха а тайпанаш ду. Тайпанийн тобананаша тукхумаш кхуллу. Масала, сан тукхум тlерлой ду, ткъа тайпан со аьрстхо ву.

DIALOGUE II: OLD MAN SPEAKING ABOUT CHECHEN NATION

Abu-Solt tells John about the Chechen nation.

It is said that the Chechen people are the descendants [came from] of the prophet Noah. A long time ago the Chechens had their own religion. Around 1500 the Chechens started converting to Islam. After that, in the 1800s the Russian Empire began taking over the Chechen lands. In those years the Chechens fought against the Russians with Imam Shamil. When the Russians took Chechnya, it became a part of the Russian Empire. During the Soviet regime Stalin deported the Chechens to Central Asia. I myself was born in Kazakhstan. When Stalin died, after spending thirteen years in Kazakhstan, the Chechens returned to their homeland. The Chechen people have many *teips*. Groups of *teips* make [create] *tukhums*. For example, my *tukhum* is *T'erloi*, and I am of the *aerstxo teip*.

Керла Дешнаш I / New Words I

шайн to yourself, to themselves (*pl.*)
зудайалор, зудайалорш (д:д) wedding
мукъам, мукъамаш (б:д) music
хелхар, хелхарш (д:д) dance (*n.*)
тов, тевнаш (й:й) party
гергара стаг, нах (в/й:б) relative
декъала blessed
барт (б) agreement, friendship
йистехь at the edge, next to, beside
ловзар, ловзарш (д:д) *event where people dance*
дуьххьара for the first time
гӀиллакх, гӀиллакхаш (д:д) customs, traditions
оьздангалла, оьздангаллаш (й:й) code of conduct
Дала барт цхьаъ бойла May God make your agreement the same (one)

Керла Хандешнаш / New Verbs

кхайкха to invite, to call someone **(кхойкху, кхайкхи, кхайкхина)**
халхад.ала to dance **(халхад.олу, халхад.ели, халхад.аьлла)**
д.истахила to have a word/conversation **(д.истахуьлу, д.истахили, д.истахилла)**
лара to respect **(лору, лери, лаьрна)**
лара а лерина *inf + present perfect, emphasizes the verb. "to really respect"*
д.овзийта to introduce **(д.овзуьйту, д.овзийти, д.овзийтина)**
тӀед.ига to lead someone, to take someone **(тӀед.уьгу, тӀед.иги, тӀед.игина)**
хьеха to teach, to advise **(хьоьху, хьийхи, хьехна)**

Керла Дешнаш II / New Words II

къам, къаьмнаш (д:д) nation
Нухь пайхамар (в) prophet Noah
зама, заманаш (й;й) period of time
дин, динш (д;д) religion
бусулба дин (д) Islam
Оьрсийн Импери (й) Russian Empire

латта, латташ (д;д) land
оьрси, оьрсий (в/й; б) Russian (*noun*)
дуьхьала against
доза, дозанаш (д:д) territory, land
дакъа, дакъош (д:д) part, piece
Юкъара Азе (й) Central Asia
даймохк, даймехкаш (б:д) fatherland
аьрстхо, аьрстхой (в:б) teip (*subgroup of clan*)
тоба, тобанаш (й:й) group
масала, масалаш (д:д) example

Керла Хандешнаш / NEW VERBS

тlеэца to accept (**тlеоьцу, тlеийци, тlеэцна**)
д.олад.ала to begin (*sing., intrans.*) (**д.олад.ало, д.олад.ели, д.олад.елла**)
д.уьйлад.ала to begin (*pl.*) (**д.уьйлад.ала, д.уьйлад.ели, д.уйьлад.елла**)
схьад,аккха to seize, to take over (*sing.*) (**схьад.оккху, схьад.аьккхи, схьад.аьккхина**)
схьад.аха to seize, take over (*pl.*) (**схьад.оху, схьад.ехи, схьад.аьхна**)
д.олад.ан to begin (*sing., trans.*) (**д.олад.о, д.олад.и, д.олад.елла**)
лата to fight (**лета, лети, летта**)
цlерад.аха to deport, to make leave (*pl.*) (**цlерад.оху, цlерад.ехи, цlерад.аьхна**)
цlадерза to return home (**цlадоьрзу, цlадирзи, цlадирзина**)
д.ина д.у to be born
кхолла to create (**кхуллу, кхоьлли, кхьоьллина**)

Граматика / GRAMMAR

Iterative Aspect of Verbs

Many Chechen verbs have different forms for simulfactive (happening one time) and iterative aspect. Iterative aspect is used for actions that take place more than once. The linguist Johanna Nichols has identified eighty Chechen verbs that distinguish simulfactive vs. iterative aspect.

For most of the verbs with aspectual pairs, the iterative aspect is formed by a change in the root vowel:

мала – мийла (*to drink more than once*)

> Со хӀинца шура **молуш** ву.
> *I am drinking milk right now.*

> Ас даиманна шура **муьйлу**.
> *I always drink milk.*

хатта – хатта (*to ask more than once*)

> Цо вай мича доьдуш дара **хаьттира**.
> *He asked where we were going.*

> Цо вай мичахь дара **хиттира**.
> *He was always asking where we were.*

харжа – хержа (*to choose more than once*)

> Ас хӀара некъ **хаьржна**.
> *I've chosen this path.*

> Ас хӀара некъ **хиржна**.
> *I've always chosen this path.*

Other verbs use a completely different stem (suppletion) to reflect iterative aspect. We've already met a few of these verbs. And as you can see, within the English translation there's an embedded sense of iterative aspect:

ала (*to say*)   баха (*to speak*)
тоха (*to hit*)   д.етта (*to beat*)

Ахь хӀу **аьлла**?   Ахь хӀу **боху**?
What did you say?   *What are you saying?*

Цо суна **туьйхира**.   Цо суна **йиттира**.
He hit me.   *He was hitting (beating) me.*

Another suppletive pair is **вада** "*to run*." Note that with a motion verb like "*to run*," the singular aspect can give a sense of suddenness or of starting the action:

Со авари гиначул тӀаьха, автобусан **тӀеведира**.
After seeing the accident, I ran to the bus.

Со паркехь **уьду**.
I run (jog) in the park.

A few rare verbs in Chechen reflect both aspect and number. One such verb is хьажа "*to look/watch*":

Со корехула ара **хьожуш** ву.
I'm looking out the window.

Тхо корехула ара **хьовсуш** ду.
We are looking out the window.

Со телевизоре **хьоьжу**.   Тхо телевизорга **хьуьсу**.
I watch TV.   *We watch TV.*

Word Building: Causative Verbs

In the first dialogue, we saw the following sentence and the verb for "*to introduce*": д.овзийта (д.овзуьйту, д.овзийти, д.овзийтина):

Сайн ненана а, ненада а, деда а **бовзийта** лаьа суна хьуна.
*I want to **introduce** you to my (maternal) grandmother and grandfather, and my (paternal) grandfather.*

Now let's look at a verb we encountered earlier, д.овза (д.евзу, д.евзи, д.евзина), "*to meet/to recognize/to know someone*":

Тхо селхана **девзи**.
*We just **met** yesterday.*

In Chechen, д.ита (д.уьйту, д.ийти, д.ийтина), which on its own means
"to leave" or *"to leave behind,"* can be added to a verb stem to form a
causative verb. Causative verbs express an action that the subject made
happen. As such, the subject will be in the Ergative case, and the direct
object in the Absolutive.

мала - малийта (*to make someone drink*)

Цо соьга шура **малийтира**.
*He made me **drink** milk.*

ала - алийта (*to make someone say*)
олуьйту (*Present Simple*)

Ас цуьнга хаза дош **олуьйту**.
*I'm **making him say** a sweet (*lit. beautiful*) word.*

Possessive Pronouns

Possessive pronouns like **сайн** or **шайн** can work with or independent
of the Genitive case of the personal pronouns. They convey the sense
of *"my own"* or *"your own"* in English. They are also used when the
subject of the phrase and the possessor of a given object are the same. In
this sense, they translate roughly to the use of *свой* in Russian.

For example, we saw in the dialogue:

Сайн ненана а, ненада а, деда а бовзийта лаьа суна хьуна.
*I want to introduce you to **my** maternal grandmother, maternal
grandfather, and paternal grandfather.*

But if we change the subject, the personal pronoun in the genitive makes
more sense:

Сан ненанана а, ненада а, деда а бовзийта лаьа **цунна** хьуна.
*He wants to introduce you to **my** maternal grandmother, maternal
grandfather, and paternal grandfather.*

This distinction is especially useful for distinguishing third person possessives:

Цунна цуьнан книга хазахета.
He likes his book. (someone else's book)

Цунна шен книга хазахета.
He likes his (own) book. (either he owns the book, or wrote it himself)

The possessive pronouns in their dependent form do not decline:

сайн *my (own)*   **тхайн / вешан** *our (own)*
хьайн *your (own)* sing.   **шайн** *your (own)* pl.
шен *his/her/its (own)*   **шайн** *their (own)*

Reflexive Pronouns

In the second dialogue in this lesson, we met reflexive pronouns in set phrases:

Со-суо Казахстанехь вина ву.
I myself was born in Kazakhstan.

As we can see, reflexive pronouns are often used for emphasis. Here they are fully declined. Note the similarities in the Genitive case between the reflexive and possessive pronouns, as well as the fact that the second person plural and third person plural are the same.

	I	you (sing.)	he/ she/it	we (exc.)	we (incl.)	you (pl.)	they
Abs.	суо	хьуо	ша	тхаьш	ваьш	шаьш	шаьш
Gen.	сайн	хьайн	шен	тхайн	вешан	шайн	шайн
Dat.	сайна	хьайна	шена	тхаьшна	ваьшна	шайна	шайна
Erg.	айс	айхь	ша	тхаьш	ваьш	шаьш	шаьш
Inst.	сайца	хьайца	шеца	тхоьца	ваьшца	шайца	шайца
Subst.	сайх	хьайх	шех	тхайх	ваьшха	шайх	шайх

Comp.	сайл	хьайл	шел	тхайл	ваьшла	шайл	шайл
Loc.	сайга	хьайга	шега	тхайга	ваьшка	шайга	шайга

Reflexive Pronouns and Relative Clauses

Compare the following two sentences:

Шен гергара нах бевзуьйтуш, зудайалош верг Джонига
вистахуьлу.
Introducing his relatives, the fiancé talks to John.

Ша гергара нах бевзуьйтуш волу, зудайалош верг Джонига
вистахуьлу.
The fiancé, who is introducing (his) relatives, is talking to John.

In the first sentence, **шен** is a possessive pronoun stating that the relatives who the fiancé is introducing are his own. In the second sentence, we see the reflexive third person pronoun in the Ergative case combined with the present gerund and д.олу. The negative form of д.олу is д.оцу. We can think of д.олу as expressing *"that, which"* or *"the person, who."* When combined with reflexive pronouns, we can create complex clauses that add extra color to what we are trying to say:

Шена даиманна деша хазахеташ волу, Джонна тlаьхари цхьа
книга йазйира.
John, who always loved reading, finally wrote a book.

Note here that we can translate the relative clause using the past tense, since the verb in the main clause is in the observed past tense. Similarly, in the below sentence, since **цкъа а** conveys a habitual aspect, we can translate the relative clause in the present tense, even though the main clause takes the future tense:

Хьайгахь **цкъа а** ахча доцуш волу, ахь-айхь массарна йаахlума
оьцур йуй?
You, who never has money (on you), will buy everyone food?

The Present Gerund

A gerund functions like an adverb, often describing how an action is done. In this lesson we saw the following sentence:

> Шен гергара нах бевзуьйтуш, зудайалош верг Джонига
> вистахуьлу.
> *Introducing his relatives, the fiancé talks to John.*

Here, the gerund бевзуьйтуш describes how or by what means the fiancé is speaking with John. The present gerund is simply formed by adding -ш to the present tense:

> Къамел деш а доьшуш а ас-сайн нохчийн мотт Iамийна.
> *By conversing and reading I learned Chechen.*

Declining Demonstrative Pronouns

In the Oblique cases, dependent demonstrative pronouns have only one extra form:

ДIогара книга хаза йу.	ДIогарчу книгехь дукха хазалла йу.
That book over there is beautiful.	*In that book there is much beauty.*

И книга хаза йу.	Оцу книгехь дуккха хазалла йу.
That book is beautiful.	*In that book there is much beauty.*

ХIара книга хаза йу.	(ХIо)кху книгехь дуккха хазалла йу.
This book is beautiful.	*In this book there is much beauty.*

When independent, xIapa is fully declined.

	this	**these**
Abs.	хIapa	хIорш
Gen.	(хIо)кхуьнан	(хIо)кхеран
Dat.	(хIо)кхунна	(хIо)кхарна
Erg.	(хIо)кхо	(хIо)кхара
Inst.	(хIо)кхуьнца	(хIо)кхаьрца

Subst.	(xlo)кхунах	(xlo)кхарах
Comp.	(xlo)кхул	(xlo)кхарел
Loc.	(xlo)кхуьнга	(xlo)кхаьрга

Упражненеш / EXERCISES

Exercise 1. *Fill in the blanks in this dialogue using the words from word box.*

доттагӏ	йистехь	Далла везийла	хазахета

Шича: Вало Джон, уьш дӏогахь стол_____ ӏаш бу.

Джон: Де дика хуьлда шун, сан цӏе Джон йу, со Мохьмадан
_____ву.

Деда: _____ Джон, сан цӏе Абу-Солт йу.
Мохьмад сан кӏента кӏант ву. Хӏорш Мохьмадан ненана
а, ненда а бу: Юнус а, цуьнан хӏусамнана Кемса.

Джон: Шу девзина_____.

Exercise 2. *Create sentences using the following new vocabulary words.*

даймохк (б;д) *n.*	депортаци (й;й) *n.*	зама (й;й) *n.*	цӏадирзира *v.*

_____

_____

_____

_____

Exercise 3. *Match the following questions to answers provided.*

1. Даймохк мичахь бу?   Со арахь ву.
2. Хьо мичахь ву?   Нохчичохь бу.
3. Депортаци хӀун йу?   Хан йу.
4. Зама хӀун йу?   Депортаци нохчий цӀерабахар йу.

Exercise 4. *Translate the sentences in Exercise 3 above.*

1. _____
2. _____
3. _____
4. _____

Exercise 5. *Translate the following sentences into Chechen.*

1. The fiancé talks to Maryam.

   _____

2. By reading I learned Chechen and Russian.

   _____

3. He likes his (own) house.

   _____

4. She made me drink coffee.

   _____

5. They made me drink tea.

   _____

Exercise 6. *Write the following times in Chechen.*

2:00 pm : _____

5:30 pm : _____

9:45 am : _____

7:40 am : _____

8:55 pm : _____

1:00 pm : _____

6:15 am : _____

7:10 pm : _____

10:25 am : _____

Exercise 7. *Read the affirmative sentences and then negate them and write in Chechen.*

1. Лоьро Хедига ахч ло. *A nurse gives money to Kheda.*

_____

2. Сан доттагӀчо соьга хеттарш до. *My friend asks questions (to me).*

_____

3. Дешархой университетехь гулло. *Students gather at university.*

_____

4. Тхан балхахь дуккха а белхалой бу. *There are many employees at our work.*

_____

5. Къеначуьнга хаза дош ала деза. *Polite words need to be used toward elderly.*

_____

6. Со Москвахь Ӏаш йу, ткъа хьо? *I live in Moscow, and you?*

_____

Корта X:
Лаьмнашка дахар

Lesson 10:
Going to the Mountains

Knowledge Check: Highlight all verbs in the dialogues that are neither singular subject nor simulfactive aspect.
Highlight constructions where gerunds are used, how would you translate these phrases into English?

Lesson Plan:
- The Past Continuous tense
- The Unreal Conditional mood
- -за and аьлла construction
- Declining definite and negative pronouns

ДИАЛОГ I

*Лаьмнашка баха Iалашо йолуш, Джон, Ваха а церан кхиболу
накъостий университетехь къамел деш бу.*

Джон: Суна хезна, кхана вай лаьмнашка гIур ду аьлла.

Ваха: ХIаъ, гIур ду. Хьо хиллий нохчийн лаьмнашкара йуьртахь?

Джон: Со лаьмнаш ганза ву, со гIалахь бен ца Iийна.

Ваха: Хьуна лаьмнаш хазахетар ду! Со жима волуш сих-сиха
воьдура цига.

Джон: Ахь хIун дора цигахь?

Ваха: Шадерриге! Аьхка малх даимана къегаш хуьлура. Со
наггахь волавелла лелара, сайн дехой болчу а воьдуш. Ас
царна кертахь дан дезачуьнца гIо дора: божол цIанйоIра,
дечиг доккхура. ХIора дийнахь бабас бежнашкара шура
йоккхуш а, котамашна йаахIума луш со хьоьжура.

Джон: Сакъоьруш хилла ахь жима волуш! Хьой, хьан дай-наний
гурахь йухадоьлхарий цига?

Ваха: ХIаъ, тхо хIора шарахь гуьйранна оьху йуьрта. Гуьйранна
догIанаш оьху, цундела тхо дукхахьолахь чохь Iа.
Цкъа хьалха ох шортта довха чай муьйлу, тIаккха тхо
телевизор хьоьжу.

Джон: Ткъа Iай хIун до аш?

Ваха: Ас бераллехь цхьа Iа бен ца даьккхина цигахь. Ло оьхура,
ткъа со лонах ловзура. Амма хIинца ох цига машен ца
хоьхку, просто телефон йетта!

Джон: Ма дика ду вай бIаьста доьлхуш долуш!

DIALOGUE I: GOING TO THE MOUNTAINS

John, Vaxa, and their other friends who are planning on going to the mountains, are talking at the university.

John: I've heard that tomorrow we will go to the mountains.

Vaxa: Yes, we will go. Have you been to a Chechen mountain village?

John: I haven't seen the mountains. I've only stayed in the city.

Vaxa: You will like the mountains! When I was little, I would often go there.

John: What would you do there? [What did you use to do there?]

Vaxa: Everything! In the summer, the sun was always shining. I sometimes would walk around, going to my father's relatives. I would help them do chores in the backyard, clean the barn and chop wood. Every day I used to watch grandma milk the cows and feed the chickens.

John: You enjoyed being young! Would you and your parents go back in autumn?

Vaxa: Yes, every year in autumn we go to the village. In autumn it rains, so we mainly stay inside. First, we drink a lot of hot tea, then we watch TV.

John: What do you do in winter?

Vaxa: In my childhood, I only spent one winter there. It would snow, and I would play in the snow. But now we don't drive the car there, we just call!

John: Well, it's great that we are going in spring!

ДИАЛОГ II

Итум-Кхаьла схьакхаьчна, Джонна а, цуьнан накъосташна ламрой го. Йуьртахь Джонна меттигер диалект хеза.

Ваха: ДIогара бIаьвнашка хьажа!

Джон: Ва-а, мел хаза ду кхузахь!

Профессор: Студентш, суна тIаьхьахIиттал, вай йуьртда волчу доьлхуш ду.

Профессорий, студентший йуьртдеца вовшакхета.

Йуьртда: Могуш-маьрша ва хьо, сан доттагI!

Профессор: Делера маршал хуьлда хьуна, Куьйра! Муха ву хьо а, хьан доьзал а? ГIарч аьлла вуй хьо сан борз?

Йуьртда: (къежаш) Аза-м бакъдацара, со къанвелла.

Профессор: ХIара дешархой йуьртара дахар гайта балийна ас. Йуьртара дахарх лаьцна дуьйцур дарий ахь хIокхарна?

Йуьртда: Делахь, алуш ду-кх, нохчи хила хала ду, амма кхузири дахар чолхе дац. Итум-Кхаьллехь цхьа азир адам ду Iаш. Бакъду, дукхахбариш са санни къани бу, къони чкъор кхузахь Iен лууш дац.

Профессор: Итум-Кхаьллера наха хIун болх бо?

Йуьртда: Божарша бажи Iу болх бо, цара устагIи лаьмнашкахь хьала а вахьа а лехку. Накхармазуй лелочара моз дохку туристашна.

Профессор: Зударша хIун до?

Йуьртда: Зударша котами а лелайо, цери хIоаш гулдо, бежан а IалашдIо.

Джон: Бераша хIун до, муха ловзу уьш?

Йуьртда: Бераша Iамчури чIари лецу, дитташ тIе схьалабовлу, гаьнгали тIехь техка а техка. Цу тIе аьхка бераш хи чохь луьйчу.

DIALOGUE II: AT THE MOUNTAINS

*Having arrived in Itum-Qaela, John and his friends see the mountaineers.
In the village, John hears the mountain dialect.*

Vaxa: Look at those towers!

John: Wow, how beautiful it is here!

Professor: Students, follow me, we are going to the head of the
             village.

The professor and students meet with the village chief, Kyira.

Kyira: Hello (may you come healthy and free), my friend!

Professor: Hello, Kyira! How are you and your family? Still strong,
          my wolf?

Kyira: *(smiling)* That is not true, I got old.

Professor: I've brought these students to show life in the village.
          Would you tell them about village life?

Kyira: Well, there is a saying, it is hard to be a Chechen, but life
          here is not hard. There are about one thousand people
          living here. It is true, the majority are old like me, the
          young generation doesn't want to live here.

Professor: What do people from Itum-Qaela do for work?

Kyira: Men work as shepherds; they drive sheep up and down the
          mountains. Beekeepers sell honey to tourists.

Professor: What do women do?

Kyira: Women take care of chickens, collect their eggs, and take
          care of cows.

John: What do the children do, how do they play?

Kyira: Children go fishing in the lake, climb trees, swing on the
          swings. In addition, in the summer the children go
          swimming.

Керла Дешнаш I / NEW WORDS I

лам, лаьмнаш (б:д) mountain
lалашо, lалашонаш (й:й) goal
кхид.олу other
йурт, йуьрташ (й:й) village
шадерриге everything
аьхке, аьхкенаш (й:й) summer
малх, малхнаш (б:д) sun
дехо, дехой (в/й:б) paternal relative
ненахо, ненахой (в/й:б) maternal relative
керта, керташ (й:й) backyard
дан дезарг, дан дезарш (д:д) chores (*lit.* what needs doing)
божал, божалш (й:й) barn
дечиг (д) wood
етт, бежнаш (б:д) cow
котам, котамаш (й:й) chicken
гуьйре, гуьйренаш (й:й) autumn, fall
догlа, догlанаш (д:д) rain
дукхахьолахь mainly
цкъа хьалха first
шортта a lot
lа, lаьннаш (д:д) winter
бералла (й) childhood
ло, лонаш (д:д) snow
бlаьсте, бlаьстенаш (й:й) spring (*season*)
просто simply

Керла Хандешнаш / NEW VERBS

къамел дан to converse (**къамел до, кьамел ди, къамел дина**)
хаза to hear (**хеза, хези, хезна**)
къага to shine (**къега, къеги, къегна**)
лела to walk (**лела, лийли, лелла**)
д.олад.елла лела to go for a walk (**д.елла лела, д.олад.елла лийли, д.олад.елла лелла**)
цlанйан to clean (**цlанйо, цlанйи, цlанйина**)
дечиг даккха to chop wood (**дечиг доккху, дечиг даьккхи, дечиг даьккхина**)

шура йаккха to milk (шура йоккху, шура йаьккхи, шура
йаьккхина)
йаахӀума йала to feed (йаахӀума ло, йаахӀума йели, йаахӀума
йелла)
хьежа to watch (*iterative*) (хьоьжу, хьийжи, хьежна)
сакъера to enjoy (сакъоьру, сакъийри, сакъерра)
йухад.аха to return, to go back (*pl.*) (йухад.оьлху, йухад.ахи,
йухад.ахна)
йухаэха to return, to go back (*iterative*) (йухаоьху, йухаихи,
йухаихна)
эха to go (*iterative, sing. and pl.*) (оьху, ихи, ихна)
мийла to drink (*iterative*) (муьйлу, мийли, мийлина)
ловза to play (ловзу, левзи, левзина)
хьахка to ride; to drive (хьохку, хьаьхки, хьаьхкина)
телефон йетта to call (*iterative*) (телефон йетта, телефон йитти,
телефон йиттина)

Керла Дешнаш II / NEW WORDS II

ламро, ламрой (в/й:б) mountaineers
меттиг, меттигаш (й:й) place
меттигера local
диалект, диалектш (й:й) dialect
бӀов, бӀевнаш (й:й) (*dialectal* бӀаьвнаш) tower
йуьртда, йуьртдай (в:б) village head
Могуш-маьрша ва хьо! May you come healthy and free!
аза-м (*dialectal:* иза-м) that/he/she/it
гӀарч strong, tough (*onomatopoeic*)
къанвалле (*dialectal:* къанвелла) to get old
дахар, дахарш (д:д) life
чолхе hard, difficult
кхузири дахар(*dialectal:* кхузара дахар) life here
азир (*dialectal:* эзар) thousand
къани (*dialectal:* кьена) old
къони (*dialectal:* къона) young
чкъор, чкъораш (д:д) skin; *here:* generation
стаг, божарий (в:б) man
бажи Ӏу, Ӏуй (в/й: б) (*dialectal:* беж Ӏу) (cow)shepherd

уьстагӀ, уьстагӀий (б:д) sheep
накхармоз, накхармозий (б:д) bee
накхармазуй лелочара (*dialectal:* **накхармозий лелорхо**) beekeeper
моз (д) honey
котами (*dialectal:* **котам (й)**) chicken, hen
цери (*dialectal:* **церан**) their; they (*in Genitive case*)
Ӏам, Ӏамнаш (б:д) lake
Ӏамчури (*dialectal:* **Ӏамчура**) from the lake
чӀари (*dialectal*: **чӀара, чӀерий (б:д)**) fish
дитт, дитташ (д:д) tree
гаьнгали, гаьнгалеш (б:д) swing
цулла совнах in addition, moreover

Керла Хандешнаш / NEW VERBS

тӀаьхьахӀотта to follow (*sing.*) (**тӀаьхьахӀутту, тӀаьхьахӀоьтти, тӀаьхьахӀоьттина**)
тӀаьхьахӀитта to follow (*pl.*) (**тӀаьхьахӀуьтту, тӀаьхьахӀитти, тӀаьхьахӀиттина**)
къанд.ала to grow old (**къанло, къанд.ели, къанд.елла**)
гайта to show (**гойту, гайти, гайтина**)
д.аладан to bring (**д.алад.о, д.алий, далийна**)
алуш (*dialectal:* **олуш**) saying
къежа to smile (**къоьжу, къийжи, къийжина**)
лаа to want (**лаьа, лии, лиина**)
лалла to drive, to herd (*sing., sing. aspect*) (**лоллу, лаьлли, лаьллина**)
лехка to drive, to herd (*pl., iterative*) (**лоьхку, лихки, лихкина**)
лахка to drive, to herd (*pl., sing. aspect*) (**лохку, лаьхки, лаьхкина**)
д.охку (*dialectal:* **д.ухку**) to sell
д.охка to sell (*sing. aspect*) (**д.ухку, д.оьхки, д.оьхкина**)
д.ихка to sell (*sing. aspect*) (**д.уьхку, д.ихки, д.ихкина**)
гулд.ан to collect (**гулд.о, гулд.и, гулд.ина**)
Ӏалашд.ан to save, to take care (**Ӏалашд.о, Ӏалашд.и, Ӏалашд.ина**)
лецу (*dialectal:* **луьйцу**) catch
лаца to catch (*sing. aspect*) (**лоцу, леци, лаьцна**)
лийца to catch (*iterative*) (**луьйцу, лийци, лийцина**)
схьалад.ала to climb (*pl.*) (**схьалад.олу, схьад.ели, схьалад.аьлла**)

схьалад.овла to climb (*pl.*) (**схьалад.овлу, схьад.евли,**

схьалад.евла)

техка to swing (*iterative*) (**техка, тихки, тихкина)**
лийча to swim, to bathe (**луьйчу, лийчи, лийчина)**

Граматика / GRAMMAR

Past Continuous Tense

The Past Continuous tense, as its name suggests, expresses an action
that was ongoing or continuous in the past. It is also called the Past
Imperfect tense. The Past Continuous tense is formed by adding the
Past tense suffix -**pa** to the Present tense form of the verb. The Past
Continuous tense in Chechen often translates to "*was x-ing,*" "*used to
x,*" or "*would x*":

> **д.о – д.ора** (*do – was doing, used to do, would do*)

> Ас царна кертахь дан дезачуьнца гӀо **до**.
> *I help them do chores in the backyard.*

> Ас царна кертахь дан дезачуьнца гӀо **дора**.
> *I used to (would) help them do chores in the backyard.*

Note, the past continuous form of "*to be*" is **хуьлура**:

> Аьхка малх даимана къегаш бу.
> *In the summer the sun is always shining.*

> Аьхка малх даимана къегаш **хуьлура**.
> *In the summer the sun **was always** shining.*

The Unreal Conditional Mood

In Lesson 7 we learned about the Real Conditional mood:

> Со нохчийн мотт Ӏамош велахь, суна книгаш оьшур йу.
> *If I am studying Chechen, I will need books.*

The Unreal Conditional mood is another "if" statement in Chechen, which conveys a statement that the speaker believes unlikely to occur. The "if" statement consists of the **-хь** suffix from the Real Conditional mood, followed by **-ара**. The verb in the main clause (apodosis) takes the future form of the verb plus **д.ара**:

> Со нохчийн мотт Iамош велахьара, суна книгаш оьшур йара.
> *If I were studying Chechen, I would need books.*

Note that in the dialogue, the "if" statement (protasis) is not necessary to convey the Conditional mood. Moreover, in a question it can soften a request, just like in English:

> Йуьртара дахарх лаьцна дуьйцур дарий ахь хIокхарна?
> *Would you tell them about life in the village?*

-за **Construction**

Adding **-за** to the infinitive form of the verb gives the sense of "*not having x-ed.*" It is similar to the negative form of the Present Perfect tense. However, it speaks more to a quality of a person, e.g., "*I am someone who has not x'd*":

> Со лаьмнаш ганза ву.
> *I haven't seen the mountains.*
> Or: *I am someone who hasn't seen the mountains.*

> Суна лаьмнаш ца гина.
> *I haven't seen the mountains.*

аьлла **Construction**

The Present Perfect form of ала, "*to say,*" has become a very useful construction for creating subordinate clauses. We saw in Lesson 6:

> Вай беркат базар гIур ду **аьлла** хета суна.
> *I like that we will go to Berkat market.*

Аьлла, like in the sentence above, is particularly useful for verbs such as "*to think,*" "*to know,*" "*to like.*" The subordinate clause can come before the main clause, like in the sentence above, or it can come after the main clause, like we saw in this lesson's dialogue:

Суна хезна, кхана вай лаьмнашка гӀур ду **аьлла**.
I've heard that tomorrow we will go to the mountains.

Declining Definite and Negative Pronouns

The declension of the pronouns **массо а** "*all*" and **хӏоп** "*each*" is straightforward:

	all	each
Abs.	массо а	хӏоп
Gen.	массеран а	хӏоранан
Dat.	массарна а	хӏоранна
Erg.	массара а	хӏорамма
Instr.	массаьрца а	хӏоранца
Subst.	массарах а	хӏораннах
Comp.	массарал а	хӏораннал
Loc.	массаьрга а	хӏоранга

The negative pronouns **цхьа а** "*no one*" and **хӏумма а** "*nothing*" follow a similar pattern:

	no one	nothing
Abs.	цхьа а	хӏумма а
Gen.	цхьаннан а	хӏуманнан а
Dat.	цхьанна а	хӏуманна а
Erg.	цхьамма а	хӏуманно а
Instr.	цхьаьнца а	хӏуманца а
Subst.	цхьаннах а	хӏуманнах а
Comp.	цхьаннал а	хӏуманнал а
Loc.	цхьаьнгга а	хӏумангга а

Упражненеш / EXERCISES

Exercise 1. *Fill in the blanks in the dialogue below using the verbs from the box.*

болх бо	луьйчу	гулдо	схьалабовлу	дохку	ловзу

Профессор: Итум-Кхаьллера наха хӀун_____?

Йуьртда: Божарша бажи Ӏу болх бо, цара устагӀи лаьмнашкахь хьала а вахьа а лехку. Накхармазуй лелочара моз_____туристашна.

Профессор: Зударша хӀун до?

Йуьртда: Зударша котами а лелайо, цери хӀоаш _____, бежан а Ӏалашдо.

Джон: Бераша хӀун до, муха _____ уьш?

Йуьртда: Бераша Ӏамчури чӀари лецу, дитташ тӀе _____, гаьнгали тӀехь техка а техка. Цу тӀе аьхка бераш хи чохь _____.

Exercise 2. *Match the Chechen words with their English translations.*

1. Лалла   to drive, to herd (*sing., sing. aspect*)
2. Гайта   to drive, to herd (*pl., iterative*)
3. Лахка   to drive, to herd (*pl., sing.*)
4. Къанд.ала   to grow old
5. Д.аладан   to bring
6. Алуш   to show
7. Лехка   *dialectal:* олуш
8. Къежа   to smile

Exercise 3. *Translate the following sentences into English.*

1. Бераша аьхка луьйчу.

_____

2. Зударша бежнаш леладо.

_____

3. Божарша уьстагӏий хьала а вахьа а лехку.

_____

4. Туристаша моз оьцу.

_____

5. Гидо Соьлжа-Гӏала гойту.

_____

Exercise 4. *Answer the following questions in Chechen in complete sentences using information from dialogues.*

1. Джон мича воьдуш ву?

_____

2. Вахас йуьртахь хӏун дора?

_____

3. Зударша йуьртахь хӏун до?

_____

4. Бераша йуьртахь хӏун до?

_____

5. Божарша йуьртахь хӏун до?

_____

Exercise 5. *Look at the table below. After translating any unfamiliar words create sentences. You can create affirmative, negative or interrogative (Yes/No) sentences.*

Subject	Adjective	+	-	?
Сан жӀаьла	ирсе			
Вайн бераш	самукъане			
Паччахьан белхалой	гӀайгӀане	ву	вац	йуй
Министерствон куьйгалхой	ойлане	йу	йац	йуй
		ду	бац	буй
Нохчийн дешархой	декъала	бу	дац	дуй
Баба	каде			
Сан деда	догцӀена			
Вайн нус	догӀаьржа			
Шун Ӏилманчаш	харцхьара			
Оьрсийн йаздархой	эсала			
Себастьян	сапаргӀат			

_____

_____

_____

_____

_____

_____

_____

_____

LESSON 10

197

Exercise 6. *Use the adjectives from the table in Exercise 5 to fill in the blanks.*

1. Сан да _____ ву.

2. Сан нана _____ йу.

3. Сан марьйиш _____ йу.

4. Тхан ваша _____ ву.

5. Вайн йиша _____ йу.

6. Сан йиши кӏант _____ ву.

7. Баби веши кӏант _____ ву.

8. Малики йоӏ _____ йу.

9. Сиражди _____ ву.

10. Жансари _____ йу.

Exercise 7. *Translate the sentences from Exercise 6.*

1. _____

2. _____

3. _____

4. _____

5. _____

6. _____

7. _____

8. _____

9. _____

10. _____

Exercise 8. *Create your own sentences describing life in a typical village.*

_____

_____

_____

_____

_____

_____

_____

_____

Корта XI:
Соьлжа-Гӏалан тур

Lesson 11:
A Tour of Grozny

Knowledge Check: Mark relative clauses in the dialogues using the д.олу construction. Also mark the gerunds. How do the two types of clauses differ?

Lesson Plan:
- Participles
- Word building: Nouns

ДИАЛОГ I

*Лаьмнашкара схьавеанчул тIаьхьа Джон а, цуьнан доттагIий а
Соьлжа-ГIалахула гидца туре боьлху.*

Гид: Вай хIинца Михаил Архангелан цIарах йолу килсан хьалха
ду, шен бухботтар 1868-чу шарахь а долуш. Соьлжа-
ГIалан бухбиллан 50 шо даьллачул тIаьхьа йоьттина
хIара килса. Шун ма-хаара, Соьлжа-ГIалан гIап
оьрсаша, Ермолов куьйгаллехь а волуш 1818 йоьттина.
1870-чу шарахь оцу гIопах гIала хилира, вайн тахана
схьагуш йолу Соьлжа-ГIала. Килса йан ахч эрмалоша а
оьрсийн йохкар-эцар лелочара делира, амма белхалой
казакш бара. Нохчийн тIом болабелча 1995-чу шарахь
килсан тхов тIера горгали буьйхира. Алссам бохам
хилира нохчийн-оьрсийн шолгIачу тIам тIехь. 2000-чу
шерашкахь Россин пачхьалкхо ахча а делла, Соьлжа-
ГIалан оьрсийн килса тойира.

Джон: Дукха нах богIий килсане?

Гид: Ши тIом бахьана долуш, оьрсий дукха ца бисина Соьлжа-
ГIалахь, цундела башха дукха нах а ца хуьлу кхузахь.

Джон: Ткъа нохчий мича боьлху ламаз дан?

Гид: Хьуна ма-хаара, дукхахболу нохчий бусулба бу, суфий.
Нохчий шина тайпана суфисташ бу, цхьаберш зикр деш
бу, ткъа вуьш зикр деш бац.

Джон: Зикр хIун йу?

Гид: Зикр бусулба божарша до, Делан цIерш йоху цара,
гобоккхий дIа а хIуьттий. Наггахь, божарий тIараш
тухуш олу зикр. ХIинца вай нохчаша ламаз дечу
"Сердце Чечни" маьждиге доьлхур ду.

DIALOGUE I: A TOUR OF GROZNY

After returning from the mountains John and his friends go on a tour through Grozny with a guide.

Guide: We are now in front of Michael the Archangel's Church, which was built in 1868. This church was built 50 years after the founding of Grozny. As you know, the Russians built the fortress when Yermolov was in charge. In 1870, the fortress became a city, which is the Grozny we see today. Yermolov and Russian traders gave money for the building of the church, but the workers were Cossacks. When the Chechen War began in 1995, the bell from the church's roof was broken. There was a lot of destruction in the Second Chechen War. In the 2000s, the Russian government gave money and Grozny's church was repaired.

John: Do a lot of people go to church?

Guide: Not many Russians were left in Grozny, due to the two wars, so not many people frequent here.

John: Where do Chechens go to pray?

Guide: As you know, most Chechens are Muslim, Sufi. Chechens are two types of Sufis, some practice the zikr, and others don't practice the zikr.

John: What is the zikr?

Guide: The Muslim men who practice the zikr chant the names of God standing in a circle. Sometimes, men chant the zikr while clapping. Now we will go to the mosque, "Heart of Chechnya," where Chechens go to pray.

ДИАЛОГ II

Джон, Ваха а гид а болалуш нохчийн маьждиган тӀекхочу.

Ваха: Суна хӀара гӀишло дика йевза! ХӀара массарна а дика девза "Сердце Чечни" йа "Нохчийчоьнан Дог" маьждиг ду.

Гид: Хьо бакъло, шуна гуш долу маьждиг, Кадыров Ахьмад-Хьаьжин цӀарах долу "Сердце Чечни" ткъа нохчийн маттахь "Нохчийчоьнан Дог" ду. ХӀара 2008-чу шарахь доьттина маьждиг Европехь уггаре доккха ду.

Джон: Дика ду, ас йоьшучу книгаш тӀера дагадогӀу суна. Чудоьлхий вай?

Джон, Ваха а Гид мачаш дӀа а йохий, маьждиган чоьхьабовлу.

Гид: Вай хӀинца маьждиган чохь ду. Маьждиган дешех бина 36 стогар бу.

Джон: Мел хаза ду хӀара маьждиг! Суна ламаз деш кӀант го дӀогахь, даиманна а догӀий адамаш кхуза ламаз дан?

Гид: ХӀаъ, ламаз дархьама даиманна богӀу кхуза уьш. ШолгӀачу гӀат тӀехь йолчу меттигехь зударша до ламаз. Бакъду, вай цига даха йиш йац.

Джон: Проблем яц, обед йан доьлхий вай?

DIALOGUE II: IN GROZNY—AT THE MOSQUE

John, Vaxa and the guide arrive at the Chechen mosque on foot.

Vaxa: I know this building very well! This is a well-known mosque called "The Heart of Chechnya" or "Chechen Heart."

Guide: You are right, the mosque you see is Kadyrov Akhmat-Khadji's "The Heart of Chechnya," or in Chechen "The Heart of Chechnya." This mosque, built in 2008, is the largest in Europe.

John: Okay, I remember it from the books I read. Shall we go in?

John, Vaxa and guide remove their shoes and walk into the mosque.

Guide: We are now inside the mosque. The mosque has 36 lamps made of gold.

John: How beautiful this mosque is! I see a praying boy over there, do people always come here to pray?

Guide: Yes, they always come here to pray. Women pray in a place on the second floor. Truly, we can't go there.

John: No problem, shall we go make lunch?

Керла Дешнаш I / New Words I

тур, турш (й:й) tour
гид, гидш (в/й:б) guide
килс, килснаш (й:й) church
бухботтар, бухботтарш (д:д) construction
гӏап, гӏепаш (й:й) fortress
куьйгалла (й) power, supervision
йохкар-эцар (д) commerce
йохкар-эцар лелорг, лелорш (в/й:б) merchant
казак, казакш (в/й:б) Cossack
тхов, тхевнаш (б:д) roof
горгали, горгалеш (б:д) bell
бохам, бохамаш (б:б) destruction
пачхьалкх, пачхьалкхш (й:й) federation
бахьна, бахьнаш (д:д) reason
дукхахд.олу majority
цхьад.ерш some
зикр, зикарш (д:д) zikr
важ, вуьш other, others (*adj.*)
маьждиг, маьждигаш (д:д) mosque

Керла Дешнаш / New Verbs

схьаган to see; to reveal (**схьаго (схьагуш), схьаги, схьагина**)
д.оха to break (*intransitive*) (**д.уху, д.уьйхи, д.оьхна**)
д.охад.ан to break (**д.охад.о, д.охад.и, д.охад.ина**
тод.ан to repair, to fix (**тод.о, тод.и, тод.ина**)
д.иса to remain (**д.уьсу, д.иси, д.исина**)
зикр дан to practice the zikr (**зикр до, зикр ди, зикр дина**)
зикр ала to chant (**зикр олу, зикр эли, зикр аьлла**)
цӏе йаккха to call the name (*sing.*) (**цӏе йоккху, цӏе йаьккхи,
                                                 цӏе йаьккхина**)
цӏерш йаха to call the names (*pl.*) (**цӏерш йогӏу, цӏерш йехи,
                                                 цӏерш йаьхна**)
гобаккха to make a circle (**гобоккху, гобаьккхи, гобаьккхина**)
хӏотта to stand; to appear (*sing. aspect*) (**хӏутту, хӏоьтти, хӏоьттина**)

хӀитта to stand; to appear (*iterative*) (хӀуьтту, хӀитти, хӀиттина)
тӀараш тоха to applaud (тӀараш туху, тӀараш туьйхи, тӀараш
         тоьхна)
тӀараш детта to applaud (*iterative*) (тӀараш доьтту, тӀараш дитти,
         тӀараш диттина)

Керла Дешнаш II / NEW WORDS II

дог, дегнаш (д:д) heart
уггаре the most
шо, шераш (д:д) year
ткъа but
архитектор, архитекторш (в/й:б) architect
сийна dark blue
стиль, стильш (й:й) style
хатӀ, хатӀш (д:д) characteristics
гӀат, гӀатш (й:й) level, floor
бакъду truly
йиш (й) opportunity
проблем, проблемш (й:й) problem
адам, адамаш (д:д) human, person
тера alike
стогар, стогарш (б:д) lamp; bulb
обед, обедш (й:й) lunch

Керла Хандешнаш / NEW VERBS

д.овза to meet, to introduce (д.евзу, д.евзи, д.евзина)
бакъlen to speak truth (бакъльоь, бакълий, бакълийна)
дагад.ан to remember (дагад.огӀу, дагад.еи, дагад.еана)
чудаха to go in (чуд.огӀу, чуд.агӀи, чуд.агӀина)
пайдаэца to benefit (пайдаоьцу, пайдаийци, пайдаэцна)

Граматика / GRAMMAR

Participles

A participle is an adjective formed from a verb. In Chechen, participles are particularly useful for forming Relative clauses. In the dialogues, we saw two types: present and past. (The third, future participle, we will also cover below.):

Ас йоьшучу книгаш тӀера дагадогӀу суна.
I remember it from the books I read.

Хӏара 2008-чу шарахь доьттина маьждиг Европехь уггаре доккха ду.
This mosque, built in 2008, is the largest in Europe.

As you can probably guess, unlike in English, the participle and/or its clause comes before the noun it describes:

Шура **молу** кӏант парке воьдуш ву.
*The boy **drinking** the milk is going to the park.*

The participle can be in either the active or passive voice, without changing form. Thus:

Кӏанта **молу шура** стол тӏехь йу.
*The milk **drunk** by the boy is on the table.*

The present participle is formed simply through the Present tense form of the verb. It has only one other form in the Oblique cases:

	Singular	**Plural**
Abs.	молу шура	молу шураш
Gen.	молучу шуран	молучу шурийн
Dat.	молучу шурана	молучу шурашна
Erg.	молучу шуро	молучу шураша
Inst.	молучу шураца	молучу шурашца
Sub.	молучу шурах	молучу шурех

Comp.	молучу шурал	молучу шурел
Loc.	молучу шурага	молучу шурашка

The past participle is formed with the Present Perfect tense. Note the different ways we can translate the participle in English:

Шура **мелла** кӀант парке воьдуш ву.
The boy, having drunk milk, is going to the park.
Or:
The boy, who drank milk, is going to the park.

КӀанта **мелла шура** стол тӀехь йу.
The milk drunk by the boy is on the table.
Or:
The milk, which was drunk by the boy, is on the table.

Like the present participle, the past participle has only two forms:

	Singular	**Plural**
Abs.	мелла шура	мелла шураш
Gen.	меллачу шуран	меллачу шурийн
Dat.	меллачу шурана	меллачу шурашна
Erg.	меллачу шуро	меллачу шураша
Inst.	меллачу шураца	меллачу шурашца
Sub.	меллачу шурах	меллачу шурех
Comp.	меллачу шурал	меллачу шурел
Loc.	меллачу шурига	меллачу шурашка

Finally, the future participle is formed with the present participle followed by **д.олу**:

Шура **молу волу** кӀант парке воьдуш ву.
The boy who will be drinking the milk is going to the park.

КӀанта **молу йолу** шура стол тӀехь ду.
The milk that will be drunk by the boy is on the table.

Again, the participle **д.олу** has only two forms. Note that we've already met д.олчу as the Locative form of д.олу in "*where*" clauses!

	Singular	**Plural**
Abs.	Молу йолу шура	Молу йолу шураш
Gen.	Молу йолчу шуран	Молу йолчу шурийн
Dat.	Молу йолчу шурана	Молу йолчу шурашна
Erg.	Молу йолчу шуро	Молу йолчу шураша
Inst.	Молу йолчу шураца	Молу йолчу шурашца
Sub.	Молу йолчу шурах	Молу йолчу шурех
Comp.	Молу долчу шурал	Молу долчу шурел
Loc.	Молу долчу шурага	Молу долчу шурашка

Word Building: Nouns

Like the suffix -p, we can add **-м** to the infinitive of verbs to create nouns. Unlike the -p suffix, which often forms a simple gerund, the **-м** suffix more often creates abstract nouns:

хаа – хаар – хаам
to know – knowing – knowledge (information)

Because -м nouns take (б:б), nouns derived from verbs that agree in noun class will start with б:

д.оха – д.охар – бохам
to break – breaking – destruction

-м nouns belong to the first declension. The following is the declension of **бохам** "*to break*":

	Sing.	**Plural**
Abs.	бохам	бохамаш
Gen.	бохаман	бохамийн
Dat.	бохамна	бохамашна

Erg.	бохамо	бохамаша
Inst.	бохамца	бохамашца
Sub.	бохамах	бохамех
Comp.	бохамал	бохамел
Loc.	бохаме	бохамашка

Упражненеш / EXERCISES

Exercise 1. *Fill in the blanks in the dialogue using the verbs from the box.*

БогӀий	боьлху	бусулба	ца бисина	цхьаберш

Джон: Дуккха а нах килсе_____?

Гид: Нохчийн ши тӀом бахьана долуш, оьрсий дукха
_____ Соьлжа-ГӀалахь, цундела башха дукха
нах а ца хуьлу кхузахь.

Джон: Ткъа нохчий мича _____ламаз дан?

Гид: Хьуна ма-хаара, дукхахболу нохчий _____
бу, суфий. Нохчий шина тайпана суфисташ бу,
_____ зикр деш бу, ткъа вуьш зикр деш бац.

Exercise 2. *Match the following questions with their answers.*

1. Нохчий муьлш бу?
2. Оьрсий килсе богӀий?
3. Нохчий маьждиге богӀий?
4. Зикр зударша дой?
5. Сердце Чечни хӀун йу?
6. Ламаз мичахь до?

a. Нохчий бусулба бу.
b. Нохчий маьждиге богӀу.
c. Оьрсий килсе богӀу.
d. Ламаз маьждигехь до.
e. Зикр зударша ца до.
f. Иза нохчийн маьждиг ду.

Exercise 3. *Translate the following phrases into English.*

1. Дуккха а нах бу кхузахь.

_____

2. Оьрсий дукха бац Соьлжа-Гӏалахь.

_____

3. Маьждиг чохь дешех бина стогар бу.

_____

4. Гидо туристашна Соьлжа-Гӏала гойту.

_____

5. Джонна маьждиг хазахета.

_____

Exercise 4. *Write the verbs in parentheses using Nominative or Ergative cases.*

1. (Со) _____ ламаз до.
2. (Тхо) _____ зикр ца до.
3. (Гид) _____ маьждиг гойтуш йу.
4. (Божарий) _____ тӏараш тухуш бу.
5. (Туристаш) _____ маьждиг хазахета.

Exercise 5. *Translate the sentences from Exercise 4.*

1._____
2._____
3._____
4._____
5._____

Exercise 6. *Use this lesson's grammar section to translate the following sentences:*

1. This mosque, built in 2008, is the largest in Europe.

_____

2. The boy drinking the milk is going to the park.

_____

3. The milk drunk by the boy is on the table.

_____

Exercise 7. *Translate the following Imperatives.*

Don't run! _____

Don't say! _____

Look! _____

Don't look! _____

Go to school! _____

Don't sleep! _____

Learn! _____

Exercise 8. *Using this lesson's examples create your own sentences.*

_____

_____

_____

_____

_____

Корта XII:
Нохчийн Литература Декьаш

Lesson 12:
Excerpts from Chechen Literature

Knowledge Check: The poem and article in this lesson are unedited literary Chechen. Try to get a feel for the syntax of Chechen poetry and formal Chechen.

Lesson Plan:
- Review: Verb conjugations

🎧 23 БАЙТ / POETRY

Хьан цIийнах йара-кх со,

Нохчийчоь, хьан цIийнах йара.

Нахана дIайийца ворхIе а ден цIе а хилла.

Хьан цIарца йаьхна со, Нохчийчоь, хьан цIарца йаьхна.

Хьешана хIоттадан комаьрша шун а сан хилла.

Хьан йуьхь ас ларйина, сайн эхь-бехк, сайн сий санна,

Къа доцучу сан сина теш хIотта Терк а ду дийна.

Хьайбахехь йагийна, да вийна мостагI санна.

Сайн кхерчах йохийна мисхал а сан боцуш бехк.

—Гайтукаева Бана

Керла Дешнаш / NEW WORDS

цIий, цIийш (д:д) blood
ворхI seven
комаьрша generous
шун, шуьннаш (д:д) tray
йуьхь, йуьхьш (д:д) face
эхь-бехк (д) shame, guilt
сий (д) dignity
къа, къинош (д:д) pity
дийна alive
мостагI, мостагIаш (в/й:б) enemy
кхерч, кхерчаш (й:й) nest, *a place where a person feels home*
бехк, бехкаш (б:д) guilt

Керла Хандешнаш / NEW VERBS

д.аха to live (деха, дехи, даьхна)
хIоттад.ан to install, to assign (хIоттад.о, хIоттад.и, хIоттад.ина)
лард.ан to guard, to protect (лард.о; лард.и; лард.ина)
теш хIотта to witness (теш хIутту, теш хIоьтти, теш хIоьттина)
д.ага to burn (*intransitive*) (д.огу, д.еги, д.аьгна)
д.ен to kill (д.оь, д.ий, д.ийна)

24 **СТАТЬЯ / ARTICLE EXCERPT**

"Нохчийн маттахь" цIе йолу поэзин суьйре.

27 апреля 2023

Цхьаьнакхетаре гулбеллера Нохчийн Пачхьалкхан Iилманан а, дешаран а министран заместительш, Зубхаджиев Мохьмад-Iела а, Усманов Ахьмад а, йаздархойн Союзан декъашхой а, иштта кхиболу хьеший а.

Суьйре дIахьош дешархоша лерамечу хьешийн тидаме йиллинера лерина кечйина программа. Цуьнан гурашкахь цара нохчийн меттан дозаллех, хазаллех лаьцна дуьйцуш йолу, махкахь гIарайевла йевзаш йолу байташ а йийцира, иллеш а элира, эшарш а лийкхира. Цхьаьнакхетар нохчийн ламастех дуьзна дара, хьешашна а чIогIа тайра иза. Цара дехар дира дешархошка шайна а, нийсархошна а йукъахь ненан мотт бийцар а, Iамор а чIагIде аьлла. Иштта, мотт дIаьбаьлча къам доцуш лоруш хилар а дийцира.

Хууш ма-хиллара, оханан беттан 25-гIа де — нохчийн меттан деза де лерина ду. Иза билгалдаьккхина вайн Мехк-Дас, Россин Турпалхочо Кадыров Ахьмад-Хьаьжин Рамзана даьккхина долчу 2007-чу шеран № 207 йолчу Указаца. Нохчийн Республикин Конституцин 10-гIа статья тIехь йаздина а ду и. Ткъа вайн махкахь иза хIора шарахь шуьйра даздеш ду.

Керла Дешнаш / New Words

цхьаьнакхетар, цхьаьнакхетарш (д:д) gathering
Ӏилма, Ӏилмаш (д:д) science
министр, министраш (в/й:б) minister
заместитель, заместительш (в/й:б) substitute (*human*)
Союз (й) Soviet
декъахо, декъашхой (в/й:б) participant
иштта and so
тидам (б) attention
программа, програмш (й:й) program
дозалла, дозаллаш (д:д) pride
байт, байташ (й:й) poetry
оханан бутт (б) April
деза *here:* holy
указ, указш (д:д) decree
шуьйра wide, widely
конституци, конституцеш (й:й) constitution
турплахо, турпалхой (в/й:б) hero
статья, статьяш (й:й) article (*newspaper*)
нийсархо, нийсархой (в/й:б) contemporary

Керла Хандешнаш / New Verbs

гулд.ала to collect, to get together **(гулло, гулд.ели, гулд.елла)**
тан to recognize, to accept **(тов, тий, тайна)**
лакха to sing; to play on instrument **(локху, лекхи, лекхна)**
гӀард.ала to become popular **(гӀард.олу, гӀард.ели, гӀардаьлла)**
д.уза to fill **(д.узу, дуьзи, дуьзна)**
билгалд.аккха to highlight **(билгалд.оккху, билгалд.аьккхи, билгалд.аьккхина)**
дехар дан to beseech **(дехар до, дехар ди, дехар дина)**
чӀагӀд.ан to strengthen **(чӀагӀ.до, чӀагӀди, чӀагӀ.дина)**
лара to respect; *here:* to dedicate **(лору, лери, лерина)**

Граматика / GRAMMAR

Verb Conjugation Review

Congratulations on reaching the end of this book! Since Chechen verbs are perhaps the most important component of learning the language, here is a review of key Chechen conjugation patterns and irregular verbs. Let's look at the different types of conjugations we have seen in this textbook, using Johanna Nichols' system for classification.

Class	Infinitive	Present	Recent Past	Present Perfect	Translation
I	лаца	лоцу	леци	лаьцна	*catch*
II	lама	lема	lеми	lемина	*learn*
III	д.аккха	д.оккху	д.аьккхи	д.аьккхина	*disrupt*
IV	латта	лаьтта	лаьтти	лаьттина	*stand*
V	мала	молу	мели	мелла	*drink*
VI	хаа	хуу	хии	хиана	*sit*
VIII	хаа	хаьа	хии	хиана	*know something*
X	хьажа	хьожу	хьаьжи	хьаьжна	*look* (sing.)
XI	кхайкха	кхойкху	кхайкхи	кхайкхина	*call*
XII	ловза	ловзу	левзи	левзина	*play*
XIII	д.овза	д.евзу	д.евзи	д.евзина	*know someone*
XVI	тоха	туху	туьйхи	тоьхна	*hit/strike*
XIX	мотта	моьтту	моьтти	моьттина	*think*
XX	д.еша	д.оьшу	д.ийши	д.ешна	*read*
XXIII	д.етта	д.оьтту	д.итти	д.иттина	*beat*
XXVI	д.ийца	д.уьйцу	д.ийци	д.ийцина	*tell*
XXX	га	го	ги	гина	*see*
XXXI	lен	lа	lий	lийна	*stay*
XXXIII	д.ен	д.оь	д.ий	д.ийна	*kill*

The verbs **дан**, **ган**, and **лаа** have irregular present continuous forms, i.e., they form irregular gerunds:

Class	Infinitive	Present	Present Continuous	Recent Past	Present Perfect	Translation
VIII	лаа	лаьа	лууш	лии	лиина	*want*
XXX	ган	го	гуш	ги	гина	*see*
XXX	д.ан	д.о	д.еш	д.и	д.ина	*do*

We have met the following irregular (irreg.) verbs, whose forms need to be memorized:

Class	Infinitive	Present	Recent Past	Present Perfect	Translation
irreg.	д.ан	д.огІу	д.еи	д.еана	*to come*
irreg.	д.ахка	д.огІу	д.аьхки	д.аьхкина	*to come* (pl.)
irreg.	д.ала	ло	д.ели	д.елла	*to give*
irreg.	д.ала	ле	д.ели	д.елла	*to die*

Упражненеш / EXERCISES

Exercise 1. *Match Chechen words with their English translations.*

1. цІий, цІийш (д:д)   nest
2. ворхІ   face
3. комаьрша   enemy
4. шун, шуьннаш (д:д)   tray
5. йуьхь, йуьхьш (д:д)   seven
6. эхь-бехк (д)   shame, guilt
7. сий (д)   dignity
8. къа, къинош (д:д)   pity
9. дийна   guilt
10. мостагІ, мостагІаш (в/й:б)   generous
11. кхерч, кхерчаш (й:й)   blood
12. бехк, бехкаш (б:д)   alive

Exercise 2. *Translate these phrases into English.*

1. Сан да гӀарваьлла поэт ву.

_____

2. Нохчаша Нохчийн Меттан де билгалдаьккхина.

_____

3. Бераша эшарш лекхира.

_____

4. Тахана оханан беттан хьалхара де ду.

_____

5. Нохчийн Меттан де Президентан указца дазадо.

_____

Exercise 3. *Fill in the blanks using verbs from the box.*

дуьйцуш йолу	йиллинера	тайра	къам доцуш	дуьзна

Суьйре дӀахьош дешархоша лерамечу хьешийн тидаме

_____ лерина кечйина программа.

Цуьнан гурашкахь цара нохчийн меттан дозаллех, хазаллех

лаьцна_____, махкахь гӀарайевла йевзаш

йолу байташ а йийцира, иллеш а элира, эшарш а лийкхира.

Цхьаьнакхетар нохчийн ламастех _____дара,

хьешашна а чӀогӀа_____иза. Цара дехар

дира дешархошка шайна а, нийсархошна а йукъахь ненан

мотт бийцар а, Ӏамор а чӀагӀде аьлла. Иштта, мотт дӀаьбаьлча

_____лоруш хилар а дийцира.

Exercise 4. *Underline all the verbs in the text in Exercise 3.*

Exercise 5. *Complete the table filling in the blanks with Imperative Positive and Negative columns.*

English	Infinitive	Imperative Positive	Imperative Negative
run	Вада / йада / дада / бада	Вадал / йадал / дадал / бадал	Ма вадал! Ма йадал! Ма дадал! Ма бадал!
give	Вала / йала / дала / бала	лол!	
say	Ала		
look	Хьажа		
listen	Ладогӏа		
go	Вагӏа / йагӏа / дагӏа / багӏа		
buy	Эца		
do	Ван / йан / дан / бан	Вел / йел / Дел / бел	
learn	Ӏамаван / Ӏамайан / Ӏамадан / Ӏамабан		
speak	Вийца / йийца / дийца / бийца		
read	Веша / йеша / деша / беша		

Exercise 6. *Compare the following animals using comparative adjectives.*

1. Пхьагал (йу) – Уьнтӏапхьид (йу) – сиха (*rabbit – turtle*)

2. Къиг (йу) – Кхокха (бу) – вон (*crow – pigeon*)

_____

3. Эмкал (йу) – Говр (йу) – лекха (*camel – horse*)

_____

4. Маймал (ду) – Вир (ду) – хьекъалла долу (*monkey – donkey*)

_____

5. Цхьогал (ду) – Хьакха (йу) – цlен (*fox – pig*)

_____

6. Сай (бу) – Гезга (йу) – хаза (*deer – spider*)

_____

Exercise 7. *Answer the following Yes/No questions in complete sentences.*

Example: Хьан да каде вуй? Хlаъ, сан да каде ву.

1. Хьан йиши кlант харцхьара вуй?_____.

2. Вайн нус догlаьржа йуй?_____.

3. Себастьян ойлане вуй?_____.

4. Нохчийн дешархой ирсе буй?_____.

5. Вайн бераш самукъане дуй?_____.

Exercise 8. *Write a paragraph about yourself and include:*

• Today's date and describe how the weather is outside, what is your mood today? What do you wear today?

• Description of yourself (present yourself, what do you do for a living, give your physical description, describe your character, how do people describe your character, what do you own and what are their physical characteristics?)

• Describe your family (present your family members, their professions, their appearance, their characters)

- Describe your home (where do you live and with who, what is the climate in your area, what does your house look like, how are the objects and their location, what is your favorite room)

- Describe what your days/weeks look like using present simple

- Describe your hobbies (what you enjoy doing/eating; what your tastes are)

- What is (are) the most important question(s) you would ask someone to know him/her?

- From the cultural context of the course or your personal knowledge, what is your favorite Chechen tradition?

Note: You should add as many details as possible, using the cases you learned and affirmative and negative sentences.

KEY TO EXERCISES

LESSON 1

Exercise 1.
1. Салам Ӏалейкум!
2. Муха йу хьо?
3. Суьйре дика хуьлда!
4. Ӏуьйре дика хуьлда!
5. Буьйсе дика хуьлда!
6. Дика де!
7. Привет!
8. Хьо нохчи вуй/йуй?

Respond to the following.
1. Далла везийла.
2. Далла йезийла.
3. Далла дезийла.
4. Далла везийла.

Exercise 2.
1. Хӏара сан кӏант **ву**.
2. Хьан цӏе хӏун **йу**?
3. Хӏара сан да **ву**.
4. Хьо муха **йу**?
5. Со Американец **ву**.
6. Хьо Американка **йу**.
7. Сан гӏуллакхаш дика **ду**.
8. Хьо мила **ву**?

Exercise 3.
Джон: Хьава! Суьйре дика хуьлда хьан! Муха йу хьо?
Хьава: **Далла везийла.** Хьан гӏуллакхаш муха ду?
Джон: Сан гӏуллакхаш дика ду, амма кӏадвелла.
Хьава: **Хӏара сан да ву.** Цуьнан цӏе Ӏарби йу.

Exercise 4.
1. Иза лор йу.
2. Сан ваша студент ву.
3. Сан доттагӏ дика лор йу.
4. Иза Америкера йу.
5. Лор Америкера ву.
6. Хьо мичара ву?
7. Кӏант кӏадвелла.
8. Иза кӏадйелла.

Exercise 5.
1. Тхо нохчий ду.
2. Вай нохчий ду.
3. Хьо американец ву.
4. Шу американцеш ду.
5. Хьо лор ву, амма тхо студенташ ду.
6. Шу кӏадделла.
7. Тхо кӏадделла.
8. Тхо нохчий ду, ткъа шу америнцеш ду.

Exercise 6.

1. Хьо нохчи вуй?
2. Иза лор йуй?
3. Вай студенташ дуй?
4. Американцш муха бу?
5. Хьо Америкера вуй?
6. Тхо хьехархой дуй?
7. И нохчи вуй?
8. Уьш американцш буй?

Exercise 7.

Good afternoon! My name is Aslan. I am a student. I am from America, but Chechen. My father is a doctor. My mother is a teacher. They are Chechens. My siblings are students. We are students. Are you Chechen? Are your siblings students? Is your father a doctor? What is his name? Where are you from?

LESSON 2

Exercise 1.

Сан цIе Джон йу. Со **нохчийн мотт** Iамош ву. Со **студент** ву. Хьава студентка **йу**. Малика цуьнан **нана** йу. Iарби Хьаван **да** ву.

Exercise 2.

1. I am a teacher.
2. You are a student.
3. Hava is a girl.
4. John is a boy.
5. Arbi is the father.
6. Malika is the mother.
7. He is a doctor.
8. We are tourists.

Exercise 3.

How are John's parents doing? They are doing good.
How many siblings does John have? John has one sister and one brother.

Exercise 4.

1. Джон турист **ву**.
2. Хьава студентка **йу**.
3. Малика лор **йу**.
4. Шалрани профессор **ву**.
5. Тхо хьехархой **ду**.
6. Йижарий кхузахь **бу**.
7. Йиша-ваша университетехь **ду**.
8. Уьш йаздархой **бу**.

Exercise 5.

1. ХIара сан йиша йу.
2. ХIара сан ваша вац.
3. ХIара сан нана йац.
4. ХIара сан да ву.
5. Со университетехь вац.
6. Хьо ишколехь йу.
7. Тхо аэропортехь ду.
8. Вай библиотекехь ду.

Exercise 6.
My name is Skyler. I live in Washingtonn state. I am not Chechen, but I speak Chechen. I am an English language teacher. I teach at a school. My students are good. Our school is in a city. My sister lives in Chechnya.

LESSON 3

Exercise 1.
1. **ХІора дийнахь** со университете йоьду.
2. Ас оьрсийн мотт **Іуьйранна** Іамабо.
3. Ахь **массо а хенахь** нохчийн мотт буьйцу.
4. Хьан доьзало **наггахь** ингалсан мотт буьйцу.
5. Ахь оьрсийн маттахь **сих-сиха** ца йаздо?
6. Джонна **даимана** нохчийн мотт буьйцу.

Exercise 2.

1. Ца воьду	5. Ца молу
2. Ца олу	6. Ца хаьа
3. Ца туху	7. Ца го
4. Ца оьцу	8. Ца доьшу

Exercise 3.

1. **Ас** нохчийн мотт буьйцу.	5. **Цо** книгаш йоьшу.
2. **Ахь** нохчийн мотт ца буьйцу.	6. **Вай** иза ца молу.
3. **Ох** оьрсийн маттахь йаздо.	7. **Цара** иза ца доьшу.
4. **Аш** оьрсийн маттахь ца йаздо.	8. **Вай** книгаш ца йазйо.

Exercise 4.
1. Со хІора дийнахь университете воьду.
2. Наггахь ас нохчийн мотт буьйцу.
3. Хьавас хІора дийнахь доьшу.
4. ШаІрани университетехь болх беш ву.
5. Ох нохчийн книгаш хІора шарахь ца йоьшу.
6. Джон Нохчийчу воьду хІора шарахь.
7. Маликас хІора шарахь доьшу.
8. Іарбис оьрсийн мотт хІора дийнахь буьйцу.

Exercise 5.
1. Цуьнан цӏе Шалрани йу.
2. Шалрани профессор ву.
3. Цуьнан доттагӏ Джон ву.

Exercise 6.

La (Winter)	Бӏаьсте (Spring)	Аьхке (Summer)	Гуьйре (Autumn)
Кхолламан	Бекарг	Асаран	Товбецан
Чиллин	Оханан	Мангалан	Эсаран
Гӏуран	Хӏутосург	Хаьттан	Лаьхьанан

Exercise 7.
1. It snows in January.
2. It is winter in December.
3. October is beautiful.

Exercise 8.
Джон: Алло, **де дика хуьлда** хьан Шалрани!

Шалрани: Далла везийла, Джон. Муха **ду хьан гӏуллакхаш**?

Джон: **Дика ду.** Хьо тахана мичахь ву?

Шалрани: Со **тахана** университетехь ву, амма кхана со ишколе воьдуш ву.

Джон: Со хьо волчу маца ван мегар ду?

Шалрани: Вторникехь, **шолгӏачу апрелехь** ван йиш йуй хьан?

Джон: Йиш ю. Со вторникехь хьо волчу университете воӏӏуш ву.

Шалрани: Дика ду, **вайшиъ библиотекехь** гура ву.

Джон: Дела **реза хуьлда**. Ӏодика йойла!

Шалрани: Гура **ду вай**!

LESSON 4

Exercise 1.
1. I have a lecture tomorrow.
2. I will go to a library tomorrow.
3. John will be at a library on Monday.
4. Sharani will give a lecture on Thursday.
5. University will open in January.
6. There will be a computer in my classroom.

Exercise 2.

1. 2:00	5. 12:35
2. 10:00	6. 3:00
3. 1:00	7. 4:06
4. 1:45	8. 3:07

Exercise 3.

1. Пхиъ даьлла
2. Йалх даьлла
3. ВорхI-ах даьлла
4. Пхийтта минот иссалгIачух йаьлла
5. Исс-ах даьлла
6. Итт минот цхьайтталгIачух йаьлла
7. Пхи минот шийтталгIачух йаьлла
8. Пхи минот йаьлча сахьт долу

Exercise 4.

1. Библиотекарь йалх даьлча схьалагIотту.
2. Цо йааxIума ворхI даьлча йуу.
3. Иза автобус тIехь бархI даьлча балха йоьду.
4. Библиотека исс-ах даьлча схьайеллало.
5. Библиотекарь суьйранна пхиъ даьлча цIа йоьду.

Exercise 5.

1. I will come.
2. I (*female*) will come.
3. They will come.
4. You will come.
5. He will study/read.
6. We will write.
7. You will speak the Chehen language.

Exercise 6.

1. Со **кхоалгIа** бер ду сан доьзаллехь.
2. Малика Iарбин **хьалхара** зуд йу.
3. Хьава **шолгIа** бер ду.
4. Джон **пхиалгIа** турист ву.

LESSON 5

Exercise 1.

Де дика хуьлда шун дешархой! Сан цIе Лайла йу, со керла дешархо йу. Со цIера Америкера йу. Сан ткъе йалх шо ду. Ас нохчийн мотт, оьрсийн мотт а, ингалс мотт а буьйцу. Суна меттанаш хазахета. Ас дика университет чекхйаьккхира Америкехь, тӀаккха со библиотеке болх бан йахара. Йуха ас жимма хьехархойн болх бира. Цул тӀаьлхьа, суна керла дешар карийра, и дешар нохчийн маттахь дара, иштта йолавелира со нохчийн мотт Ӏамабан. Йуха со Нохчийчу йеара сайн дикка нохчийн мотт Ӏамабан.

Exercise 2.

1. Ас хи мели.
2. Ахь гӀо ди.
3. Цара чӀепалгаш дии.
4. Вай баркал эли.
5. Цо книга йийши.
6. Цунна компьютер ги.
7. Лизина хан хии.
8. Бешто библиотеке вахи.

Exercise 3.

1. Маликина аудиотори гира.
2. Студенташа довха чай мелира.
3. Вежарий цӀено чу бахара.
4. Ох шура йийцира.
5. Уьш цӀахь бара.
6. Хьуна иза университетехь гира
7. Хьехархо студенташка вистахилира.
8. Аш кехат йаздира.

Exercise 4.

1. **Дешархой** ишколе бахара.
2. Хьо нохчийн **маттахь** доьшуш ву.
3. Ваха шен **деца** гӀалайукъе (town center) веара.
4. Цара **вежаршца** пикник йо аьхка хӀора шарахь

Exercise 5.

1. Students went to school.
2. You are reading in Chechen language.
3. Vaxa went to town center with his dad.
4. They have picnic with brothers every year in summer.

Exercise 6.

1. Малахьа-малал
2. Хьажахьа-хьажал
3. Дийцахьа-дийцал
4. Ма дийцахьа- ма дийцал
5. Алахьа- алал
6. ДӀахӀоттахьа-дӀахӀоттал
7. Охьахаахьа-охьахаал
8. Тиллахьа-тиллал

Exercise 7.

1. Хьо хьаьнца Іаш ву? Со сайн **ненца** Іаш ву.
   Who do you live with? I live with my mother.
2. Хьо университете хьаьнца воьду? Со университете
   накъостаца воьду.
   Who are you going to the university with? I am going to the
   university with my companion.
3. Хьо балха стенца воьду? Со балха **автобусца** воьду.
   How do you go to work? I go to work by bus.
4. Хьо кафе хьаьнца воьду? Со кафе **доттагІчуьнца** воьду.
   Who are you going to the cafe with? I go to the cafe with my friend.
5. Ахь чай стенца молу? Ас чай **тортаца** молу.
   With what do you drink tea? (*lit.* with what) I drink my tea with cake.

Exercise 8.

1. Ас чай шекарца молу.
2. Тхо балха машенца доьлху.
3. Цунна шекарца чай деза.
4. Со сайн ненца базара воьду.
5. Цо нохчийн мотт книгаца Іамабо.

Lesson 6

Exercise 1.

English	Absolutive	Substantive	Comparative	Declension
language	мотт	маттах	маттал	First Declension Ablaut
father	да	дех	дел	Second Declension Ablaut
brothers	вежарий	вежарех	вежарел	Third Declension
book	книга	книгах	книгел	First Declension
sister	йиша	йишах	йишал	Third Declension
teacher	хьехархой	хьехархойх	хьехархойл	Fourth Declension

Exercise 2.

1. Джон кІантал диках ву.
2. ХІара помидорш йезах йу картогел.

3. Хьава сол кӀадйелла йу.
4. Сан хьехархо массарел а хьекъал долуш йу.
5. Сан квартира хьан цӀенол йоккха йу.

Exercise 3.
1. Хьавана чорп дикахета – f
2. Ӏарбина квартира дикахете – b
3. Суна помидорш дикахета – е
4. Вайна копаст дикахета – а
5. Маликина жижиг мерзахета – с
6. Тхуна ловзар хазахета – d

Exercise 4.
1. Соьгахь копаст йу.
2. Соьгахь ахча ду.
3. Цуьнгахь книжка йац.
4. Туьканахь жижиг дац.
5. Базарахь помидорш йу.
6. Беркатехь картолш йу.
7. Тхоьгахь шура йу.
8. Цаьргахь чӀепалгаш дац.

Exercise 5.
1. Суна **цӀенош** дикахета, амма **петарш** дика ца хета.
2. Суна **копаст** мерзахета, амма **картолш** мерза ца хета.
3. Суна **Нохчийчоь** хазахета, амма **Африка** хаза ца хета.
4. Суна **Малика** дикахета.
5. Суна **нохчийн мотт** хазахахета.

Exercise 6.
1. 40 4. 38
2. 50 5. 80
3. 30

Exercise 7.
1. Throw away
2. Throw toward (*speaker*)
3. Throw down
4. Throw beneath
5. Throw upward
6. Throw onto

Exercise 8.
Али:　Жижигах хӀун доьху?
Хаважи: Жижигах **ши бӀе** сом доьху.
Али:　ХьаьжкӀех хӀун доьху?
Хаважи: ХьаьжкӀех **бӀе** сом доьху.

Али: **Наьрсех** хӀун доьху?
Хаважи: **Наьрсех шовзткъе** сом доьху.
Али: **Iежех** хӀун доьху?
Хаважи: **Iежех кхузткъе сом** доьху.

LESSON 7

Exercise 1.
1. цӀен – b
2. Iаьржа – c
3. кӀайн – a

Exercise 2.
1. Цициган **йоккха** муцӀар йу.
2. Оьпин **доца** лергаш ду.
3. Дехкан **деха** цӀога ду.
4. Сан жӀала **дерстан** ду.

5. Вон стаг **ваьсса** стаг ву.
6. Шура **йораха** йу.
7. Бер **дерзина** ду.
8. Жима йоӀ **йерзина** йу.

Exercise 3.
1. хаза – хазаниг – хазанаш
2. дика – диканиг – диканаш
3. оьзда – оьзданиг – оьзданаш
4. эсала – эсалниг – эсалнаш

5. деха – деханиг – деханаш
6. доца – доцаниг – доцанаш
7. мерза – мерзаниг – мерзанаш

Exercise 4.
1. Суна цунах **лаьцна** хӀумма а ца хаьа.
2. Хьан можа коч йуй? **ЦӀениг** йац хьан?
3. **Тхойшиъ** йуьртахь ву.
4. Сан когаш **баккхий** бу.

Exercise 5.
1. Every month elderly get out.
2. I have big eyes.
3. You have small teeth.

4. Is our cat thin?
5. Is your nose small?

Exercise 6.
1. Тахана малх хьаьжна.
2. Тахана хӀутосурган цхьайтталгӀа де ду.

3. Тахана йовха йу.
4. Селхана догІа деара.
5. Селхана шийла де дара.
6. Кхана тахана санна хенанхІоттам хир йу.

Exercise 7.

Грозный — Соьлжа-ГІала

Аргун — Орга-ГІала / Устрада ГІала

Гудермес — Гуьмсе

Шали — Шела

Урус-Мартан — Хьалха-Марта / МартантІе

Курчалой — Курчалой-гІала / Куьшалойл

Ачхой-Мартан — Іашхой-Марта / ТІаьхьа-Марта / ТІехьа-Марта

Наур — Невр / Новр-гІала

Lesson 8

Exercise 1.
1. тІекхосса – *to throw on*
2. дІаэца – *to take away/buy*
3. кІелад.аха – *to go beneath*
4. хьалад.аккха – *to take out*

Exercise 2.
1. The food is in the kitchen.
2. Malika is under the tree.
3. Arbi is on the chair.
4. John is next to me.
5. Batteries are under the window.
6. The window is next to the bed.
7. The picture is above the bed.
8. The apartment is on the second floor.

Exercise 3.
1. Хьажа – b
2. Дада – a
3. Дала – d
4. Саца – c

Exercise 4.

Джон: **Дела реза хуьлда** сан гІуллакхе хьажарна.

Агент: ХІумма дац, Дела реза массарна а хуьлда. Вайшиъ хІинца хьалхара квартире хьожур ву. ХІара квартира Мамсурова урамехь йу, **гӀалан йуккъехь** уггаре хазачу меттехь. Вай гӀишлон арахь лаьтташ ду.

Джон: И хаза здани йу! Маса **квартира** йу оцу гӀишлон?

Агент: Ткъе квартира бен йац. Зданин тӀехьа ткъе бархӀалгӀа маршрутка а соцу. Кхузара маршруткан **соцунгӀа** йолчу подъезд чухула воьду.

Exercise 5. *Answers will vary*

Exercise 6.
1. Сан цициг ду.
2. Сан кхо жӀала ду.
3. Тхан биъ етт бу.
4. Церан бархӀ газа йу.

5. Хьан ши ваша ву.
6. Сан пхи йиша йу.
7. Цуьнан йиъ котам йу.
8. Цуьнан исс шо ду.

Exercise 7.
1. Со университете **хӀора дийнахь** йоьду.
2. Со базар **хӀора кӀиранахь** йоьду.
3. Тхо кино хьожу **хӀора баттахь**.
4. Аса **хӀора шарахь** сайн цӀеран болх хуьйцу.
5. Аса сайн доттагӀчунна **наггахь** гӀо до.

Lesson 9

Exercise 1.

Шича: Вало Джон, уьш дӀогахь стол **йистехь** Ӏаш бу.

Джон: Де дика хуьлда шун, сан цӀе Джон йу, со Мохьмадан **доттагӀ** ву.

Деда: **Далла везийла** Джон, сан цӀе Абу-Солт йу. Мохьмад сан кӀента кӀант ву. ХӀорш Мохьмадан ненана а, ненда а бу: Юнус а, цуьнан хӀусамнана Кемса.

Джон: Шу девзина **хазахета**.

Exercise 2. *Answers will vary*

Exercise 3.
1. Даймохк мичахь бу?
2. Хьо мичахь ву?
3. Депортаци хӀун йу?
4. Зама хӀун йу?

Нохчичохь бу.
Со арахь ву.
Депортаци нохчий цӀерабахар йу
Хан йу.

Exercise 4.
1. Where is your homeland? In Chechnya.
2. Where are you? I am outside.
3. What is deportation? Deportation is taking Chechens from their homes.
4. What is *зама*? It is time.

Exercise 5.
1. Зудйалориг Марьямига вистхуьлу.
2. Дешарца Iемира суна нохчийн а оьрсийн а меттанаш.
3. Цунна шен цIено хазахета.
4. Цо малийтира соьга кофе.
5. Цара малийтира соьга чай.

Exercise 6.
2:00 pm : Ши сахьт даьлла / Шиъ даьлла
5:30 pm : Пхиъ-ах даьлла
9:45 am : Пхийтта минот йаьлча итт долу
7:40 am : Ткъе минот йаьлча бархI долу
8:55 pm : Пхи минот йаьлча исс долу
1:00 pm : Сахьт даьлла / Цхьа сахьт даьлла
6:15 am : Пхийтта минот ворхIалгIачух йаьлла
7:10 pm : Итт минот бархIалгIачух йаьлла
10:25 am : Ткъе пхи минот цхьайтталгIачух йаьлла

Exercise 7. Affirmative / Negative
1. Лоьро Хедига ахч ло. / Лоьро Хедига ахч ца ло.
2. Сан доттагIчо соьга хеттарш до. / Сан доттагIчо соьга хеттарш ца до.
3. Дешархой университетехь гулло. / Дешархой университетехь ца гулло.
4. Тхан балхахь дуккха а белхалой бу. / Тхан балхахь дуккха а белхалой бац.
5. Къеначуьнга хаза дош ала деза. / Къеначуьнга хаза дош ала ца деза.
6. Со Москвахь Iаш йу, ткъа хьо? / Со Москвахь Iаш йац, ткъа хьо?

LESSON 10

Exercise 1.

Профессор: Итум-Кхаьллера наха хlун **болх бо**?

Йуьртда: Божарша бажи lу болх бо, цара устагlи лаьмнашкахь хьала а вахьа а лехку. Накхармазуй лелочара моз **дохку** туристашна.

Профессор: Зударша хlун до?

Йуьртда: Зударша котами а лелайо, цери хlоаш **гулдо**, бежан а lалашдо.

Джон: Бераша хlун до, муха **ловзу** уьш?

Йуьртда: Бераша lамчури чlари лецу, дитташ тlе **схьалабовлу**, гаьнгали тlехь техка а техка. Цу тlе аьхка бераш хи чохь **луьйчу**.

Exercise 2.
1. Лалла — to drive, to herd (*singular, singular aspect*)
2. Гайта — to show
3. Лахка — to drive, to herd (*plural, singular*)
4. Къанд.ала — to grow old
5. Д.аладан — to bring
6. Алуш — *dialectal:* олуш
7. Лехка — to drive, to herd (*plural, iterative*)
8. Къежа — to smile

Exercise 3.
1. Children swim in summer.
2. Women take care of cows.
3. Men take sheep up (hill) and down.
4. Tourists buy honey.
5. Guide shows Grozny.

Exercise 4.
1. Джон лаьмнашка воьдуш ву.
2. Вахас йуьртахь волавелла лелара.
3. Зударша йуьртахь котамаш лелайо.
4. Бераша йуьртахь ловзу.
5. Божарша йуьртахь болх бо.

Exercises 5–8. *Answers will vary.*

Lesson 11

Exercise 1.

Джон:　Дуккха а нах килсе **богІий**?

Гид:　Нохчийн ши тІом бахьана долуш, оьрсий дукха **ца бисина**. Соьлжа-ГІалахь, цундела башха дукха нах а ца хуьлу кхузахь.

Джон:　Ткъа нохчий мича **боьлху** ламаз дан?

Гид:　Хьуна ма-хаара, дукхахболу нохчий **бусулба** бу, суфий. Нохчий шина тайпана суфисташ бу, **цхьаберш** зикр деш бу, ткъа вуьш зикр деш бац.

Exercise 2.

1. Нохчий муьлш бу?
2. Оьрсий килсе богІий?
3. Нохчий маьждиге богІий?
4. Зикр зударша дой?
5. Сердце Чечни хІун йу?
6. Ламаз мичахь до?

a. Нохчий бусулба бу.
c. Оьрсий килсе богІу.
b. Нохчий маьждиге богІу.
e. Зикр зударша ца до.
f. Иза нохчийн маьждиг ду.
d. Ламаз маьждигехь до.

Exercise 3.

1. There are many people here.
2. There are not many Russians in Grozny.
3. There is golden lamp in mosque.
4. The guide shows Grozny to tourists.
5. John likes the mosque.

Exercise 4.

1. **Ас** ламаз до.
2. **Ох** зикр ца до.
3. **Гид** маьждиг гойтуш йу.

4. **Божарий** тІараш тухуш бу.
5. **Туристашна** маьждиг хазахета.

Exercise 5.

1. I pray.
2. We do zikr.
3. The guide is showing the mosque.

4. The men are applauding.
5. The tourists like the mosque.

Exercise 6.

1. 2008-чу шарахь доьттина маьждиг Европехь уггаре доккха ду.

2. Шура молу клант парке воьдуш ву.
3. Кланта мелла шура стол тlехь йу.

Exercise 7.

Don't run!	Ма вада!
Don't say!	Ма ала!
Look!	Хьажа!
Don't look!	Ма хьажа!
Go to school!	Ишколе гlo!
Don't sleep!	Ма вижа!
Learn!	Деша!

LESSON 12

Exercise 1.
1. цlий, цlийш (д:д) *blood*
2. ворхl *seven*
3. комаьрша *generous*
4. шун, шуьннаш (д:д) *tray*
5. йуьхь, йуьхьш (д:д) *face*
6. эхь-бехк (д) *shame/guilt*
7. сий (д) *dignity*
8. къа, къинош (д:д) *sin/pity*
9. дийна *alive*
10. мостагl, мостаглаш (в/й:б) *enemy*
11. кхерч, кхерчаш (й:й) *nest/a place where a person feels home*
12. бехк, бехкаш (б:д) *guilt*

Exercise 2.
1. My father is a famous poet.
2. The Chechens highlighted the Chechen Language Day.
3. Children sang songs.
4. Today is the first of April.
5. The Chechen Language Day is celebrated by president's order.

Exercise 3.
Суьйре дlахьош дешархоша лерамечу хьешийн тидаме
йиллинера лерина кечйина программа. Цуьнан гурашкахь
цара нохчийн меттан дозаллех, хазаллех лаьцна **дуьйцуш йолу**,

махкахь гӀарайевла йевзаш йолу байташ а йийцира, иллеш а элира, эшарш а лийкхира. Цхьаьнакхетар нохчийн ламастех дуьзна дара, хьешашна а чӀогӀа тайра иза. Цара дехар дира дешархошка шайна а, нийсархошна а йукъахь ненан мотт бийцар а, Ӏамор а чӀагӀде аьлла. Иштта, мотт дӀаьбаьлча къам доцуш лоруш хилар а дийцира.

Exercise 4. *See underlined verbs above.*

Exercise 5.

English	Infinitive	Imperative Positive	Imperative Negative
run	бада / йада / дада / бада	Вадал / йадал / дадал / бадал	Ма вадал! Ма йадал! Ма дадал! Ма бадал!
give	бала / йала / дала / бала	лол!	Ма лол!
say	Ала	Алал!	Ма алал!
look	Хьажа	Хьажал	Ма хьажал
listen	ЛадогӀа	ЛадогӀал!	Ла ма догӀал!
go	багӀа / йагӀа / дагӀа / багӀа	ГӀол!	Ма гӀол!
buy	Эца	Эцал!	Ма эцал!
do	бан / йан / дан / бан	Вел / йел / дел / бел	Ма д.ел!
learn	Ӏамаван / Ӏамайан/ Ӏамадан / Ӏамабан	Ӏамад.ел!	Ма Ӏамад.ел!
speak	бийца / йийца / дийца / бийца	Д.ийцал!	Ма дийцал!
read	бешӀа / йеша / деша / беша	Д.ешал!	Ма дешал!

Exercise 6.

1. Пхьагал (йу) - УьнтІапхьид (йу) - сиха
   Пхьагал уьнтІапхьидал сиха йу.

2. Къиг (йу) - Кхокха (бу) - вон
   Къиг кхокхел вон йу.

3. Эмкал (йу) - Говр (йу) - лекха
   Эмкал говрал лекха йу.

4. Маймал (ду) - Вир (ду) - хьекъал долуш
   Маймал вирал хьекъал долуш ду.

5. Цхьогал (ду) - Хьакха (йу) – цІен
   Цхьогал хьакхел цІен ду.

6. Сай (бу) - Гезга (йу) - хаза
   Сай гезгал хаза йу.

Exercise 7.

1. Хьан йишин кІант харцхьара вуй? ХІаъ, сан йишин кІант
   харцхьара ву.

2. Вайн нус догІаьржа йуй? ХІан-хІа, вайн нус догІаьржа йу.

3. Себастьян ойлане вуй? ХІаъ, Себастьян ойлане ву.

4. Нохчийн дешархой ирсе буй? ХІаъ, вайн дешархой ирсе бу.

5. Вайн бераш самукъане дуй? ХІаъ, вайн бераш самукъане ду.

Chechen–English Glossary

А а

августе (б:д) August
автобус, автобусаш (й:й) bus
агенствон офис, офисаш (й:й) agency office
адам, адамаш (д:д) human, person
аза-м *dialectal:* иза-м
азир *dialectal:* эзар
ала to say (олу; олуш; эли)
алуш *dialectal:* олуш
Американец, Американцеш (д:д) American, Americans
Америкера from America
амма but
апрел (б:д) April
арахула лела to walk around (арахула лела; арахула лели)
арахь outside
арендовать д.ан to rent (арендовать д.о, арендовать д.и, арендовать д.ина)
архитектор, архитекторш (в/й:б) architect
ас ма-аллара as I said
атта easy
аудитори, аудитореш (й:й) auditorium
ахча (дӀа)далан to pay (ахча дӀало; ахча дӀадели; ахча дӀаделла)
ахча даккха to earn money (ахча доккху; ахча даьккхи)

Аь аь

аьрстхо, аьрстхой (в:б) taip (*subgroup of clan*)
аьхке, аьхкенаш (й:й) summer

аьшпаш/пуьтш (б) (*n.; only pl.*) lies

Б б

бал, баьлаш (б:д) cactus
бажи Ӏу, Ӏуй (в/й: б) *dialectal:* (беж) Ӏу (cow) shepherd
байт, байташ (й:й) poetry
баккъала real
бакъду truly
бакълен to speak truth (бакълоь, бакълий, бакълийна)
бакъо, бакъонаш (й:й) rule, law; policy; rights
барам, барамаш (б:д) size
баркалла thank you
барт (б) agreement; friendship
барт бан to agree (барт бо, барт би, барт бина)
батарейка, батарейкаш (й:й) European-style heating installations
баха to tell; to speak (боху; бехи; баьхна)
бахьна, бахьнаш (д:д) reason
башха not very, not too
баьццара green
бежанан жижиг (д) beef
бен ца only
бералла (й) childhood
бехк ма била excuse me; unfortunately
бехк, бехкаш (б:д) guilt
библиотека, библиотекаш (й:й) library
билгалд.аккха to highlight (билгалд.оккху, билгалд.аьккхи, билгалд.аьккхина)

божал, божалш (й:й) barn
бой, бойнаш (й:й) curtains
болх б.еш working
болх, белхаш (б:д) work, job
борз (в) term of endearment for men
борз, берзалой (й:й) wolf
бос, беснаш (б:д) color
бохам, бохамаш (б:б) destruction
бусулба дин (д) Islam
бухахь underneath
бухботтар, бухботтарш (д:д)
  construction
баьрг тоха to take a look (баьрг
  туху, баьрг туьйхи, баьрг тоьхна)
баьсте, баьстенаш (й:й) spring
  (season)
блов, блевнаш (й:й) tower (dialectal
  баьвнаш)

В в

Ваалалейкум ассалам *response to*
  "Салам лалейкум"
важ, вуьш other, others (*adj.*)
Вай Дела Oh my god
вайшиъ (в/й) the two of us
  (*inclusive; exclusive is* тхойшиъ)
ваша, вежарий (в:б) brother
вешин йоьl-йоl, вешин йоьl-йоlрий
  (й:б) brother's granddaughter
вешин кlант, вешин кlентий
  (в:б) nephew *(brother's son)*
вешин кlент-кlант, вешин кlент-
  кlентий (в:б) brother's grandson
вовшахкхета to get together, to
  meet (вовшахкхета, вовшахкхийти,
  вовшахкхетта)
вон bad

Г г

гайта to show (гойту, гайти, гайтина)
ган to see, to meet (го; гуш; ги; гина)
гаьнгали, гаьнгалеш (б:д) swing

гергара стаг, нах (в/й:б) relative
гид, гидш (в/й:б) guide
глобус, глобусш (й:й) globe
гобаккха to make a circle (гобоккху,
  гобаьккхи, гобаьккхина)
горгали, горгалеш (б:д) bell
гулд.ала to collect; to get together
  (гулло, гулд.ели, гулд.елла)
гулд.ан to collect (гулд.о, гулд.и,
  гулд.ина)
Гура ду вай! See you!
Гуттар а дика ду-кх! Excellent!
гуьйре, гуьйренаш (й:й) autumn

Гl гl

гlорта to try; to attempt (гlерта,
  гlоьрти, гlоьртина)
гlала, гlаланаш (й:й) city, town
гlант, гlентш (д:д) chair
гlап, гlепаш (й:й) fortress
гlард.ала to become popular
  (гlард.олу, гlард.ели, гlардаьлла)
гlарч strong, tough
гlат, гlатш (й:й) level, floor
гlиллакх, гlиллакхаш (д:д)
  custom, tradition
гlишло, гlишлош (й:й) building;
  tower
гlо (д) help, assistance
гlо дан to help (д.о; д.еш; д.и)
гlуллакх, гlуллакхаш (д:д) affair,
  affairs (*business*)
гlуткха, гlуткхаш (д:д) drawer

Д д

д.аа to eat (д.уу; д.ууш; д.ии)
д.ага to burn (*intrans.*) (д.огу, д.еги,
  д.аьгна)
д.айн light
д.аккхий big (*pl.*)
д.ала to finish; to cost (д.олу; д.ели;
  д.елла)

д.аладан to bring (д.алад.о, д.алий, далийна)

д.ан to do (д.о; д.и; д.ина)

д.ан to come (д.оггу; д.еа; д.еана)

д.атта to bake (д.отту; д.етти; д.еттина)

д.аха to go (д.оьду; д.ахи; д.ахина), (pl.) (д.оьлху; д.ахи; д.ахана); to live (деха, дехи, даьхна)

д.ахало to be able to go (д.ахало; д.ахад.аьлли; д.ахад.елла)

д.ахка to come (pl.) (д.оггу; д.аьхки; д.аьхкина)

д.аьсса empty

д.еза expensive; heavy

д.еза to need; to love (д.еза; д.ийзи; д.езна)

д.екъана gaunt

д.ела to laugh, to smile (д.оьлу; д.ийли)

д.ен to kill (д.оь, д.ий, д.ийна)

д.ерстан fat

д.еха long

д.еша to read (д.оьшу; д.иши; д.ишина)

д.ийца to speak (д.уьйцу; д.ийци; д.ийцина)

д.ина д.у be born

д.иса to remain (д.уьсу, д.иси, д.исина)

д.истахила to have a word, to converse (д.истахуьлу, д.истахили, д.истахилла)

д.ихка to sell (iterative aspect) (д.уьхку, д.ихки, д.ихкина)

д.овза to meet; to recognize (д.евзу, д.евзи, д.евзина)

д.овзийта to introduce (д.овзуьйту, д.овзийти, д.овзийтина)

д.овха warm, hot

д.оккха big

д.олад.ала to begin (sing., intrans.) (д.олад.ало, д.олад.ели, д.олад.елла)

д.олад.ан to begin (sing., trans.) (д.олад.о, д.олад.и, д.олад.ина)

д.олад.елла лела to go for a walk (д.елла лела, д.олад.елла лийли, д.олад.елла лелла)

д.оллу planning to

д.орах cheap

д.отта to build (д.утту, д.оьтти, д.оьттина)

д.оха to break (intrans.) (д.уху, д.уьйхи, д.оьхна)

д.охад.ан to break (trans.) (д.охад.о, д.охад.и, д.охад.ина

д.охка to sell (sing. aspect) (д.ухку, д.оьхки, д.оьхкина)

д.оца short

д.уза to fill (д.узу, дуьзи, дуьзна)

д.уьйлад.ала to begin (pl., intrans.) (д.уьйлад.ала, д.уьйлад.ели, д.уйьлад.елла)

да, дай (в:б) father

даар, даарш (д) food

дагад.ан to remember (дагад.оггу, дагад.еи, дагад.еана)

дагард.ан to count (дагард.о; дагард.и; дагард.ина)

даиманна always

даймохк, даймехкаш fatherland

дакъа, дакъош (д:д) part; piece

дам (д) flour

дан дезарг, дан дезарш (д:д) chores

да-нана (д) parents

дахар, дахарш (д:д) life

дахьийта to send (дохьуьйту, дахьийти, дахьийтна)

Де дика хуьлда! Hello!

де, денош (д:д) day, days

деваша, девежарий (в:б) uncle (from father's side)

деда, дедай (в:б) grandfather (father's father)

дейиша, дейижарий (й:б) aunt

(*from father's side*)

декабрь (б:д) December

декъа dry

декъала blessed

декъахо, декъашхой (в/й:б) participant

денана, денаной (й:б) grandmother (*father's mother*)

дера of course, definitely

дерзина naked

дехар дан to beseech (**дехар до, дехар ди, дехар дина**)

дехка rotten

дехо, дехой (в/й:б) paternal relative

дечиг (д) wood

дечиг даккха to chop wood (**дечиг доккху, дечиг даьккхи, дечиг даьккхина**)

дешаран книга, книгаш (й:й) textbook

дешархо, дешархой (в/ й:б) student, pupil, learner

диалект, диалектш (й:й) dialect

диван, диванш (й:й) sofa

дийна alive

дика good

Диканца дуккха д.ехийла! May you live long and well!

дин, динш (д:д) religion

дитт, дитташ (д:д) tree

дог, дегнаш (д:д) heart

догІа, догІанаш (д:д) rain

догІаьржа (*adj.*) mean

доза, дозанаш (д:д) territory, land

дозалла, дозаллаш (д:д) pride

дукхахд.олу majority

дукхахьолахь mainly

дуткъа thin

дуьхьала against

дІавуьжу чоь, чоьнаш (й:й) bedroom

дІад.аита to send (with someone) (**дІадоуьту, дІадаити, дІадаитна**)

дІад.алан to give away (**дІало; дІад. ели; дІад.елла**)

дІад.аха to go up (**дІад.оьду; дІад. ахи: дІад.ахина**)

дІайазд.ан to write down (**дІайазд.о; дІайазд.и; дІайазд.ина**)

дІахІотта to stand up (**дІахІутту; дІахІоьтти; дІахІоьттина**)

дІогахь over there

Е е

еара Thursday

ерригге all

етт, бежнаш (б:д) cow

Ж ж

жижиг, жижигаш (д:д) meat

жима (*sing.*) small (**кегий** *pl.* small)

жиманиг the small one

жимах д.олу the youngest

жоп д.ала to answer (**жоп ло, жоп д.ели, жоп д.елла**)

жоп, жоьпаш (д:д) answer

З з

забар йан to joke (**забар йо; забар йи; забар йина**)

закладка, закладкаш (й:й) bookmark

зал, залш (й:й) living room

зама, заманаш (й:й) period of time

заместитель, заместительш (в/й:б) substitute (*human*)

здани, зданеш (й:й) building

зезаг, зезагаш (д:д) flower

зикр, зикарш (д:д) zikr

зикр ала to chant the zikr (**зикр олу; зикр эли; зикр аьлла**)

зикр дан to practice the zikr (**зикр до; зикр ди; зикр дина**)

зуда, зударий (й:б) woman

зудайалор, зудайалорш (д:д) wedding

И и

ингалсан мотт (б) English language
инзаре very
интернет, интернетш (й:й) internet
ирча ugly
исбаьхьа very beautiful, amazing
истори, истореш (й:й) history
ишкап, ишкапш (й:й) closet,
   cabinet, bookshelf
иштта and so
июль (б:д) July
июнь (б:д) June

Й й

йааxlума йала to feed (**йааxlума ло;**
   йааxlума йели; йааxlума йелла)
йааxlума йан to cook (**йааxlума йо;**
   йааxlума йи; йааxlума йина)
йеттшура (й) kefir
йистехь at the edge, next to, beside
йиш (й) opportunity
йиша, йижарий (й:б) sister
йиша-ваша (д:б) siblings
йишин йоьl-йоl, йишин йоьl-йоlрий
   (й:б) sister's granddaughter
йишин кlант, йишин кlентий
   (в:б) nephew *(sister's son)*
йишин кlент-кlант, йишин кlент-
   кlентий (в:б) sister's grandson
йовхо, йовхонаш (й:й) heat
йоьl-йоl, вешин йоьl-йоlрий (й:б)
   granddaughter
йоl, йоlарий (й:б) daughter
йохкархо, йохкархой (в/й:б) seller
йохкар-эцар (д) commerce
йохкар-эцар лелорг, лелорш
   (в/й:б) merchant
йуккъехь in the middle
йурт, йуьрташ (й:й) village
йухад.аха to return, go back *(pl.)*
   (**йухад.оьлху, йухад.ахи, йухад.ахна**)
йухаэха to return, go back *(iterative)*

(**йухаоьху, йухаихи, йухаихна**)
йуьртда, йуьртдай (в:б) village
   head
йуьхь, йуьхьш (д:д) face

К к

Казак, Казакш (в/й:б) Cossack
картол, картолш (й:й) potato
квартира, квартираш (й:й)
   apartment
кегий small *(pl.)*
керла new
керта, керташ (й:й) backyard
кехат, кехатш (д:д) paper
кечд.ан to prepare, decorate (**кечд.о,**
   кечд.и, кечд.ина)
кийла, кийланаш (й:й) kilogram
кийча ready
килс, килснаш (й:й) church
комаьрша generous
компьютер, компьютерш (й:й)
   computer
конституци, конституцеш (й:й)
   constitution
контракт, контарктш (д:д)
   contract
концелярски хlуманаш (й) school
   supplies
копаст, копастш (й:й) cabbage
кор, кораш (д:д) window
котам, котамаш (й:й) chicken
котаман жижиг (д) chicken *(meat)*
коьрта important
кружка, кружкаш (й:й) mug, cup
куз, кузанаш (б:б) carpet
кухни, кухнеш (й:й) kitchen
куьг йаздан to sign (**куьг йаздо;**
   куьг йазди; куьг йаздина)
куьзг, куьзганаш (д:д) mirror
куьзганаш (д) glasses, eyeglasses
куьйгалла (й) power

Кх кх

кхаара Wednesday
кхайкха to invite, to call someone (кхойкху, кхайкхи, кхайкхина)
кхана tomorrow
кхерч, кхерчаш (й:й) nest; a place where a person feels home
кхехка to boil (кхехка; кхихки; кхихкина)
кхидолу other
кхин дӏа а et cetera, and so on
кхолла to create (кхуллу; кхоьлли; кхьоьллина)
кхуза here

Кӏ кӏ

кӏиранде Sunday
кӏадд.елла, кӏадй.елла tired
кӏайн white
кӏайн у, кӏайн аннаш (д:д) whiteboard
кӏалд, кӏалдш (й:й) cottage cheese
кӏант, кӏентий (в:б) son
кӏелахь under, underneath
кӏент-кӏант, йишин кӏент-кӏентий (в;б) grandson

Къ къ

къа, къинош (д:д) pity
къага to shine (къега; къеги; къегна)
къам, къаьмнаш (д:д) nation
къамел дан to talk, to discuss (къамел до; къамел ди; къамел дина)
къанд.ала to grow old (къанло; къанд.ели; къанд.елла)
къежа to smile (къоьжу; къийжи; къийжина)
къена old
къинхетаме kind, charitable
къинхьегаме hardworking
къолам, къоламаш (б:д) pencil
къона young

Л л

лаа to want (лаьа; лии; лиина)
лакха to sing; to play on instrument (локху; лекхи; лекхна)
лалла to drive, to herd (*sing.*) (лоллу; лаьлли; лаьллина)
лам, лаьмнаш (б:д) mountain
лами, ламеш (б:д) stair
ламро, ламрой (в/й:б) mountaineers
лара to respect; to dedicate (лору; лери; лаьрна)
лард.ан to guard, to protect (лард.о; лард.и; лард.ина)
лата to fight (лета; лети; летта)
латта to stand (лаьтта; лаьтти; лаьттина)
латта, латташ (д:д) land
латтсурт, латтсуьрташ (д:д) map
лаха to look for (лоху; лехи; лехна)
лахка to drive, to herd (*pl.*) (лохку; лаьхки; лаьхкина)
лаца to catch (лоцу; леци; лаьцна)
лекха tall
лекци, лекцеш (й:й) lecture
лела to walk (лела; лийли; лелла)
лелад.ан to take care of; to use; to wear (лелад.о; лелад.и; лелад.ина)
лехка to drive, to herd (*pl., iterative*) (лоьхку; лихки; лихкина)
лийца to catch (*iterative*) (луьйцу; лийци; лийцина)
лийча to swim, to bathe (луьйчу; лийчи; лийчина)
литература, литератураш (й:й) literature
ло, лонаш (д:д) snow
ловза to play (ловзу; левзи; левзина)
ловзар, ловзарш (д:д) event
лоха short
лоьмар, лоьмарш (й:й) number

М м

май (б:д) May (*month*)
майра brave
мала to drink (молу; мели; мелла)
малойолуш lazy
малх, малхнаш (б:д) sun
март (б:д) March (*month*)
Марша воглийла! Welcome!
маршо, маршонаш (й:й) freedom
маса? how many?
масала, масалаш (д:д) example
масийтта a few
массо а хенахь always
мах, мехаш (б:д) price
маца when
маьждиг, маьждигаш (д:д) mosque
маьнга, маьнгеш (б:д) bed
мебель, мебельш (й:й) furniture
мегар ду okay (*lit.* it's possible)
мел how
мел, мелаш (б:д) chalk
мерза delicious, tasty
мерзахета to like (taste) (мерзахета; мерзахийти; мерзахийтина)
меттиг, меттигаш (й:й) place
меттигера local
мийла to drink (*iterative*) (муьйлу; мийли; мийлина)
министр, министраш (в/й:б) minister
мичара from where
могӏа, могӏанаш (б:д) row
могшалла, могшаллонаш (й:й) health
можа yellow
моз (д) honey
мостагӏ, мостагӏаш (в/й:б) enemy
мотт, меттанаш (б:д) language
мукъам, мукъамаш (б:д) music
муха how
муьлха which

Н н

наггахь sometimes
наг-наггахь from time to time
накхармоз, накхармозий (б:д) bee
накъост, накъостий (в/й:б) companion
нана, наной (й:б) mother
нел, неларш (й:й) door
ненана, ненананой (й:б) grandmother (*mother's mother*)
ненахо, ненахой (в/й:б) maternal relative
ненваша, ненвежарий (в:б) uncle (*from mother's side*)
ненда, ненадай (в:б) grandfather (*mother's father*)
ненйиша, ненйижарий (й:б) aunt (*from mother's side*)
нийсархо, нийсархой (в/й:б) contemporary
ноутбук, ноутбукш (й:й) laptop
нохчалла (й) traditional Chechen code of conduct
Нохчи (в:й) Chechen (*person*)
Нохчийчоь (й) Chechnya
ноябрь (б:д) November
Нухь пайхамар (в) Noah

О о

обед, обедш (й:й) lunch
октябрь (б:д) October
оршот Monday
остановка, остановкаш (й:й) bus stop
оханан бутт (б) April
охьахаа to sit down (охьахуу; охьахууш; охьахии)

Оь оь

Оьгӏазе gloomy, sad
Оьздангалла, Оьздангаллаш (й:й) code of conduct

Оьрси, Оьрсий (в/й:б) Russian *(person)*
Оьрсийн Импери (й) Russian Empire
Оьрсийн мотт (б) Russian *(language)*

П п

пайдаэца to benefit (пайдаоьцу; пайдаийци; пайдаэцна)
папка, папкаш (б:д) binder
паргlат comfortable, relaxed
парта, парташ (й:й) desk
паспорт, паспорташ (д:д) passport
пачхьалкх, пачхьалкхш (й:й) federation
петар, петарш (й:й) apartment
подъезд, подъездаш (й:й) building entrance
помидор, помидорш (й:й) tomato
портфель, портфельш (б:д) backpack
проблем, проблемш (й:й) problem
программа, програмш (й:й) program
просто simply
профессор, профессорш (в:б) professor

Пl пl

пlераска Friday

Р р

расписани, расписанеш (й:й) schedule
ручка, ручкаш (й:й) pen

С с

сагlа, сагlанаш (д:д) alms
садала to relax; to enjoy oneself (садолу; садоьли; садоьлна)
сакъера to enjoy (сакъоьру; сакъийри; сакъерра)
самукъане funny, fun

сахьт, сахьтш (д:д) hour; clock, watch
саца *(pl.)* to stop (совцу; севци; севцина); *(sing.)* (соцу; сеци; сецина)
сацам бан to decide (сацам бо, сацам би, сацам бина)
семестр, семестрш (й:й) semester
сени/прихожи, прихожеш (й:й) hall
сентябрь (б:д) September
сий (д) dignity
сийна blue
сих-сиха often
совгlат, совгlаташ (д:д) present
советан lедал, lедалш (д:д) Soviet times
соцунгlа, соцунгlаш (й:й) bus stop
союз, союзш (й:й) Soviet
стаг, божарий (в:б) man
статья, статьяш (й:й) article
стёрка, стёркаш (й:й) eraser
стешха cowardly
стиль, стильш (й:й) style
стогар, стогарш (б:д) lamp
стол, стоьлш (й:й) table
студент, студенташ (в:б) student, students
сурт, суьрташ (д:д) picture, photo
сутар greedy
Суьйре дика хуьлда хьан! Good evening!
схьаган to see; to reveal (схьаго; схьаги; схьагина)
схьад,аккха to seize, take over *(sing.)* (схьад.оккху; схьад.аьккхи; схьад.аьккхина)
схьад.аха to seize, take over *(pl.)* (схьад.оху; схьад.ехи; схьад.аьхна)
схьакард.ан to find (схьакард.о; схьакард.и; схьакард.ина)
схьакхача to arrive (схьакхочу; схьакхечи; схьакхаьчна)

схьалад.аккха to raise; to take up
(схьалад.оккху; схьаьлад.аьккхи;
схьаладаьккхина)

схьалад.ала to rise, to go up
(схьалад.олу; схьалад.ели;
схьалад.аьлла)

схьалад.овла to rise (*pl.*) (схьалад.
овлу; схьад.евли; схьалад.евла)

схьалаца to catch; to hold
(схьалоцу; схьалеци; схьалаьцна)

схьаэца to buy up; to take up
(схьаоьцу; схьайци; схьаэцна)

Т т

тайпа different; type of

тайп-тайпана different

тан to recognize; to accept (тов, тий,
тайна)

тахана today

таьхьо later

телефон йетта to call (*iterative*)
(телефон йетта; телефон йитти;
телефон йиттина)

тептар, тептарш (д:д) copybook,
notebook

тера alike

техка to swing (*iterative*) (техка;
тихки; тихкина)

тидам (б) attention

тийна quiet

ткъа and, but

тоба, тобанаш (й:й) group

тод.ан to repair, to fix (тод.о; тод.и;
тод.ина)

тур, турш (й:й) tour

турплахо, турпалхой (в/й:б) hero

туька, туьканаш (й:й) store

тхов, тхевнаш (б:д) roof

Тl тl

тlараш детта to applaud (*iterative*)
(тlараш доьтту; тlараш дитти;

тlараш диттина)

тlараш тоха to applaud (тlараш
туху; тlараш туьйхи; тlараш
тоьхна)

тlаьхьахlитта to follow (*pl.*)
(тlаьхьахlуьтту; тlаьхьахlитти;
тlаьхьахlиттина)

тlаьхьахlотта to follow (*sing.*)
(тlаьхьахlуьтту; тlаьхьахlоьтти;
тlаьхьахlоьттина)

тlед.ига to lead someone, to take
someone (тlед.уьгу; тlед.иги; тlед.
игина)

тlехулахь above, on top

тlехь on

тlехьа behind

тlеэца to accept (тlеоьцу, тlеийци,
тlеэцна)

тlом, тlемаш (б:д) war

тlоьрмиг (б:д) backpack; bag

У у

у, аннаш (д:д) blackboard; board

уггаре the most

указ, указш (д:д) decree

уллехь near, close, next to

**университет, университеташ
(й:й)** university

урам, урамаш (б:д) street

урок, урокаш (й:й) class, lesson

Уь уь

уьстагl, уьстагlий (б:д) sheep

Ф ф

фамили, фамилеш (й:й) last name

февраль (б:д) February

филологи (й) philology

Х х

хаа to know (хаьа; хии; хиина); to
sit (хуу; хии; хиина)

хаза *(v.)* to hear (хеза; хези; хезна)
хаза *(adj.)* beautiful
хала difficult
халхад.ала to dance (халхад.олу; халхад.ели; халхад.аьлла)
хан, хенаш (й:й) time
харжа to choose (хоржу; хаьржи; хаьржина)
хасстом, хасстоьмаш (б:д) vegetable
хатI, хатIш (д:д) characteristics
хаттар дан to ask (хаттар до; хаттар ди; хаттар дина)
хаттар, хаттарш (д:д) question
хелхар, хелхарш (д:д) dance
хенахIоттам; погода (й) weather
хи, хиш (д:д) water
хила to be *(iterative)*; to become (хуьлу; хили; хилла)
хох, хохаш (б:д) onion

Хь хь

хьажа *sing.* to look, to watch (хьожу; хьаьжи; хьаьжна); *(pl.)* (хьовсу, хьевси, хьевсина)
хьалха before, ago; in front
хьалхара first
хьахка to ride; to drive (хьохку; хьаьхки; хьаьхкина)
хьахо to advise, to recommend (хьоьху; хьийхи; хьийхина)
хьежа to watch *(iterative)* (хьоьжу; хьийжи; хьежна)
хьекъале smart
хьеха to teach, to advise (хьоьху; хьийхи; хьехна)
хьехархо, хьехархой (в/й:б) teacher
хьешан чоь, чоьнш (й:й) guest room

ХI хI

хIара this
хIитта to stand; to appear *(iterative)* (хIуьтту; хIитти; хIиттина)
хIотта to stand; to appear (хIутту; хIоьтти; хIоьттина)
хIун what
хIунда why
хIунда аьлча because
хIора every
хIан-хIа no
хIаъ yes
хIоттад.ан to install; to assign (хIоттад.о; хIоттад.и; хIоттад.ина)
хIунда аьлча because

Ц ц

ца not
цигахь there
цкъа а never, not once
цкъа хьалха first
цулла совнах in addition, moreover
цунна тIе in addition
цхьад.ерш some
цхьаъ one
цхьаьнакхетар, цхьаьнакхетарш (д:д) gathering

ЦI цI

цIе, цIераш (й:й) name
цIадерза to return home (цIадоьрзу; цIадирзи; цIадирзина)
цIанйан to clean (цIанйо; цIанйи; цIанйина)
цIе йаккха to call the name (цIе йоккху; цIе йаьккхи; цIе йаьькхина)
цIен red
цIена clean
цIерад.аха to deport, to make leave *(pl.)* (цIерад.оху; цIерад.ехи; цIерад.аьхна)
цIий, цIийш (д:д) blood

Ч ч

чехкха fast, quick

чкъор, чкъораш (д:д) generation; skin

чолхе hard, difficult

чохь inside

чуд.ан to come in (**чуд.огІу; чуд.еи; чуд.еана**)

чуд.аха to go in (**чуд.огІу, чуд.агІи, чуд.агІина**)

чухула through

чуьра from inside

ЧІ чІ

чІагІд.ан to strengthen (**чІагІ.до; чІагІди; чІагІ.дина**)

чІара, чІерий (б:д) fish

чІогІа very

Ш ш

шадерриге everything

шадолу each

шело, шелонаш (й:й) cold

шийла cold

шинара Tuesday

шифоньер, шифоньерш (й:й) wardrobe, closet

шича, шичой (в/й:б) cousin

шо, шераш (д:д) year

шортта a lot

шот Saturday

штат, штаташ (й:й) state

шун, шуьннаш (д:д) tray

шур, шуреш (й:й) milk

шура йаккха to milk (**шура йоккху; шура йаьккхи; шура йаьккхина**)

шуьйра wide

Э э

экономика (й) economy

эха to go (*iterative*) (**оьху; ихи; ихна**)

эхь-бехк (д) shame, guilt

эца to buy; to take (**оьцу; ийци; эцна**)

эша to must; to need (**оьшу; ийши; эшна**)

Ю ю

Юкъара Азе (й) Central Asia

Я я

январь (б:д) January

І і

Іам, Іамнаш (б:д) lake

Іодика йойла! Goodbye!

Іаьржа black

Іен to stay, to remain (**Іа; Іи; Іийна**)

Іа, Іаьннаш (д:д) winter

Іалашд.ан to save; to take care (**Іалашд.о; Іалашд.и; Іалашд.ина**)

Іалашо, Іалашонаш (й:й) goal

Іама to study; to learn (**Іема; Іеми; Іаьмма**)

Іилма, Іилмаш (д:д) science

Іовдал fool

ENGLISH–CHECHEN GLOSSARY

A a

a lot шортта

above тӀехулахь/тӀехула

accept *(v.)* тан (тов, тий, тайна); тӀеэца (тӀеоьцу, тӀеийци, тӀеэцна)

advise *(v.)* хьахо (хьоьху, хьийхи, хьийхина)

affair гӀуллакх, гӀуллакхаш (д:д)

against дуьхьала

agency office агенствон офис, офисаш (й:й)

agree *(v.)* барт бан (барт бо, барт би, барт бина)

agreement барт (б)

alike тера

alive д.ийна

all ерригге

alms сагӀа, сагӀанаш (д:д)

always даиманна; массо а хенахь

amazing исбаьхьа

American американец, американцеш (д:д)

and ткъа

answer *(v.)* жоп д.ала (жоп ло, жоп д.ели, жоп д.елла)

answer *(n.)* жоп, жоьпаш (д:д)

apartment квартира, квартираш (й:й); петар, петарш (й:й)

applaud *(v.)* тӀараш тоха (тӀараш туху, тӀараш туьйхи, тӀараш тоьхна); *iterative* тӀараш детта (тӀараш доьтту; тӀараш дитти; тӀараш диттина)

April апрель (б), оханан бутт (б)

architect архитектор, архитекторш (в/й:б)

arrive *(v.)* схьакхача (схьакхочу, схьакхечи, схьакхаьчна)

article статья, статьяш (й:й)

ask *(v.)* хаттар дан (хаттар до, хаттар ди, хаттар д.ина)

assign *(v.)* хӀоттад.ан (хӀоттад.о, хӀоттад.и, хӀоттад.ина)

attention тидам (б)

auditorium аудитори, аудитореш (й:й)

August августе (б:д)

aunt *(father's side)* дейиша, дейижарий (й:б); *(mother's side)* ненйиша, ненйижарий (й:б)

autumn гуьйре, гуьйренаш (й:й)

B b

backpack портфель, портфельш (б:д)

backyard керта, керташ (й:й)

bad вон

bag тӀоьрмиг (б:д)

bake *(v.)* д.атта (д.отту, д.етти, д.еттина)

barn божал, божалш (й:й)

bathe *(v.)* лийча (луьйчу, лийчи, лийчина)

beautiful хаза

because хӀунда аьлча

become *(v.)* хила (хуьлу, хили, хилла) *also "to be" (iterative)*

become popular *(v.)* гӀард.ала (гӀард.олу, гӀард.ели, гӀардаьлла)

bed маьнга, маьнгеш (б:д)
bedroom дӏавуьжу чоь, чоьнаш (й:й)
bee накхармоз, накхармозий (б:д)
beef бежанан жижиг (д)
before хьалха
begin *(v.) sing., intrans.* д.олад.ала (д.олад.ало, д.олад.ели, д.олад. елла); *pl., intrans.* д.уьйлад.ала (д.уьйлад.ала, д.уьйлад.ели, д.уйьлад.елла); *sing., trans.* д.олад. ан (д.олад.о, д.олад.и, д.олад.ина)
behind тӏехьа
bell горгали, горгалеш (б:д)
benefit *(v.)* пайдаэца (пайдаоьцу, пайдаийци, пайдаэцна)
beseech дехар дан (дехар до, дехар ди, дехар дина)
big *sing.* д.оккха; *pl.* д.аккхий
binder папка, папкаш (б:д)
black ӏаьржа
blackboard у, аннаш (д:д)
blessed декъала
blood цӏий, цӏийш (д:д)
blue сийна
boil *(v.)* кхехка (кхехка; кхихки; кхихкина)
bookmark закладка, закладкаш (й:й)
born *(v.) (as in "to be born")* д.ина д.у
brave майра
break *(v.) intrans.* д.оха (д.уху, д.уьйхи, д.оьхна); *trans.* д.охад.ан (д.охад.о, д.охад.и, д.охад.ина)
bring *(v.)* д.аладан (д.алад.о, д.алий, далийна)
brother ваша, вежарий (в:б)
brother's granddaughter вешин йоьл-йоӏ, вешин йоьл-йоӏрий (й:б)
brother's grandson вешин кӏент-кӏант, вешин кӏент-кӏентий (в:б)
build *(v.)* д.отта (д.утту, д.оьтти, д.оьттина)
building здани, зданеш (й:й); гӏишло, гӏишлош (й:й)

building entrance подъезд, подъездаш (й:й)
burn *(v.) intrans.* д.ага (д.огу, д.еги, д.аьгна)
bus автобус, автобусаш (й:й)
bus stop остановка, остановкаш (й:й); соцунгӏа, соцунгӏаш (й:й)
but амма, ткъа
buy *(v.)* эца (оьцу; ийци; эцна)
buy up *(v.)* схьаэца (схьаоьцу, схьаийци, схьаэцна)

C c

cabbage копаст, копастш (й:й)
cabinet ишкап, ишкапш (й:й)
cactus бал, баьлаш (б:д)
call *(v.) iterative* телефон йетта (телефон йетта; телефон йитти; телефон йиттина)
carpet куз, кузанаш (б:б)
catch *(v.)* лаца (лоцу, леци, лаьцна); *iterative* лийца (луьйцу, лийци, лийцина)
chair гӏант, гӏентш (д:д)
chalk мел, мелаш (б:д)
chant the zikr *(v.)* зикр ала (зикр олу, зикр эли, зикр аьлла)
characteristic хатӏ, хатӏш (д:д)
cheap д.орах
Chechen *person* Нохчи (в:й); *language* Нохчийн мотт (б)
Chechnya Нохчийчоь (й)
chicken котам, котамаш (й:й)
chicken meat котаман жижиг (д)
child бер, бераш (д:д)
childhood бералла (й)
choose *(v.)* харжа (хоржу, хаьржи, хаьржина)
chop wood *(v.)* дечиг даккха (дечиг доккху, дечиг даьккхи, дечиг даьккхина)
chores дан дезарг, дан дезарш (д:д)

church килс, килснаш (й:й)
circle *(v.)* гобаккха (гобоккху, гобаьккхи, гобаьккхина)
city гӏала, гӏаланаш (й:й)
class урок, урокаш (й:й) *(also* lesson)
clean *(adj.)* цӏена
clean *(v.)* цӏанйан (цӏанйо, цӏанйи, цӏанйина)
clock сахьт, сахьтш (д:д)
closet ишкап, ишкапш (й:й)
code of conduct оьздангалла, оьздангаллаш (й:й)
cold *(adj.)* шийла
cold *(n.)* шело, шелонаш (й:й)
collect *(v.)* *intran.* гулд.ала (гулло, гулд.ели, гулд.елла); *trans.* гулд.ан (гулд.о, гулд.и, гулд.ина)
color бос, беснаш (б:д)
come *(v.) sing.* д.ан (д.огӏу, д.еа, д.еана); *pl.* д.ахка (д.огӏу, д.аьхки, д.аьхкина)
come in *(v.)* чуд.ан (чуд.огӏу, чуд.еи, чуд.еана)
comfortable паргӏат
commerce йохкар-эцар (д)
companion накъост, накъостий (в/й:б)
computer компьютер, компьютерш (й:й)
constitution конституци, конституцеш (й:й)
construction бухботтар, бухботтарш (д:д)
contemporary нийсархо, нийсархой (в/й:б)
contract контракт, контарктш (д:д)
cook *(v.)* йаахӏума йан (йаахӏума йо, йаахӏума йи, йаахӏума йина)
Cossack Казак, Казакш (в/й:б)
cottage cheese кӏалд, кӏалдш (й:й)
count *(v.)* дагард.ан (дагард.о; дагард.и; дагард.ина)

cousin шича, шичой (в/й:б)
cow етт, бежнаш (б:д)
cowardly стешха
create *(v.)* кхолла (кхуллу; кхоьлли; кхьоьллина)
cup кружка, кружкаш (й:й)
curtain бой, бойнаш (й:й)
custom гӏиллакх, гӏиллакхаш (д:д), *(also* tradition)

D d

dance *(v.)* халхад.ала (халхад.олу, халхад.ели, халхад.аьлла)
dance *(n.)* хелхар, хелхарш (д:д)
daughter йол, йоларий (й:б)
day де, денош (д:д)
December декабрь (б:д)
decide *(v.)* сацам бан (сацам бо, сацам би, сацам бина)
decorate *(v.)* кечд.ан (кечд.о, кечд.и, кечд.ина)
decree указ, указш (д:д)
delicious мерза
deport *(v.) trans. pl.* цӏерад.аха (цӏерад.оху, цӏерад.ехи, цӏерад.аьхна)
desk парта, парташ (й:й)
destruction бохам, бохамаш (б:б)
dialect диалект, диалектш (й:й)
different тайп-тайпана
difficult хала; чолхе
dignity сий (д)
do *(v.)* д.ан (д.о; д.и; д.ина) *(also* to make)
door неӏ, неӏарш (й:й)
drawer гӏуткха, гӏуткхаш (д:д)
drink *(v.)* мала (молу, мели, мелла); *iterative* мийла (муьйлу, мийли, мийлина)
drive *(v.)* хьахка (хьохку, хьаьхки, хьаьхкина)
dry декъа

E e

each шадолу

earn money *(v.)* ахча даккха (ахча доккху, ахча даьккхи, ахча даьккхина)

easy атта

eat *(v.)* д.аа (д.уу, д.ууш, д.ии)

economy экономика (й)

empty д.аьсса

enemy мостагІ, мостагІаш (в/й:б)

English *(language)* ингалсан мотт (б)

enjoy *(v.)* сакъера (сакъоьру, сакъийри, сакъерра)

eraser стёрка, стёркаш (й:й)

et cetera кхин дІа а

event ловзар, ловзарш (д:д)

every хІора

everything шадерриге

example масала, масалаш (д:д)

Excuse me! Бехк ма била!

expensive д.еза

F f

face йуьхь, йуьхьаш (д:д)

fast чехкха

fat д.ерстан

father да, дай (в:б)

fatherland даймохк, даймехкаш

February февраль (б:д)

Federation пачхьалкх, пачхьалкхш (й:й)

feed *(v.)* йаахІума йала (йаахІума ло, йаахІума йели, йаахІума йелла)

few масийтта

fight *(v.)* лата (лета, лети, летта)

fill *(v.)* д.уза (д.узу, дуьзи, дуьзна)

find *(v.)* схьакард.ан (схьакард.о, схьакард.и, схьакард.ина)

finish *(v.)* д.ала (д.олу, д.ели, д.елла)

first хьалхара

fish чІара, чІерий (б:д)

floor гІат, гІатш (й:й)

flour дам (д)

flower зезаг, зезагаш (д:д)

follow *sing.* тІаьхьахІотта (тІаьхьахІутту, тІаьхьахІоьтти, тІаьхьахІоьттина); *pl.* тІаьхьахІитта (тІаьхьахІуьтту, тІаьхьахІитти, тІаьхьахІиттина)

food даар, даарш (д)

fortress гІап, гІепаш (й:й)

freedom маршо, маршонаш (й:й)

Friday пІераска (д)

friendship барт (б)

from inside чуьра

from time to time наг-наггахь

from where мичара

fun самукъане

funny самукъане

furniture мебель, мебельш (й:й)

G g

gathering цхьаьнакхетар, цхьаьнакхетарш (д:д)

gaunt д.екъана

generation чкъор, чкъораш (д:д)

generous комаьрша

gift совгІат, совгІаташ (д:д)

give *(v.)* д.ала (ло, д.ели, д.елла)

give away *(v.)* дІал.ала (дІало, дІал. ели, дІал.елла)

glasses (eyeglasses) куьзганаш (д)

globe глобус, глобусш (й:й)

go *(v.) sing.* д.аха (д.оьду, д.ахи, д.ахина); *pl.* д.аха (д.оьлху, д.ахи, д.ахана); *iterative* эха (оьху, ихи, ихна)

go for a walk *(v.)* д.олад.елла лела (д.елла лела, д.олад.елла лийли, д.олад.елла лелла)

go in *(v.)* чуд.аха (чуд.огІу, чуд.агІи, чуд.агІина)

go up *(v.)* дІад.аха (дІад.оьду, дІад. ахи, дІад.ахина)

goal Iалашо, Iалашонаш (й:й)
good дика
Goodbye! Iодика йойла!
granddaughter йоьI-йоl, вешин йоьI-йоlрий (й:б)
grandfather *(father's father)* деда, дедай (в:б)
grandfather *(mother's father)* ненда, ненадай (в:б)
grandmother *(father's mother)* денана, денаной (й:б)
grandmother *(mother's mother)* ненана, ненананой (й:б)
grandson кIент-кIант, йишин кIент-кIентий (в;б)
greedy сутар
green баьццара
group тоба, тобанаш (й:й)
grow old *(v.)* къанд.ала (къанло, къанд.ели, къанд.елла)
guard *(v.)* лард.ан (лард.о, лард.и, лард.ина)
guest хьаша, хьеший (в/й:б)
guest room хьешан чоь, чоьнш (й:й)
guide гид, гидш (в/й:б)
guilt бехк, бехкаш (б:д)

H h

hardworking къинхьегаме
have a word *(v.)* д.истахила (д.истахуьлу, д.истахили, д.истахилла)
health могшалла, могшаллонаш (й:й)
hear *(v.)* хаза (хеза, хези, хезна)
heart дог, дегнаш (д:д)
heat йовхо, йовхонаш (й:й)
heating батарейка, батарейкаш (й:й)
heavy д.еза
Hello! Де дика хуьлда!
help *(v.)* гIо дан (д.о, д.еш, д.и)

help *(n.)* гIо (д)
herd *(v.)* *sing.* лалла (лоллу, лаьлли, лаьллина); *pl.* лахка (лохку, лаьхки, лаьхкина); *pl. iterative* лехка (лоьхку, лихки, лихкина)
here кхуза
hero турплахо, турпалхой (в/й:б)
highlight *(v.)* билгалд.аккха (билгалд.оккху, билгалд.аьккхи, билгалд.аьккхина)
history истори, истореш (й:й)
honey моз (д)
hot д.овха
hour сахьт, сахьтш (д:д)
how муха
how many маса
how much мел
human адам, адамаш (д:д)

I i

important коьрта
in чохь
in addition цунна тIе
in front хьалха
inside чохь
install *(v.)* хIоттад.ан (хIоттад.о, хIоттад.и, хIоттад.ина)
internet интернет, интернетш (й:й)
introduce *(v.)* д.овзийта (д.овзуьйту, д.овзийти, д.овзийтина)
invite *(v.)* кхайкха (кхойкху, кхайкхи, кхайкхина)
Islam бусулба дин (д)

J j

January январь (б:д)
job болх, белхаш (б:д)
joke забар йан (забар йо, забар йи, забар йина)
July июль (б:д)
June июнь (б:д)

K k

kefir йеттшура (й)
kill *(v.)* д.ен (д.оь, д.ий, д.ийна)
kilogram кийла, кийланаш (й:й)
kind къинхетаме
kitchen кухни, кухнеш (й:й)
know *(v.)* хаа (хаьа, хии, хиина)

L l

lake лам, ламнаш (б:д)
lamp стогар, стогарш (б:д)
land латта, латташ (д:д)
language мотт, меттанаш (б:д)
laptop ноутбук, ноутбукш (й:й)
last name фамили, фамилеш (й:й)
later таьхьо
laugh *(v.)* д.ела (д.оьлу, д.ийли, д.ийлина)
law бакъо, бакъонаш (й:й)
lazy малойолуш
lead someone *(v.)* тӏед.ига (тӏед. уьгу, тӏед.иги, тӏед.игина)
learn лама (лема, леми, лаьмма)
lecture лекци, лекцеш (й:й)
lesson урок, урокаш (й:й) *(also* class)
level гӏат, гӏатш (й:й) *(also* floor)
library библиотека, библиотекаш (й:й)
lie *(n.)* аьшпаш (б); пуьтш (б)
life дахар, дахарш (д:д)
light д.айн
like the taste *(v.)* мерзахета (мерзахета, мерзахийти, мерзахийтина)
literature литература, литератураш (й:й)
live *(v.)* д.аха (деха, дехи, даьхна)
living room зал, залш (й:й)
local меттигера
long д.еха
look *(v.) sing.* хьажа (хьожу, хьаьжи, хьаьжна); *pl.* хьажа (хьовсу, хьевси, хьевсина)
look for *(v.)* лаха (лоху, лехи, лехна)
love *(v.)* д.еза (д.еза, д.ийзи, д.езна),
lunch обед, обедш (й:й)

M m

mainly дукхахьолахь
majority дукхахд.олу
make *(v.)* д.ан (д.о; д.и; д.ина)
man стаг, божарий (в:б)
map латтсурт, латтсуьрташ (д:д)
March *(month)* март (б:д)
maternal relative ненахо, ненахой (в/й:б)
May *(month)* май (б:д)
mean *(adj.)* догӏаьржа
meat жижиг, жижигаш (д:д)
meet *(v.)* вовшахкхета (вовшахкхета, вовшахкхийти, вовшахкхетта)
merchant йохкар-эцар лелорг, лелорш (в/й:б)
middle йуккъехь
milk *(n.)* шур, шуреш (й:й)
milk *(v.)* шура йаккха (шура йоккху, шура йаьккхи, шура йаьккхина)
minister министр, министраш (в/й:б)
mirror куьзг, куьзганаш (д:д)
Monday оршот
moreover цулла совнах
mosque маьждиг, маьждигаш (д:д)
most (the ...) уггаре
mother нана, наной (й:б)
mountain лам, лаьмнаш (б:д)
mountaineer ламро, ламрой (в/й:б)
mug кружка, кружкаш (й:й)
music мукъам, мукъамаш (б:д)
must *(v.)* эша (оьшу, ийши, эшна)

N n

naked дерзина
name цӏе, цӏераш (й:й)

nation къам, къаьмнаш (д:д)

near уллехь

need *(v.)* д.еза (д.еза, д.ийзи, д.езна); эша (оьшу, ийши, эшна)

nephew *(brother's son)* вешин кӀант, вешин кӀентий (в:б)

nephew *(sister's son)* йишин кӀант, йишин кӀентий (в:б)

nest кхерч, кхерчаш (й:й)

never цкъа а

new керла

next to йистехь

no хӀан-хӀа

Noah Нухь пайхамар (в)

not ца

not very башха

notebook тептар, тептарш (д:д)

November ноябрь (б:д)

number лоьмар, лоьмарш (й:й)

O o

October октябрь (б:д)

of course дера

often сих-сиха

OK/okay мегар ду, дика ду

old къена

on тӀехь

one цхьаъ

onion хох, хохаш (б:д)

only бен ца

opportunity йиш (й)

other важ, вуьш; кхидолу

outside арахь

P p

paper кехат, кехатш (д:д)

parents да-нана (д)

part (piece) дакъа, дакъош (д:д)

participant декъахо, декъашхой (в/й:б)

passport паспорт, паспорташ (д:д)

paternal relative дехо, дехой (в/й:б)

pay *(v.)* ахча (дӀа)далан (ахча дӀало, ахча дӀадели, ахча дӀаделла)

pen ручка, ручкаш (й:й)

pencil къолам, къоламаш (б:д)

person адам, адамаш (д:д)

philology филалоги (й)

photo сурт, суьрташ (д:д)

picture сурт, суьрташ (д:д)

pity къа, къинош (д:д)

place меттиг, меттигаш (й:й)

planning to д.оллу

play *(v.)* (~ a game) ловза (ловзу, левзи, левзина); (~ an instrument) лакха (локху, лекхи, лекхна)

poetry байт, байташ (й:й)

potato картол, картолш (й:й)

power куьйгалла (й)

practice the zikr *(v.)* зикр дан (зикр до, зикр ди, зикр дина)

prepare *(v.)* кечд.ан (кечд.о, кечд.и, кечд.ина)

price мах, мехаш (б:д)

pride дозалла, дозаллаш (д:д)

problem проблем, проблемш (й:й)

professor профессор, профессорш (в:б)

program программа, програмш (й:й)

Q q

question хаттар, хаттарш (д:д)

quick чехкха

quiet тийна

R r

rain догӀа, догӀанаш (д:д)

raise *(v.)* схьалад.аккха (схьалад. оккху, схьалад.аьккхи, схьаладаьккхина)

read *(v.)* д.еша (д.оьшу, д.иши, д.ишина)

ready кийча

real баккъала

reason бахьна, бахьнаш (д:д)

recognize *(v.)* д.овза; тан (тов, тий, тайна)

recommend *(v.)* хьахо (хьоьху, хьийхи, хьийхина)

red цlен

relative гергара стаг, нах (в/й:б)

relax *(v.)* садала (садоlу, садоьли, садоьлна)

religion дин, динш (д:д)

remain *(v.)* д.иса (д.уьсу, д.иси, д.исина); лен (lа, lи, lийна)

remember *(v.)* дагад.ан (дагад.оrlу, дагад.еи, дагад.еана)

rent *(v.)* арендовать д.ан (арендовать д.о, арендовать д.и, арендовать д.ина)

repair *(v.)* тод.ан (тод.о, тод.и, тод.ина)

respect *(v.)* лара (лору, лери, лаьрна)

return *(v.)* йухад.аха (йухад.оьду, йухад.ахи, йухад.ехна)

return home *(v.)* цlадерза (цlадоьрзу, цlадирзи, цlадирзина)

reveal *(v.)* схьаган (схьаго, схьаги, схьагина)

rise *(v.) sing.* схьалад.ала (схьалад.олу, схьалад.ели, схьалад.аьлла); *pl.* схьалад.овла (схьалад.овлу, схьад.евли, схьалад.евла)

roof тхов, тхевнаш (б:д)

rotten дехка

row моrlа, моrlанаш (б:д)

rule бакъо, бакъонаш (й:й)

Russia Россин Пачхьалкх (й)

Russian *(person)* Оьрси, оьрсий (в/й:б)

Russian *(language)* Оьрсийн мотт (б)

S s

sad оьгlазе

Saturday шот

save *(v.)* lалашд.ан (lалашд.о, lалашд.и, lалашд.ина)

say *(v.)* ала (олу, олуш, эли)

schedule расписани, расписанеш (й:й)

school ишколе, ишколеш (й:й)

school supplies концелярски хlуманаш (й)

science lилма, lилмаш (д:д)

see *(v.)* ган (го, гуш, ги, гина)

See you! Гура ду вай!

seize *(v.) sing.* схьад,аккха (схьад. оккху, схьад.аьккхи, схьад. аьккхина); *pl.* схьад.аха (схьад. оху, схьад.ехи, схьад.аьхна)

sell *(v.)* д.охка (д.ухку, д.оьхки, д.оьхкина); *iterative* д.ихка (д.уьхку, д.ихки, д.ихкина)

seller йохкархо, йохкархой (в/й:б)

semester семестр, семестрш (й:й)

send *(v.)* дахьийта (дохьуьйту, дахьийти, дахьийтна)

September сентябрь (б:д)

shame эхь-бехк (д)

sheep уьстаrl, уьстаrlий (б:д)

shine *(v.)* къага (къега, къеги, къегна)

short д.оца; лоха

show *(v.)* гайта (гойту, гайти, гайтина)

siblings йиша-ваша (д:б)

sign *(v.)* куьг йаздан (куьг йаздо, куьг йазди, куьг йаздина)

simply просто

sing *(v.)* лакха (локху, лекхи, лекхна)

sister йиша, йижарий (й:б)

sister's granddaughter йишин йоьl-йоl, йишин йоьl-йоlрий (й:б)

sister's grandson йишин кlент-кlант, йишин кlент-кlентий (в:б)

sit *(v.)* хаа (хуу, хии, хиина)

sit down *(v.)* охьахаа (охьахуу, охьахии, охьахиина)

size барам, барамаш (б:д)
skin чкъор, чкъораш (д:д)
small *sing.* жима; *pl.* кегий
smart хьекъале
smile *(v.)* д.ела (д.оьлу, д.ийли, д.ийлина)
snow ло, лонаш (д:д)
sofa диван, диванш (й:й)
some цхьад.ерш
sometimes наггахь
son кӀант, кӀентий (в:б)
speak *(v.)* баха (боху, бехи, баьхна); д.ийца (д.уьйцу, д.ийци, д.ийцина)
speak the truth *(v.)* бакъален (бакъолоь, бакъалий, бакъалийна)
spring *(season)* бӀаьсте, бӀаьстенаш (й:й)
stair лами, ламеш (б:д)
stand *(v.)* хӀитта (хӀуьтту, хӀитти, хӀиттина); латта (лаьтта, лаьтти, лаьттина)
stand up *(v.)* дӀахлотта (дӀахлутту, дӀахлоьтти, дӀахлоьттина)
state штат, штаташ (й:й)
stay лен (ла, ли, лийна)
stop *(v.)* саца (соцу, сеци, сецина); *pl.* саца (совцу, севци, севцина)
store туька, туьканаш (й:й)
street урам, урамаш (б:д)
strengthen *(v.)* чӀагӀд.ан (чӀагӀд.о, чӀагӀд.и, чӀагӀд.ина)
strong гӀарч
student *(college)* студент, студенташ (в:б); *(pupil, learner)* дешархо, дешархой (в/й:б)
study *(v.)* Ӏама (Ӏема, Ӏеми, Ӏаьмма)
style стиль, стильш (й:й)
substitute *(human)* заместитель, заместительш (в/й:б)
summer аьхке, аьхкенаш (й:й)
sun малх, малхнаш (б:д)
Sunday кӀиранде

swim *(v.)* лийча (луьйчу, лийчи, лийчина)
swing *(n.)* гаьнгали, гаьнгалеш (б:д)
swing *(v.)* *iterative* техка (техка, тихки, тихкина)

T t

table стол, стоьлш (й:й)
taip *(subgroup of clan)* тайп, тайпаш (д:д)
take *(v.)* эца (оьцу, ийци, эцна)
take a look *(v.)* бӀаьрг тоха (бӀаьрг туху, бӀаьрг туьйхи, бӀаьрг тоьхна)
take care of *(v.)* лелад.ан (лелад.о, лелад.и, лелад.ина)
talk *(v.)* къамел дан (къамел до, къамел ди, къамел дина)
tall лекха
teach *(v.)* хьеха (хьоьху, хьийхи, хьехна)
teacher хьехархо, хьехархой (в/й:б)
tell *(v.)* баха (боху, бехи, баьхна)
territory доза, дозанаш (д:д)
textbook дешаран книга, книгаш (й:й)
thank you баркалла
there цигахь; **over there** дӀогахь
thin дуткъа
this хӀара
through чухула
Thursday еара
time хан, хенаш (й:й); **(period of ~)** зама, заманаш (й:й)
tired кӀадд.елла
today тахана
tomato помидор, помидорш (й:й)
tomorrow кхана
tour тур, турш (й:й)
tower гӀишло, гӀишлош (й:й)
tradition гӀиллакх, гӀиллакхаш (д:д)
tray шун, шуьннаш (д:д)
tree дитт, дитташ (д:д)

truly бакъду
try *(v.)* гӀорта (гӀерта, гӀоьрти, гӀоьртина)
Tuesday шинара
type тайпа

U u

ugly ирча
uncle *(father's side)* деваша, девежарий (в:б)
uncle *(mother's side)* ненваша, ненвежарий (в:б)
under кӀелахь
underneath бухахь
university университет, университеташ (й:й)
use *(v.)* лелад.ан (лелад.о, лелад.и, лелад.ина)

V v

vegetable хасстом, хасстоьмаш (б:д)
very инзаре; чӀогӀа
village йурт, йуьрташ (й:й)
village head йуьртда, йуьртдай (в:б)

W w

walk *(v.)* лела (лела, лийли, лелла)
want *(v.)* лаа (лаьа, лии, лиина)
war тӀом, тӀемаш (б:д)
wardrobe шифоньер, шифоньерш (й:й)
warm д.овха
watch *(v.) sing.* хьажа (хьожу, хьаьжи, хьаьжна); *pl.* хьажа (хьовсу, хьевси, хьевсина)

watch *(n.)* сахьт, сахьтш (д:д)
water хи, хиш (д:д)
wear *(v.)* лелад.ан (лелад.о, лелад.и, лелад.ина)
weather хенахӀоттам; погода (й)
wedding зудайалор, зудайалорш (д:д)
Wednesday кхаара
Welcome! Марша вогӀийла!
what хӀун
when маца
which муьлха
white кӀайн
whiteboard кӀайн у, кӀайн аннаш (д:д)
why хӀунда
wide шуьйра
window кор, кораш (д:д)
winter Ӏа, Ӏаьннаш (д:д)
wolf борз, берзалой (й:й)
woman зуда, зударий (й:б)
wood дечиг (д)
write *(v.)* йазд.ан (йзд.о, йазд.и, дӀайазд.ина)

Y y

year шо, шераш (д:д)
yellow можа
yes хӀаъ
young къона

Z z

zikr зикр, зикарш (д:д)

Audio Track List

 Audio files available at:
https://www.hippocrenebooks.com/beginners-online-audio.html

Track 1: Lesson 1, Dialogue 1: "At the Grozny Airport"
Track 2: Lesson 1, Dialogue 2: "Meeting a Friend"
Track 3: Lesson 2, Dialogue 1: "At Hwava's Home"
Track 4: Lesson 2, Dialogue 2: "At the Table"
Track 5: Lesson 3, Dialogue 1: "At Hwava's House"
Track 6: Lesson 3, Dialogue 2: "On the Phone"
Track 7: Lesson 4, Dialogue 1: "At the University"
Track 8: Lesson 4, Dialogue 2: "At the Library"
Track 9: Lesson 5, Dialogue 1: "Meeting Another Student"
Track 10: Lesson 5, Dialogue 2: "In the Classroom"
Track 11: Lesson 6, Dialogue 1: "At the Market"
Track 12: Lesson 6, Dialogue 2: "At the Stall"
Track 13: Lesson 7, Dialogue 1: "At the Store"
Track 14: Lesson 7, Dialogue 2: "At the Bookstore"
Track 15: Lesson 8, Dialogue 1: "Renting an Apartment"
Track 16: Lesson 8, Dialogue 2: "Renting an Apartment"
Track 17: Lesson 9, Dialogue 1: "At the Wedding"
Track 18: Lesson 9, Dialogue 2: "Old Man speaking about the Chechen Nation"
Track 19: Lesson 10, Dialogue 1: "Going to the Mountains"
Track 20: Lesson 10, Dialogue 2: "At the Mountains"
Track 21: Lesson 11, Dialogue 1: "A Tour of Grozny"
Track 22: Lesson 11, Dialogue 2: "Grozny: at the Mosque"
Track 23: Lesson 12, Recording 1: "Excerpt from Chechen Literature: Poetry"
Track 24: Lesson 12, Recording 2: "Newspaper Article"

Other recordings: Chechen Alphabet